christian
social
ethics

christian social ethics

Perry C. Cotham
editor

BAKER BOOK HOUSE
Grand Rapids, Michigan

Copyright 1979 by
Baker Book House Company
ISBN: 0-8010-2424-2
Library of Congress Catalog Card Number: 78-068118
Printed in the United States of America

Contents

Preface

My purpose in this project was to assemble a group of evangelical scholars to discuss the relationship of the church to the larger society and/or to confront certain contemporary issues from a Christian perspective. The first five chapters of this volume deal with general principles and perspectives in Christian social ethics. The remaining chapters treat some specific problems; obviously, no effort has been made to discuss all major socio-political issues. Each contributor is an experienced writer and distinguished by previous interest and training in his or her particular subject matter.

This volume grew out of an earlier project in Christian ethics that for various reasons did not materialize. I would, however, like to acknowledge those writers who prepared special material for that volume: Joel Anderson, Anthony Ash, Karen Wells Borden, Don Haymes, Allen Isbell, Thomas Langford, Hubert G. Locke, Edward Macleod, Arthur Lee Smith, Derwood Smith, and John P. Vanderpool.

It is hoped that these studies will increase our understanding of God's Word and human needs. May the church intensify whatever efforts are necessary to fulfill her social responsibilities.

Perry C. Cotham
June, 1978

PERRY C. COTHAM

1

INTRODUCTION
The Ethic of Escapism
Versus The Ethic of Involvement

Perhaps the most persistent and vexing issue facing the Christian community is its relationship to the surrounding social environment. How should Christians relate to nonbelievers? How involved should disciples of Christ become in the institutions and affairs of non-Christian men and women? What is the meaning of ministry in the world and how much influence should Christians attempt to exert on social and political processes outside their community of faith? How politically and socially active should Christians become in the problems of people all about them? How and in what way can the religious community be a moral community?

These related questions have been posed, answered, and acted upon (or not acted upon, as the case may be) in various ways throughout church history. The answers worked out in any given period of history have depended as much on the legal and social status of the church as upon most other factors. George W. Forell has identified three basic patterns of social teaching which have emerged in the course of history and which have been elaborated in various ways in the Christian church. These patterns he calls the *separation*, the *domination*, and the *integration*.

Separation

The separation pattern is characterized by the effort of the

9

Christian community to remain as detached and as uninvolved as possible with the secular world. Such detachment has meant that, whenever feasible, actual geographic segregation is practiced in order to avoid any "contaminating" contact with people in the world at large. Still practiced by minority sects today, such a behavior pattern is only possible when the withdrawn community is a very small group. Rural life has lent itself to this policy of isolation most easily. As western societies became larger, more complex, and interdependent, it became more difficult for the entire Christian community, or even religious bodies within Christendom, to withdraw successfully from the world.

Domination

The domination pattern was attempted as soon as the Christian church attained a position of power. When political leaders openly affiliated themselves with the church, they made an effort to use their power to enforce a Christian pattern of morality upon all citizens in the land and eventually to excommunicate nonconformists and heretics. Once it became so established, this Christian world view naturally influenced the cultivation of all arts and sciences, and its mark is still felt through the institutions its spirit helped to found.

Americans have flirted with the domination pattern; throughout American history efforts were made by both Protestants and Catholics to employ the law as a tool to force conformity in the larger community to certain moral standards. But America has been a melting pot of many peoples and cultures, and the founding fathers wisely moved to protect dissent and the free exercise of religion in the First Amendment. Because of these rights (admittedly, more zealously guaranteed by the federal court system than by the general public), the domination pattern has never been allowed to take hold of the entire nation.

Historically, the price exacted of dissenters in the successful domination of Christian thought and practice has been a heavy one. Dissenters have been suppressed, even persecuted. If they were tolerated, they were often sequestered in ghettos in order to eliminate all unnecessary contact with the Christian world.

Integration

The integration pattern is based on the premise that if the

Christian faith is to survive it is imperative that it live in meaningful contact with the non-Christian world. This "dialogical"
relationship with the world does not mean abandonment or compromise of traditional Christian doctrine; instead, it means mature
application of Jesus' dictum that his disciples are to be *in the
world*, although not of the world.

A look at American church history indicates that evangelicals
have been ambivalent about their role in and relationship to the
world. Timothy L. Smith and David O. Moberg have written of
the evangelical social activism of the late nineteenth century; they
point out that evangelicals played a major role in both social welfare and social reconstruction. Among the organizations
evangelicals helped to found were the Salvation Army, the
Florence Crittenton homes, schools for immigrants, industrial
training institutes, antislavery and temperance societies, and
many associations, programs, and services for the under-
privileged and culturally deprived. Evangelicals also established
schools and colleges at the heart of whose curricula was a concern
for "moral philosophy" and "the moral government of God."
They believed that God's universal sovereignty made it imperative to conform all aspects of society to God's moral law and
so, instead of confining themselves to individual acts of charity,
they attempted to get at the root causes of frustration, suffering,
and poverty.

The early twentieth century saw evangelicals completely shift
their attitude away from social and political activism, a shift that
has been called "the great reversal." Support for some of the
institutions and programs waned and many projects were
abandoned. New Testament ethics were deemed to be largely, if
not entirely, individualistic. Old, persistent problems like the li-
quor traffic and alcoholism were attacked almost exclusively in
terms of personal salvation, without regard for social conditions.
The causes for this almost 180-degree turn were several: renewed
concern for biblical doctrine, the continuing ideological conflict
between the fundamentalists and modernists, the association of
social activism with the social gospel (which was deemed to be
little more than humanistic optimism), and the movement of
evangelical activists into the liberal camp.

The great reversal is now being reversed. Events in recent years
have compelled evangelicals to look again at their cherished
positions in light of the Scriptures. Many painfully reached the
conclusion that the principles of *laissez-faire* capitalism,

Americanism, and status quoism had given more substance and direction to their ethical position *vis-à-vis* the world than had considerations of love, justice, and mercy.

Perhaps more than any other issue, the challenge of race relations to the conservative conscience served as a catalyst to reconsider the old position and defenses. The civil rights turmoil that began in the late 1950s could not be ignored by church leaders, nor by many rank and file church members. There was little alternative other than to agree with Kyle Haseldon, a Baptist and editor of *Christian Century*, when he adapted the words of Martin Luther and noted that "when the white Christian church looks at itself in the mirror of race, the reflection which comes back to it is clearly and unmistakably the countenance of a sinner."

Today there is a lay Christian movement that has taken root and is burgeoning within established church circles. It is an optimistic quest for ways to be a Christian in the world as well as in the church. This quest is reflected in the abundant literature and in the social and political activism among conservatives and evangelicals in the last ten to fifteen years. Many evangelical leaders have come to see that the ethic of escapism and withdrawal from the world is a self-serving retreat from the full demands of genuine discipleship. Public Christian ministry is now aimed at more than simply winning additional converts, restorations, and public confessions. The world of many Christians can no longer be divided into rigidly isolated areas—political, social, economic, civil, religious—with the pulpit and church in general addressing itself only to matters ecclesiastical. For one does not have to discount the value and power of collective individual piety in order to justify acting through and upon group relationships in institutions that develop and shape character.

The impact of the Great Commission of Jesus Christ is being more fully felt. Faithfulness in this world, it is now realized, means that the Christian joins with others in the continuing struggle for social justice. One need not opt for the utopian, frenzied activism of liberal churchmen of the past, nor choose the passivity and dedication to the status quo of so many culture-denying fundamentalists. The Christian life is one of balance and perspective, and social and political involvement must be firmly rooted in the Word of God. The Christian activist must never forget Paul's dictate to the Colossian Christians: "Whatever you are doing, whether you speak or act, do everything in the name of the Lord Jesus, giving thanks to God the Father through him" (3:17).

And so the Christian acts in the world in which he did not ask to be born, bringing to bear a ministry of witness in the world in which he decides to be born again. The shape of his ministry and the nature of his opposition, ideological or otherwise, are determined in large part by the nature of the problems and status of the institutions in his immediate community.

Just as the first-century church did not choose to be called into being by God at that particular point in history—under the shadow of an unpredictable, totalitarian Roman empire and with the opposition of Gnosticism and mystery religions of the Gentiles—so Christians today do not choose the issues thrust upon them by a modern, pluralistic society. But there is no virtue in an easy escapism. The committed disciple will not concede that his faith in its pure strength and pristine form encounters any opponent for which it is no match.

There are no challenges in social justice and morality too deep, too enormous, or with too much momentum for a Christian commitment to resolution. New Testament faith contends that God in his Son has encountered and can conquer varied evils and injustices, and through his Holy Spirit and people can overthrow their defenses and structures, whatever their form, in any age. This premise underlies the evangelical's activism in all areas of life and refutes the contention, stated or implied, that Christianity is basically impotent or inept in the face of great challenges and must therefore await the climax of history for all accounts to be settled.

Christians recognize at least four generalizations about their commitment to activism.

Faith in God

First, Christian action begins with the fact of the existence of God. Upon God and his infinite grace depend our faith, our life, our world, and our salvation. We are loved by him and thus motivated to love others; we are saved by him and thus freed to work for the salvation of others. God made the world and all things therein and then charged man with the responsibility of caretaking.

Our faith in God leads us to develop other vital traits of the Christian character. One such trait is hope; action based on faith in God is action in hope. This is not the hope of the utopian idealists of past reform periods or the hope of premillenialists awaiting an imminent perfecting of all earthly systems. Instead, our hope assures us that history and our personal lives have theme and purpose running through them and that God's goal will ultimately be realized.

One need not be overcome by the frustration and confusion that are stirred by the complexities and intransigence of the modern social order. Political institutions and social processes that seem impenetrable and erratic are not beyond the power of God's redeeming activity. Hope makes us affirmative, despair can be conquered, even "when hope seems hopeless" (cf. Rom. 4:18). Hope enables us to find possibility as well as difficulty, capacity for regeneration and renewal as well as realism about corruption.

Equally important, our faith in God and finite understanding of his grace lead us to humility, one of the fruits of God's Spirit that informs our action. Such humility is not an easy abandonment of goals in the face of setbacks, or discouragement about our chances for success. It is not a diffident and apologetic demeanor when encountering the rigors of the world. Rather, it is a mindset that tempers and shapes the substance and style of all that we attempt to do in the name of Jesus Christ.

Such humility flows from our acknowledgment of God's prior order, prior power, and prior gift of grace, out of which our motivation to action springs. Humility is a function of gratitude—gratitude for the richness of God's grace and his bestowal of blessings. Humility is also a function of the true knowledge of self. In humility the Christian activist realizes he may be guilty of hypocrisy, may practice "selective morality," or may become absorbed with symbolic victories to the extent that substantive concerns are slighted. In humility he realizes that when he acts in relationship to his fellowman, he cannot escape sin. He knows that the greater his involvement in a conflict, and the more its resolution will affect his status, the more likely he is to conceal the true nature of his action behind the mask of transcendent values or high-flown moral ideology. To the Christian, immoral activities, immoderate desires, and the failure to exercise self-discipline are sinful; but he is also aware that evil includes man's desire to employ his most sacred values and highest faculties as tools of his own selfishness, sometimes without awareness that he is doing so.

The Life of Christ

Second, Christian action is directed by the pattern of Jesus Christ, who revealed God to sinful man in concrete ways. The Christian faith holds that Jesus of Nazareth was the Son of God and that his own ministry was a revelation of the nature and will of his Father. Jesus established a community of believers, the church, in order that the work and ministry he began might be continued by the guidance of his Holy Spirit. Indeed, the Christian social activist follows a Master who addressed his ministry and his teaching to the greatest issues of body, mind, and soul, and who came to heal the estrangements of man from God, of man from man, and of the individual personality from himself.

For the multitudes who accept his life and teachings as authoritative in their lives today, Jesus Christ may function as a type of spiritual Rorschach test in which his followers see what they want to see or have almost been programmed to see. Pulpit ministers frequently reflect upon the fact that the Son of Man was a preacher and that he sent his apostles into the world to preach the word and immerse believers. And this is true; the importance and role of the preaching ministry must not be diminished in our time. But some alternative ways of looking at Jesus, though often good in themselves for expressing various aspects of his depth and mystery as a person, may lead us astray. An older image of Jesus is that of the ideal human whose life was an exalted expression of what humanity should struggle to become. To youth Jesus is proclaimed the model of moral purity and to mature Christians he is the paradigm of the faithful and omnipresent friend.

More damaging is a tendency to picture Jesus from the portraits that have been painted throughout the centuries which envision him as a mild, almost sickly, meek and gentle do-gooder. The New Testament image of Christ is not a "stained glass window" type of servant. We see the Savior as a real person stained with dust, sweat, tears, and finally, blood. He was a strong man of action who was most specific in his commands and answers to those who sought to understand him. He had a full and unequivocal response to those who suffered and there can be no denying that in his ministry he identified more with the people who were societal outcasts, the poor, the sick, and the victims of oppression than with those who were prosperous and well-situated.

Christ's theology included an important teaching ministry but it entailed much more than uttering words. It meant demonstrating the love of his Father by innumerable concrete actions. There is no doubt that these signs and wonders were intended to provide acceptable bases for faith in Jesus as the Son of God, but to deny that Christ used his power simply for the sake of helping others because he was motivated by pure love is to miss a vital portion of the meaning of his example. Truly he was, in the words of Dietrich Bonhoeffer, "the man for others."

His disciples were directed both explicitly and implicitly to act upon the issues for which he expressed concern: the quality of family life, hunger, sickness, oppression, injustice, and even loneliness. These are and will continue to remain controversial issues today, for they are part and parcel of the human condition. If we are truly Christ's disciples, do we not invalidate his gospel by espousing an ethic of escapism from these and similar problems to which he addressed himself?

The teachings of the Old Testament and, in particular, of Israel's prophets made it clear that the calling of God included the solemn responsibility of enriching and cleansing all aspects of the Hebrew physical and spiritual existence. The first-century church did not diminish but magnified this concern. While the church was a new community of believers which had emerged in history out of the life of Christ, the saving action of God and the gift of the Holy Spirit, it was also both a continuation and a consummation of the covenant community of Israel and was intended to bring salvation to all peoples, races, and nations.

We are familiar with the sacrificial benevolence and service of the early Christians, the collection of funds to help brethren in the grips of famine, the example of Christians such as Dorcas, and the acts of healing and resurrection accomplished through the apostles. The early Christians saw that, in the words of Paul, the "new man" or "new being" with life in the Spirit brought about a radical transformation of the whole of human existence. The early church was effective, even under conditions that parallel those in totalitarian nations today, not because it was primarily a social institution, but because it understood that genuine discipleship demanded far-reaching concomitant social involvement.

Justice

Third, Christian action in the world seeks nothing less than social justice. "Let justice roll on like a river," Amos quotes the

Lord as saying, "and righteousness like an ever-flowing stream" (5:24). For the Christian citizen, there is no uncertainty about the role of justice in restoring and maintaining the sense of human community; indeed, justice *is* community, in the full sense of the word. Justice is giving to every person his due. To H. N. Wieman, justice means free and equal access to the sources of human fulfillment. Social justice should be that manifestation of fairness and love which aims directly at the good of a group of persons, and incidentally at the good of each person in the group. The goal of social justice is restoration and maintenance of solidarity and community.

The preamble to the U. S. Constitution and certain of its amendments summon citizens to justice and make explicit its minimal demands. The church, informed and inspired by the good news of Jesus Christ, possesses a unique perspective that reaffirms the centrality and efficacy of justice in interpersonal and societal affairs. But the disciple also encounters the reality of sin—especially greed, covetousness, the lust for power— operating in political societies, in social institutions as well as in the hearts of men. Since governments are maintained by sinful people, the disciple discovers legal arrangements which favor some people and deny others full access to the resources for human potential; he sees public officials captivated by private interests, not only by overt pressure, but often by the subtle, albeit pervasive influence of money.

Sin is the root of social inequities, discrimination, and structural arrangements that exploit, oppress, or deprive people. If the reformers of a century ago seemed to deal with effects rather than causes of social injustice, perhaps the very complexity of institutional structures explains their approach as much as their alleged compromise with the entrenched powerholders.

We have noted already that social and political institutions and processes are not static. Social justice is clearly not to be reached by some mechanical formula. The intelligent Christian activist is aware that justice is more of an art than an exact science, and that it requires an uncommon measure of knowledge and practical wisdom. But the very premise on which this volume was planned is that the children of God do not—must not—acquiesce in the endless quest for justice simply because the challenges are great, the solutions are complex, or because the particular shape of justice must be constantly reworked as new forces rise on the political scene. Consequently, Christian ethicists need to be well read in the social sciences and informed by the perspective of history.

Considerations of justice cut across every facet of society. What about international justice, fraught with complexities and ambiguities of over 150 political societies seeking their own version of national interest? What about distributive justice in a finite world where the vision of infinite progress is now a perilous illusion? How shall the material gifts from God—the sources of energy, the raw materials, the water, air, and fertile earth—be rendered available so all his creatures now and in the future may have fair access and lead meaningful lives? And what about the criminal justice system? Can it reconcile and serve consistently the functions of societal retribution, rehabilitation, and restoration to create an ordered community? Are community and solidarity advanced or weakened by our mass media? Is abortion a just solution to the problems of undesired pregnancy? What do we owe to the aged? What are just measures for the poor, the destitute, the underprivileged, the hungry?

These are some of the issues that contributors to this volume have confronted. The inseparability of public policy and morality, obviously, will lead these writers to do more than mouth generalizations about Christian values or sprinkle religious rhetoric with pious platitudes and innocuous references to a just God. Their desire is to help laymen in the church and in positions of social responsibility to interpret their duty in light of the full demands of the gospel.

Love

Finally, Christian action is motivated by love. Jesus asserted: " 'Love the Lord your God with all your heart, with all your soul, with all your mind.' That is the greatest commandment. It comes first. The second is like it: 'Love your neighbor as yourself.' Everything in the Law and the prophets hangs on these two commandments" (Matt. 22:37-40). The manner in which the Christian strives to establish and administer human justice is conditioned by his membership in the body of Christ, a community of people both loved and loving. Even Reinhold Niebuhr, with all his realistic warnings about the "impossible possibility" of love in the social order, assumes it as the Christian ideal. The law of love is involved in all approximations of justice, he noted, and not only as the source of the norms of justice, but as an ultimate perspective by which their limitations are discovered.

Love is an internal norm that guides Christian thought and action. Love ministers and does not attempt to rule. Love's effectiveness lies in its power and not in its claim to power. Love bestows upon one's neighbor more than he deserves, just as God's grace gives to us more than we deserve. Love overcomes the neighbor's evil by doing good. In a sense, love is impulsive and indiscriminate; the love which is no respecter of persons bestows its blessings freely and without consideration of merit or status.

Action in love seeks the good of others in concrete ways within the realm of the possible. What justice seeks is also sought by love. Love can transform a system of justice so that it meets its purpose more effectively. Love and justice go together, but self-sacrificial love is not halted by the boundaries of justice, as God made painfully clear to the world at Calvary. The love of God empowers his children to act lovingly in all relationships of which they are a part; it is indefatigable in pursuit of human solidarity. Love continues to come into play after the demands of justice have been satisfied, supplementing them by its own free gift.

The Christian cannot concur with those who argue that the love for neighbor of which Jesus spoke is impractical and irrelevant in seeking social justice, especially when considering the needs of a class, race, or nation of people. Admittedly, when we deal with larger societies and groups within a society, neighbor-love cannot be effected directly and individually. But by furthering justice for these groups, neighbor-love can be given indirectly and collectively. Unlike romantic love or the ties of close friendship, neighbor-love does not require direct relationship with a person—it requires *de minimis* the willingness to treat another, directly or indirectly, as a person. The neighbor-love and enemy-love of which Jesus spoke is not primarily a sentiment or an emotion; it is a concrete conviction to affirm the equality of others, to respect their God-given rights, and to serve their needs. Viewed accordingly, love does not depend on a personal, emotional relationship with each member of a group. A neighbor-love that does not seek social justice is but sentimental and vain rhetoric.

A Christian who is faithful in this world joins with others in the continuing struggle for justice. His proclamation of the good news is preceded and authenticated by specific deeds and decisions that humanize truth and energize moral idealism. The ultimate test of morality in spiritual life is not solely the values

and ideals we proclaim, but what we have the ability and courage
to carry out. The Christian activist should never forget the ad-
monition of an Old Testament prophet: "And what doth the Lord
require of thee, but to do justly, and to love mercy, and to walk
humbly with thy God?" (Mic. 6:8).

2

Old Testament Foundations of Social Justice

In his haste to examine Christian ethics, the student of the Scriptures may move too rapidly to New Testament sources. In the first chapter of Genesis, we are confronted with the straight fact that our world, our life, and our faith begin with God. This is where the Christian must commence his pursuit of responsible answers to the complex situations he faces in the world. This essay is based on three principles which the Bible considers to be self-evident. These principles are only very rarely stated explicitly, but many biblical affirmations and truths have no foundation apart from them.

Human Nature

First, man's nature is basically the same in all periods of history. His precise behavior may differ from one generation to another, but the characteristics which produce this behavior are the same. Thus, if the Old Testament truly contains God's evaluation of man, its analysis of man's nature must be as correct and valid as that of the New Testament. It is because Paul accepted this principle that he wrote these words to the Corinthian Christians concerning the Israelites who escaped from Egypt under Moses and wandered in the wilderness:

Now these things are warnings for us, not to desire evil as they did.

Do not be idolaters as some of them were; as it is written, 'The people sat down to eat and drink and rose up to dance.' We must not indulge in immorality as some of them did, and twenty-three thousand fell in a single day. We must not put the Lord to the test, as some of them did and were destroyed by serpents; nor grumble, as some of them did and were destroyed by the Destroyer. Now these things happened to them as a warning, but they were written down for our instruction, upon whom the end of the ages has come (I Cor. 10:6-11).

God's Nature

Second, God's nature and character are unchanging. He was no less God in Old Testament times than he was in the days of Jesus and Paul, or than he is in modern times.[1] To be sure, he acts differently in different circumstances because each situation has its own unique set of complex problems, but his actions are motivated by the same nature and character. The old clichés that the God of the Old Testament was a God of wrath and the God of the New Testament is a God of love, and that the God of the Old Testament was a God of justice and the God of the New Testament is a God of grace are completely foreign to biblical teaching. As to the former, the New Testament frequently announces that God's wrath will come upon sinners, as, for example, when Paul says to the Thessalonians:

This is evidence of the righteous judgment of God, that you may be made worthy of the kingdom of God, for which you are suffering—since indeed God deems it just to repay with affliction those who afflict you, and to grant rest with us to you who are afflicted (II Thess. 1:5-7),

and the Old Testament repeatedly exalts God's love, as, for example, when Moses declares to Israel:

It was not because you were more in number than any other people that the Lord set his love upon you and chose you, for you were the fewest of all peoples; but it is because the Lord loves you (Deut. 7:7-8).

---

[1]"The unity between the testaments . . . results . . . from the fact that the Bible is concerned throughout with God and with his dealings with mankind. It is one and the same God who is present and active in the history of Israel, in Jesus Christ, and in the Spirit-led life and witness of the apostolic church." Floyd V. Filson, "The Unity between the Testaments," in *The Interpreter's One-Volume Commentary on the Bible*, ed. Charles M. Laymon (Nashville: Abingdon Press, 1971), p. 992.

And with regard to the latter, both Testaments teach that justice *and* grace are vital aspects of God's character. In commenting on the rejection of the Jews and the acceptance of the Gentiles, Paul states:

> Note then the kindness and the severity of God: severity toward those who have fallen, but God's kindness to you, provided you continue in his kindness; otherwise you too will be cut off. And even the others, if they do not persist in their unbelief, will be grafted in, for God has the power to graft them in again (Rom. 11:22-23).

The same balanced picture of God's nature occurs in the Ten Commandments:

> I the Lord your God am a jealous God, visiting the iniquity of the fathers upon the children to the third and the fourth generation of those who hate me, but showing steadfast love to thousands of those who love me and keep my commandments (Exod. 20:5-6).

In the Old Testament (as in the New), God's justice is depicted as an expression of his grace and mercy. He punishes man *because* he loves him (Prov. 3:11-12, quoted in Heb. 12:5-6). Thus, it is God's grace (not his justice) which is the *prime* motivation in the Old Testament. Frequently God is extolled in the Old Testament in words such as these:

> The Lord, the Lord, a God merciful and gracious, slow to anger, and abounding in steadfast love and faithfulness, keeping steadfast love for thousands, forgiving iniquity and transgression and sin, but who will by no means clear the guilty, visiting the iniquity of the fathers upon the children and the children's children, to the third and fourth generation (Exod. 34:6-7; see also Num. 14:18; Neh. 9:17; Pss. 86:15; 103:8; 145:8; Joel 2:12-13; Jonah 4:2).[2]

And, as Robert Kennett writes:

> Justice and mercy are not antagonistic, for neither can have its perfect

---

[2]In the Old Testament, "anger is not the habitual attitude of Yahweh. Habitually Yahweh is inclined to show covenant love, and his anger is the exceptional eruption. Yahweh's anger endures only for a moment; his covenant love endures for life (Ps. 30:6)." John L. McKenzie, S. J., "Aspects of Old Testament Thought," in *The Jerome Biblical Commentary*, ed. Raymond E. Brown, Joseph A. Fitzmyer, and Roland E. Murphy (Englewood Cliffs, N.J.: Prentice-Hall, 1969) 2:753.

work unless it be combined with the other. Jehovah is judge to punish the wicked and to vindicate the righteous: yet He is not extreme to mark what is done amiss: for in Him truth can never be severed from mercy, but might and gentleness, holiness and compassion meet together.[3]

God's Activity

Third, the way God acts among men and the way he expects them to treat their fellows are basically the same throughout the Bible. It is true, of course, that as he acted anew, God gave men new ways of commemorating and proclaiming his mighty deeds. This explains why the Passover Feast was so central to the Israelite, but the Lord's Supper is so central to the Christian.

Behind these external details is a consistent theological underpinning which firmly binds the two testaments together. For example, Jeremiah declares that regular attendance at worship in the Jerusalem temple, correct procedure in offering sacrifices, and all other acts of worship are unacceptable to God unless they come from a heart and life ruled by God (see, e.g., Jer. 3:21—4:4; 7:1-26; 9:25-26). Similarly, Paul teaches that singing, making melody, preaching, and partaking of the Lord's Supper are all vain if they do not issue from a genuine heart and life (see respectively Eph. 5:19; Col. 3:16; I Cor. 11:17-34).

In light of these three principles, a study of Old Testament teaching on social justice is of primary importance for one who takes the Bible seriously as a guide for his own life. Indeed, the Old Testament teaching on this subject depicts accurately the divine message.[4] Filson correctly and succinctly says:

> Since the Reformation certain small groups have been ready to discount or discard the OT and be content with the NT as the sole Christian scripture. Individuals have maintained that the OT is antiquated or sub-Christian and so is no legitimate part of the church's scripture. Such views imply that there is no essential unity between the testaments and that the NT alone forms the Christian canon. The church as a whole has always rejected such proposals. It has included both testaments in the Bible and found a deep unity between them.

---

[3]R. H. Kennett, "The Contribution of the Old Testament to the Religious Development of Mankind," in *The People and the Book*, ed. Arthur Samuel Peake (Oxford: At the Clarendon Press, 1925), p. 390.

[4]As the Old Testament teaching is presented in what follows, it should become clear that in essence it is no different from the New Testament teaching on this subject.

This church position has roots in the NT itself. Not simply by quoting the OT as scripture but also by continually accepting and reasserting OT content and ideas the NT attests the unity between the testaments. To reject the OT or to deny its basic unity with the NT not merely casts doubt on the OT but also charges the NT with being deeply in error, for to the NT writers the OT is truly scripture; to them it is an indispensable witness to God, his work, and his will for men. These NT writers think that their message is in basic accord with the OT.[5]

God's Concern for Social Justice

The very first affirmation in Scripture is that God created all that is (Gen. 1). In distinction from the rest of created life, "God created man in his own image, in the image of God he created him" (Gen. 1:27). One cannot take the Bible seriously if he fails to respect his fellowmen as creatures made in the image of God. His attitude toward all men, whether they be rich or poor, black or white, friend or foe, young or old, must be governed by this biblical affirmation. The *reason* given by one biblical writer in forbidding a man to kill his fellow (an extreme act of social injustice) is that he is created in the image of God (Gen. 9:6).[6] Other acts of social injustice are wrong for the same reason.

God created man as he is, and man has no control over the needs which his creatureliness forces upon him. At the same time, God did not leave man alone to supply his own needs, for this is beyond man's ability. God is greatly concerned for and continually cares for man whom he has created.

---

[5]Filson, "The Unity between the Testaments," p. 989. I highly recommend Filson's entire article for readers interested in a balanced study of this issue.

[6]Admittedly, the meaning of the statement "God created man in his own image" in Gen. 1:27 is interpreted in other ways. However, the context of Gen. 1:26ff.; 9:1ff.; and Ps. 8 (which clearly carries the same concept, even though it does not use the expression "image of God") makes the interpretation suggested here most likely. For a scholarly discussion of the major views and problems, see Norman W. Porteous, "Image of God," in *The Interpreter's Dictionary of the Bible*, ed. G. A. Buttrick, 4 vols. (Nashville: Abingdon Press, 1962) 2:682-85. Porteous's interpretation is fundamentally the same as mine. For example, he remarks: "The manner in which the creation of man is introduced in 1:26 and the fact that the passage 9:1-7 implies that human life has a greater sanctity than animal life and that this difference is linked with the image of God imply that the writer intends by the phrase 'image of God' to express in some way *man's peculiar dignity*," p. 683. And again, "Ps. 8 implies *dignity* and authority and nobility of appearance as God's gift to man to fit him for his cultural task (cf. Gen. 1:26, 28)" p. 684.

A man can be rich or intelligent or powerful *only* if God causes or allows him to be so. The psalmist says:

> Be not afraid when one becomes rich,
>   when the glory of his house increases.
> For when he dies he will carry nothing away;
>   his glory will not go down after him.
> Though, while he lives, he counts himself happy,
>   and though a man gets praise when he does well for himself,
> he will go to the generation of his fathers,
>   who will never more see the light.
> Man cannot abide in his pomp,
>   he is like the beasts that perish (Ps. 49:16-20;
>   see also Job 1:21; Eccles. 5:15; I Tim. 6:6-10).

God explicitly warns the rich and those in power that if they afflict the underprivileged, he himself will intervene and see that the oppressors are punished. Note the following words:

> You shall not afflict any widow or orphan. If you do afflict them, and they cry out to me, I will surely hear their cry; and my wrath will burn, and I will kill you with the sword, and your wives shall become widows and your children fatherless (Exod. 22:22-24).

If God is so concerned that social justice be done, the idea that social justice is not "religious" is erroneous. It also follows that one cannot be "like God" in his attitude and action unless he advocates and promotes social justice and does all he can to stop social injustices.[7] One whose attitude is godlike respects the poor man because he is made in God's image. He is moved with compassion for him, he puts himself in his place, and he does all he can to help him overcome his problems and needs. "He who oppresses a poor man insults his[8] Maker, but he who is kind to the needy honors him" (Prov. 14:31).

----

[7] See V. H. Fletcher, "The Shape of Old Testament Ethics," *Scottish Journal of Theology* 24 (1971): 47-73, esp. 57-61.

[8] One cannot be certain whether "his" refers to the oppressor or to the poor. The oppressor would insult his Maker (God) by flaunting God's desire that a man treat the poor with kindness and consideration. Or, God would be insulted if a man mistreated his fellowman who is poor. "In either case the familiar duty is based on *religious* grounds, but in the latter case . . . there is the implied recognition of a common humanity—*the needy man is not merely an object of passing sympathy, he is respected as a creation of the divine wisdom.*" C. H. Toy, *Proverbs*. The International Critical Commentary, ed. Samuel Rolles Driver, Alfred Plummer, and Charles A. Briggs (New York: Charles Scribner's Sons, 1904), p. 299, italics mine.

God is concerned about and cares for the needs of man because this is a fundamental facet of his nature—this is the way he *really feels*. He does not have to be coerced into loving man and into providing for his needs. Central to God's very character is his compassion and liberality. He does not give man the minimum which he requires, but he gives to him abundantly, and when man receives it much is left over. One who is truly like God manifests a similar spirit, even though his capacity to give is much less than God's. "When a rich man and a poor man meet, [Let them remember that] the Lord has made them both (Prov. 22:2).[9] As Crawford Toy says, "There are social differences among men—but all men, as creatures of God, have their rights, and their mutual obligations of respect and kindness."[10]

God's messengers in Old Testament times frequently emphasized that God had acted and was acting in a special way toward his chosen people Israel. They did so (among other reasons) to stimulate the Israelites to treat others in like manner. Thus, one account of the injunction to keep the sabbath states that the reason for such a law was to allow the servants of the Israelites to rest. God's people had learned by bitter experience in Egypt what it was to be slaves, and they were not to allow themselves to treat others in an inhumane way:

> Six days you shall labor, and do all your work; but the seventh day is a sabbath to the Lord your God; in it you shall not do any work, you, or your son, or your daughter, or your manservant, or your maidservant, or your ox, or your ass, or any of your cattle, or the sojourner who is within your gates, that your manservant and your maidservant may rest as well as you. You shall remember that you were a servant in the land of Egypt, and the Lord your God brought you out thence with a mighty hand and an outstretched arm; therefore the Lord your God commanded you to keep the sabbath day (Deut. 5:13-15).

In one account of the law governing the release of slaves in the

---

[9]This is the translation of R. B. Y. Scott, *Proverbs, Ecclesiastes*. The Anchor Bible, ed. William Foxwell Albright and David Noel Freedman (Garden City, N. Y.: Doubleday, 1965), p. 127. Scott points out that there are at least three possible interpretations of the first line: "(a) . . . they share a common humanity, (b) . . . God has willed their station in life, and may reverse it, or (c) . . . personal worth is more important than wealth," (p. 128). All of these views are in harmony with the point being made here.

[10]Toy, *Proverbs*, p. 414.

seventh year, Israelites are admonished to treat these slaves as
God had treated them in Egypt:

> If your brother, a Hebrew man, or a Hebrew woman, is sold to you,
> he shall serve you six years, and in the seventh year you shall let him
> go free from you. And when you let him go free from you, you shall
> not let him go empty-handed; you shall furnish him liberally out of
> your flock, out of your threshingfloor, and out of your winepress; as
> the Lord your God has blessed you, you shall give to him. You shall
> remember that you were a slave in the land of Egypt, and the Lord
> your God redeemed you; therefore I command you this today (Deut.
> 15:12-15).

The Israelites were commanded to love strangers and to treat
them as they would have wanted to be treated when they were
strangers in the land of Egypt.

> When a stranger sojourns with you in your land, you shall not do him
> wrong. The stranger who sojourns with you shall be to you as the
> native among you, and you shall love him as yourself; for you were
> strangers in the land of Egypt (Lev. 19:33-34; see also Exod. 22:21;
> 23:9; Deut. 10:18-19).[11]

It follows from these passages (and there are many similar
passages in the Old Testament) that two major principles which
were to motivate the attitude and behavior of Israelites were: "Do
unto others as God has done unto you,"[12] and "Love your
fellowman as you love yourself." It is true that many Israelites
did not have right attitudes or behave in a godlike manner toward
their fellows, but this does not nullify the responsibility which
God's message concerning these matters placed upon them. In
the same way, the failure of many Christians to apply New Testa-

---

[11]See the excellent essays by Millar Burrows, "The Social Institutions of Israel,"
in *Peake's Commentary on the Bible*, ed. Harold Henry Rowley and Matthew Black
(New York: Thomas Nelson and Sons, 1963), 134-41, esp. pp. 138-39; and Norman
W. Porteous, "The Care of the Poor in the Old Testament," in *Living the Mystery*:
Collected Essays (Naperville, Ill.: Allenson, 1968), p. 149.

[12]"As Jehovah has dealt with His people, so He desires that His people should
deal one with another. Those to whom much is given, of them shall much be required. . . . Those who look to Him for justice must themselves be just. It is not
the least glory of the Old Testament that it sets forth an ideal of justice far superior
to the ordinary morals of those who profess and call themselves Christians." Kennett, "The Contribution of the Old Testament," p. 391. See C. U. Wolf, "Poor," in
The Interpreter's Dictionary of the Bible, 3: 843-44; and Fletcher, "The Shape of Old
Testament Ethics," pp. 50, 52-57.

ment principles to their lives and hearts does not negate those principles.

Man's Self-Centeredness and Social Injustice

It is possible to determine the ways that man treated his fellows in Israel during the various periods of Old Testament history not only from descriptions of such behavior, but also from laws, prophetic oracles, poetic laments, and so forth. These make sense only if the matters discussed in them were actually being practiced during that time. Using these two criteria, a great deal of information may be gleaned from pertinent texts concerning social injustices in ancient Israel. (Limits of space permit only a few observations.)

According to the Old Testament, the root of social injustice is the heart. These lines from the Psalms are typical:

> The wicked plots against the righteous,
>   and gnashes his teeth at him (Ps. 37:12).

> Deliver me, O Lord, from evil men;
>   preserve me from violent men,
> who plan evil things in their heart,
>   and stir up wars continually (Ps. 140:1-2).

> Incline not my heart to any evil,
>   to busy myself with wicked deeds
> in company with men who work iniquity;
>   and let me not eat their dainties (Ps. 141:4).[13]

Time and again this principle is applied to a specific situation. Two examples may suffice.

(1) Apparently it was a common practice in Israel for judges to take bribes from the rich and decide the case to his advantage. In denouncing such a practice, the Old Testament is not content to condemn the overt act of accepting a bribe, but traces it to *greed* in the judge's heart. "He who is greedy for unjust gain makes trou-

---

[13]For an excellent treatment of the importance of the "intention" of the heart lying behind the overt act in Old Testament teaching, see B. Gemser, "Gesinnungs-ethik im Psalter," *Oudtestamentische Studiën* 13 (1963): 1-20; and "The Object of Moral Judgment in the Old Testament," *Adhuc Loquitur* (1968): 78-95 (first published in Dutch, 1961).

ble for his household, but he who hates bribes will live" (Prov. 15:27; see also Ps. 10:3; Jer. 6:13; 8:10).

(2) Old Testament legal codes specify several ways that Israelites were to help the poor. But these do not stop with material aid ("lend him [the poor man] sufficient for his need, whatever it may be" Deut. 15:8), but also demand that he who gives to the poor must do so with a genuine attitude of love and concern ("you shall not harden your heart or shut your hand against your poor brother. . . . You shall give to him freely, and your heart shall not be grudging when you give to him" Deut. 15:7, 10). God is just as concerned about inner motives and intentions in Old Testament times as he is in the New.

Although not always the case, attitudes such as greed and grudgery often characterize the man in high position. His life is absorbed with securing and maintaining a certain measure of wealth, power, or fame for himself. And if he must hurt his fellowmen (usually the poor or underprivileged or defenseless) to achieve the goal which he has set for himself, he is ready to do so. He will sacrifice anything or anyone to see that his goal is achieved. Fundamentally, it is this attitude which lies behind social injustice.

Social injustice may manifest itself in a wide variety of ways. Different economic and political systems issue in different malpractices, but the principles involved are the same. This may be illustrated by a few examples.

(1) In ancient Israel, a rich man brought false charges against a poor man to destroy his reputation, thus putting the rich man in a position to seize his property or possessions (Exod. 23:1-3, 6-8; I Kings 21:1-16). In modern times, an employer receives an accusation against one of his employees from a financial supporter of the company. Without investigating the veracity of the accusation, he fires the employee to keep the financial supporter happy.

(2) In ancient Israel, a merchant sold a fraudulent quantity ("making the ephah small") of an inferior grade of wheat ("the refuse of the wheat") at an excessive price ("making the shekel great") to his unsuspecting or defenseless customers (Amos 8:5-6). In modern times, a large automobile repair shop overcharges an out-of-town customer whose car breaks down on the highway and who is stranded without it.

(3) In ancient Israel, a rich man loaned money to a poor man to pay a debt. When the poor man could not repay it within an allotted period of time, the rich man confiscated the poor man's

possessions and property and sold him into slavery in order to retrieve his money (Amos 2:6-7; 4:1; 5:11). In modern times, a wealthy banker seizes a poor man's home when the poor man is unable to repay the money borrowed from the bank because he has incurred an unexpected hospital debt due to sickness in the family.

(4) In ancient Israel, the prophet Amos announced that the northern kingdom would be overthrown by an enemy army because those in positions of power were taking advantage of the poor and helpless. The king of Israel (Jeroboam II) and the priest of Bethel (Amaziah) accused Amos of conspiring against the land, forbade him to preach at Bethel again, and drove him out of the country (Amos 7:7-17). In modern times, a preacher in a local church speaks out against injustices which whites inflict on blacks and calls on his congregation to follow the teachings of Christ and of the New Testament to break down racial barriers which divide mankind. He is told by the leaders of the congregation that such preaching is not acceptable in this church, and that he must either quit preaching on such "unscriptural matters" (!) and preach only "the gospel," or else he will have to begin looking for another pulpit. Or, a teacher at a church-related college emphasizes that the search for truth is a never-ending task of the Christian, and advocates that church traditions must be abandoned if and when they contradict biblical truth. The school administrators and the head of his department advise him that while his position is sound, they cannot tolerate it or allow the churches to know that they share it for fear that support for the school might suffer. They state that if he persists in teaching such things, he will be asked to submit his resignation, since his position is hurting the reputation of the school.[14]

---

[14]Such unethical "religious" practices place the sincere man of God who has the responsibility of raising a family, serving God, and helping the church grow spiritually in an ethical dilemma. The problem is ably described by Raymond Calkins, "The First and Second Books of Kings," in *The Interpreter's Bible*, ed. G. A. Buttrick, 12 vols. (Nashville: Abingdon Press, 1954) 3: 179-80: "Take the case of a teacher. As such, he is dedicated to the imparting of truth. But the school where he teaches is subjected to certain pressure groups which insist that he shall give a desired color to the content of his teaching. In order to hold his position he gives consideration to pleasing those groups. Thereupon he ceases to be the free agent that Spinoza was when he refused to accept the chair of philosophy at Heidelberg because it might curb his independence of thought. Or consider a minister of the gospel. As a minister, he is ordained to preach the word of God as sincerely as he can know it. But he asks himself, 'What good is it to proclaim God's word if I

Social Justice in the Old Testament

Because God acted mightily in Israel's behalf, he engaged his people in an inescapable encounter with himself which demanded their positive response to his acts. The compassionate nature of his deeds for them offered them no alternative but to act in the same manner toward one another and toward others.[15] Indeed, the Old Testament contains a great deal of teaching on social justice.

(1) *Legal Material.* The three major law codes in the Old Testament (Exod. 20:22—23:33; Lev. 17—26; and the Book of Deuteronomy)[16] and replete with injunctions which are intended to promote social justice. A few examples may be noted.[17] If a master beats a slave to death while punishing him, he must be punished (Exod. 22:20). If he puts out his eye or knocks out his

---

have few to hear it? Am I not the pastor of a congregation, and must I not seek to give my message in such a way that it will win acceptance by my people?' Yet in trying to get his words across, it is so easy to allow his concern for their acceptability to soften the truth! To be a servant of one's parishioners and also a prophet of one's God is no easy task, and unless one is very careful he lets the people he serves put a mortgage on his soul."

[15]Porteous, "Ritual and Righteousness," in *Living the Mystery*, pp. 67-68, expresses this thought admirably when he writes concerning Amos: "To the Hebrew prophet the encounter of man with God was the encounter of person with Person and was a summons to truly ethical behaviour. . . . Ethical behaviour is a consequence of man's becoming fully personal through the realization of his immediate relationship to the will and purpose of God. . . . The encounter with God, just because it is ethically conditioned, does not leave a man in solitude, but is creative of community. . . . When religion is conceived, not as a function of human nature but as the commerce of God with man, then it is inseparable from ethics. . . . When God meets a man He does not allow him to by-pass his neighbour."

[16]In scholarly circles, these groups of legal material are called, respectively, the "Book of the Covenant" (because of the reference to it by this name in Exod. 24:7), the "Holiness Code" (because of the repeated statement "You shall be holy; for I the Lord your God am holy," as in Lev. 19:2; 20:7; 26; etc.) and the "Deuteronomic Code."

[17]For a much fuller treatment see Porteous, "The Care of the Poor," pp. 146-52; G. J. Botterweck, " 'ebyôn," in *Theological Dictionary of the Old Testament*, ed. G. J. Botterweck and H. Ringgren, rev. ed., trans. John T. Willis (Grand Rapids: Eerdmans, 1977) 1:27-41; and Terry Lee Brown, "The Poor in the Legal Literature of the Old Testament" (master's thesis, Abilene Christian College, 1972). The scholarly approach consists of studying each law code separately, noting the similarities and differences among them, and attempting to explain these. The nature and length of this essay, however, prohibits such an approach.

tooth while punishing him, he must set the slave free (Exod. 22:26-27). When a master releases a slave who has served him seven years, he is not to send him away empty-handed, but is to furnish him liberally out of his flock, threshingfloor, and winepress (Deut. 15:13-14). A runaway slave is not to be returned to his master or treated harshly, but is to be allowed to live where he chooses (Deut. 23:15-16). A hired servant, whether he be an Is-raelite or a sojourner, is to be treated kindly and is to be paid on the day that he does his work before the sun goes down (Deut. 24:14-15; Lev. 19:13).

God's people are not to wrong or to oppress a stranger or afflict a widow or an orphan (Exod. 22:21-22; 23:9; Lev. 19:33-34). They must not pervert justice due to the sojourner, orphan or poor man. They are not to take a widow's garment in pledge, make false charges against the innocent, or take bribes and subvert the cause of those who are in the right (Exod. 23:6-8; Deut. 10:18; 19:16-21). The man of God is to love, feed, and clothe orphans, widows, and sojourners (Deut. 10:18).

When a godly man lends money to a poor man, he is not to ex-act interest from him (Exod. 22:25-27; Deut. 23:19-20; Lev. 25:35-38), because the purpose of lending him money is to help relieve his poverty, not to increase it. If a poor man is unable to repay the debt in seven years, the lender is to release him from it (Deut. 15:1-2).

One reason the Israelites are to keep the Sabbath is to give their servants an opportunity to rest from their labors (Exod. 23:12; Deut. 5:12-15). At harvest time farmers are to leave sheaves of barley or wheat in the field, olives on the trees, and grapes on the vines so that widows, orphans, sojourners, and poor might come and find food (Deut. 24:19-22; Lev. 19:9-10; 23:22). Every seventh year, farmers are to leave their fields and orchards fallow to provide food for the needy (Exod. 23:10-11; Lev. 25:2-7).

The Book of Deuteronomy in particular emphasizes the im-portance of treating one's fellowman justly and lovingly. In his special study of this subject, Weinfeld writes:

> The primary aim of the Deuteronomic author is the instruction of the people in humanism. . . . In Deuteronomy the author's primary con-cern is the protection of *man*, and primarily the man whose means of protection are limited.[18]

---

[18]M. Weinfeld, "The Origin of the Humanism in Deuteronomy," *Journal of Bib-lical Literature* 80 (1961): 242-43.

Perhaps one of the strongest statements in the entire Old Testament on social justice appears in Deuteronomy 15:7-11:

> If there is among you a poor man, one of your brethren, in any of your towns within your land which the Lord your God gives you, you shall not harden your heart or shut your hand against your poor brother, but you shall open your hand to him, and lend him sufficient for his need, whatever it may be. Take heed lest there be a base thought in your heart, and you say, 'The seventh year, the year of release is near,' and your eye be hostile to your poor brother, and you give him nothing, and he cry to the Lord against you, and it be sin in you. You shall give him freely, and your heart shall not be grudging when you give to him; because of this the Lord your God will bless you in all your work and in all that you undertake. For the poor will never cease out of the land; therefore I command you, You shall open wide your hand to your brother, to the needy and to the poor, in the land."

Beyond what was said earlier about this passage, verse 7 is most challenging when it suggests that property does not really belong to man, but to the Lord (". . . your land which the Lord your God gives you"). Man is therefore not to use it selfishly, but to help the poor and to supply the needs of others.

Even punishments prescribed for persons guilty of certain crimes are intended to promote social justice. A noteworthy example of this appears in laws calling for punishment of "an eye for an eye and a tooth for a tooth." This is applied to harm brought to a pregnant woman in the course of a fight between two men (Exod. 21:22-23), to a man that disfigures his neighbor (Lev. 24:19-20), and to a legal witness who testifies maliciously against his fellowman with the intention of harming him (Deut. 19:16-21). Admittedly the punishment in the third instance is more severe because of the malicious intent of the offender, but still this punishment

> was not intended to justify private retaliation out of personal spite; but it was designed on the one hand *to insure that those who were guilty of the same offense should not receive punishments of unequal severity* according to the caprice of individual judges, and on the other to fix a limit to the extent of the punishment judicially inflicted.[19]

(2) *Narratives.* Many narratives in the Old Testament betray the author's chagrin at injustices and/or his concern that justice be done.

---

[19]Kennett, "The Contribution of the Old Testament," p. 393, italics mine.

Laban promises to give his daughter Rachel to Jacob if he will work for him seven years, but he gives him Leah instead, and then agrees to give him Rachel only if he will work for him seven additional years (Gen. 29:15-30). When Jacob's flocks and herds prosper and Laban's decline, he exchanges them (Gen. 30:29-43). During the twenty years that Jacob serves Laban, Laban changes his wages tèn times (Gen. 31:41-42).

While Uriah the Hittite is at Rabbah in Ammon fighting for Israel, David takes his wife and commits adultery with her. He then recalls Uriah from the battlefield and tries to get him to go home to his wife, but in vain; then he has Joab put Uriah in the thick of a skirmish at Rabbah and see that he is killed (II Sam. 11:2-17). In due time, Nathan the prophet comes to David and tells him the famous parable of the rich man who fed an unexpected visitor at his home with a poor man's little ewe lamb (II Sam. 12:1-4). David expresses the very heart of Old Testament ethical ideals when he condemns the unjust actions of the rich man (and unknowingly himself) in this manner: "The man who has done this deserves to die; . . . because he did this thing, and because he had no pity" (II Sam. 12:5-6). Note the concern for the inner motivation (pity, compassion) as well as for the overt act.

At the suggestion of Jezebel, Ahab has two men bring charges of crimes punishable by death against the poor farmer Naboth. Ahab desires to procure the vineyard which Naboth refused to sell or trade to the king because it was the family inheritance. The prophet Elijah confronts the king and charges him with doing what is evil in the sight of the Lord (I Kings 21:1-21).

The same Ahab has the prophet Micaiah cast into prison because he refuses to predict that Ahab would defeat the Syrians at Ramoth-gilead, the message which Ahab wanted to hear and which the popular prophets were proclaiming (I Kings 22:1-28).

Elijah provides food for a widow in Zarephath of Phoenicia and brings her only son back to life (I Kings 17:8-24).

Elisha helps a widow of one of the sons of the prophets pay her debts just at the time that her creditors were about to take her two children as slaves because she was unable to meet her obligations (II Kings 4:1-7).

In spite of the fact that Ruth was a Moabitess, Boaz treated her kindly and saw to it that her needs were supplied (Ruth 2:1-16).

Numerous stories such as these occur throughout the Old Testament. It is significant for the purpose of the present study that they all show the deep concern for social justice so prevalent in the Old Testament.

(3) *The Prophets.* The prophetic literature abounds in texts which call for social justice and decry social injustices.[20] Here attention is called to some of the most noteworthy passages.

The prophets of the eighth century B.C. (Amos and Hosea in North Israel and Isaiah and Micah in South Judah) lived in a period of military and economic expansion equal to, if not excelling, Israel's prosperity under Solomon. This provided the kind of atmosphere conducive to all sorts of social injustices, and the prophets cried out against them. Amos denounces the rich and powerful "because they sell the righteous for silver, and the needy for a pair of shoes—they that trample the head of the poor into the dust of the earth, and turn aside the way of the afflicted" (Amos 2:6-7; see also Amos 8:4-6). Amos summons Assyria and Egypt to observe the corruption which had gripped Israel when he cries:

> Assemble yourselves upon the mountains of Samaria,
> and see the great tumults within her,
> and the oppressions in her midst.
> They do not know how to do right, says the Lord,
> those who store up violence and robbery in their
> strongholds (Amos 3:9-10).

He speaks out against the wealthy women of Samaria "who oppress the poor, who crush the needy, who say to their husbands, 'Bring, that we may drink!' " (Amos 4:1). He calls sinners to repentance, saying:

---

[20]The literature on this subject is voluminous. Here mention may be made of H.-J. Kraus, "Die prophetische Botschaft gegen das soziale Unrecht Israels," *Evangelische Theologie* 15 (1955): 295-307; E. Hammershaimb, "On the Ethics of the Old Testament Prophets," *Supplements to Vetus Testamentum* 7 (1960): 75-101; R.B.Y. Scott, *The Relevance of the Prophets*, chap. 8, "The Prophets and the Social Order" (New York: Macmillan, 1968), pp. 171-92; H. Donner, "Die soziale Botschaft der Propheten im Lichte der Gesellschaftsordnung in Israel," *Oriens Antiquus* 2 (1963): 229-45; F. N. Jasper, "Reflections on the Moral Teaching of the Prophets," *Scottish Journal of Theology* 21 (1968): 462-76; Porteous, "The Basis of the Ethical Teaching of the Prophets," in *Living the Mystery*, pp. 47-60; O. H. Steck, "Prophetische Kritik der Gesellschaft," *Christentum und Gesellschaft* (1969): 46-62; G. Fohrer, "Zur Einwirkung der gesellschaftlichen Struktur Israels auf seine Religion," in *Near Eastern Studies in Honor of William Foxwell Albright*, ed. Hans Goedicke (Baltimore: John Hopkins Press, 1971), pp. 169-85; and K. Koch, "Die Entstehung der sozialen Kritik bei den Profeten," in *Probleme biblischer Theologie: Gerhard von Rad zum 70. Geburtstag*. ed. H. W. Wolff (Munich: C. Kaiser, 1970), pp. 236-57.

> Seek the Lord and live . . . ,
> O you who turn justice to wormwood,
>   and cast down righteousness to the earth! (Amos 5:7;
>   see also 6:12).

Against people who feel they can "get away" with all sorts of social crimes, the Lord announces through the prophet:

> I know how many are your transgressions,
>   and how great are your sins—
> you who afflict the righteous, who take a bribe,
>   and turn aside the needy in the gate (Amos 5:12).

The "religious piety" of those who neglected and/or oppressed the poor was disgusting to God, and he exclaims:

> I hate, I despise your feasts,
>   and I take no delight in your solemn assemblies.
> Even though you offer me your burnt offerings and
>   cereal offerings,
>   I will not accept them,
> and the peace offerings of your fatted beasts
>   I will not look upon.
> Take away from me the noise of your songs;
>   to the melody of your harps I will not listen.
> But let justice roll down like waters,
>   and righteousness like an everflowing stream
>   (Amos 5:21-24).

Isaiah of Jerusalem delivers similar oracles. He also reproves those who try to hide their social injustices behind a cloak of worship. After specifically denouncing their empty multitude of sacrifices, regularity of worship, and vanity of prayer (Isa. 1:10-15), he says:

> Wash yourselves; make yourselves clean;
>   remove the evil of your doings from before my eyes;
> cease to do evil,
>   learn to do good;
> seek justice,
>   correct oppression;
> defend the fatherless,
>   plead for the widow (Isa. 1:16-17; see also vv. 21-23).

He declares God's deep concern for the poor:

> The Lord enters into judgment
>   with the elders and princes of his people:

"It is you who have devoured the vineyard,
  the spoil of the poor is in your houses.
What do you mean by crushing my people,
  by grinding the face of the poor?"
    says the Lord God of hosts (Isa. 3:14-15).

Isaiah's famous "Song of the Vineyard" (Isa. 5:1-7) is directed
against the injustice and unrighteousness in Judah (see esp. v. 7).
His "woes" in 5:8-23 are directed primarily against social injustices. Note in particular the final "woe" in this series:

Woe to those who are heroes at drinking wine,
  and valiant men in mixing strong drink,
who acquit the guilty for a bribe,
  and deprive the innocent of his right! (Isa. 5:22-23).

A similar "woe oracle" occurs in Isaiah 10:1-2:

Woe to those who decree iniquitous decrees,
and the writers who keep writing oppression,
to turn aside the needy from justice
  and to rob the poor of my people of their right,
that widows may be their spoil,
  and that they may make the fatherless their prey!

Many such oracles were spoken by Isaiah and by his contemporary
Micah. Perhaps the most pointed oracle by the prophet Micah occurs in Micah 2:1-2:

Woe to those who devise wickedness
and work evil upon their beds!
When the morning dawns, they perform it,
  because it is in the power of their hand.
They covet fields, and seize them;
  and houses, and take them away;
they oppress a man and his house,
  a man and his inheritance (See also 2:8-9;
    3:9-11; 6:9-13; 7:1-6).

The prophets just before, during, and after the Babylonian exile
of Judah (587 B.C.) faced similar circumstances and delivered
similar oracles. Jeremiah cries out:

Wicked men are found among my people;
  they lurk like fowlers lying in wait.
They set a trap;
  they catch men.
Like a basket full of birds,
  their houses are full of treachery;

therefore they have become great and rich,
    they have grown fat and sleek.
They know no bounds in deeds of wickedness;
    they judge not with justice
the cause of the fatherless, to make it prosper,
    and they do not defend the rights of the needy.
Shall I not punish them for these things? says the Lord,
    and shall I not avenge myself
on a nation such as this? (Jer. 5:26-29).

On one occasion, King Jehoiakim forces a group of carpenters and painters to build him a beautiful house in Jerusalem without pay. Jeremiah does not hesitate to rebuke Jehoiakim for such gross injustice, and to shame him for failing to act justly as his father Josiah did:

Woe to him who builds his house by unrighteousness,
and his upper rooms by injustice;
who makes his neighbor serve him for nothing,
and does not give him his wages;
who says, 'I will build myself a great house
    with spacious upper rooms,'
and cuts out windows for it,
    paneling it with cedar,
    and painting it with vermilion.
Do you think you are a king
    because you compete in cedar?
Did not your father eat and drink
    and do justice and righteousness?
    Then it was well with him.
He judged the cause of the poor and needy;
    then it was well.
Is not this to know me? says the Lord,
But you have eyes and heart
    only for your dishonest gain,
for shedding innocent blood
    and for practicing oppression and violence
      (Jer. 22:13-17).

It is noteworthy that Jeremiah declares that one cannot know God without advocating and practicing social justice.

Of the numerous passages on social justice in the Book of Ezekiel, the following is most challenging:

If a man is righteous and does what is lawful and right—if he does not eat upon the mountains or lift up his eyes to the idols of the house of Israel, does not defile his neighbor's wife or approach a woman in the time of her impurity, does not oppress any one, but restores to the debtor his pledge, commits no robbery, gives his bread to the hungry and covers the naked with a garment, does not lend at interest or take any increase, withholds his hand from iniquity, executes true justice between man and man, walks in my statutes, and is careful to observe my ordinances—he is righteous, he shall surely live, says the Lord God (Ezek. 18:5-9).

In other words, Ezekiel *defines* a righteous man as one who promotes and supports social justices of all kinds.

But perhaps one of the most interesting and unique texts in the entire Old Testament dealing with social justice is found in Isaiah 58. Here God's people are attempting to secure the Lord's favor and blessing by fasting. As one begins reading verse 3, he hears the people saying to God:

> Why have we fasted, and thou seest it not?
> Why have we humbled ourselves, and thou takest no
>   knowledge of it?

to which the Lord replies:

> Behold, in the day of your fast you seek your own pleasure,
>   and oppress all your workers.
> Behold, you fast only to quarrel and to fight
>   and to hit with wicked fist.
> Fasting like yours this day
>   will not make your voice to be heard on high.
> Is such the fast that I choose,
>   a day for a man to humble himself?
> Is it to bow down his head like a rush,
>   and to spread sackcloth and ashes under him?
> Will you call this a fast,
>   and a day acceptable to the Lord?
> Is not this the fast that I choose:
>   to loose the bonds of wickedness,
>   to undo the thongs of the yoke,
> to let the oppressed go free,
>   and to break every yoke?
> Is it not to share your bread with the hungry,
>   and to bring the homeless poor into your house;
> when you see the naked, to cover him,
>   and not to hide yourself from your own flesh?
>   (Isa. 58:3-7).

(4) *The Psalms and the Wisdom Literature.* Like the prophetic literature, the psalms and the wisdom literature (especially Job and Proverbs) are replete with warnings against social injustices and exhortations to treat one's fellows righteously. Psalm 37 contains many statements along this line:

> The wicked draw the sword and bend their bows,
>   to bring down the poor and needy,
>   to slay those who walk uprightly;
> their sword shall enter their own heart,
>   and their bows shall be broken (vv. 14-15).

> I have been young, and now am old;
>   yet I have not seen the righteous forsaken
>   or his children begging bread.
> He is ever giving liberally and lending,
>   and his children become a blessing.
> Depart from evil, and do good;
>   so shall you abide for ever.
> For the Lord loves justice;
>   he will not forsake his saints (vv. 25-28).

> The wicked watches the righteous,
>   and seeks to slay him.
> The Lord will not abandon him to his power,
>   or let him be condemned when he is brought to trial
>   (vv. 32-33).

Psalm 41 begins with these words:

> Blessed is he who considers the poor!
> The Lord delivers him in the day of trouble;
> the Lord protects him and keeps him alive;
>   he is called blessed in the land;
>   thou dost not give him up to the will of his enemies
>   (vv. 1-2; see also Ps. 72:1-4, 12-14).

Job's speech of vindication (Job 29—31) reflects a very high ethical standard. For example, he says:

> I delivered the poor who cried,
>   and the fatherless who had none to help him.
> The blessing of him who was about to perish came upon me,
>   and I caused the widow's heart to sing for joy.
> I put on righteousness, and it clothed me;
>   my justice was like a robe and a turban.
> I was eyes to the blind,
>   and feet to the lame.
> I was a father to the poor,
>   and I searched out the cause of him whom I did not know
>   (Job 29:12-16).

Again he declares:

> If I have rejected the cause of my manservant or my maidservant,

when they brought a complaint against me;
what then shall I do when God rises up?
   When he makes inquiry, what shall I answer him?
Did not he who made me in the womb make him?
   And did not one fashion us in the womb?
If I have withheld anything that the poor desired,
   or have caused the eyes of the widow to fail,
or have eaten my morsel alone,
   and the fatherless has not eaten of it
(for from his youth I reared him as a father,
   and from his mother's womb I guided him);
if I have seen any one perish for lack of clothing,
   or a poor man without covering;
if his loins have not blessed me,
   and if he was not warmed with the fleece of my sheep;
if I have raised my hand against the fatherless,
   because I saw help in the gate;
then let my shoulder blade fall from my shoulder,
   and let my arm be broken from its socket (Job 31:13-22).

The Book of Proverbs denounces one who is poor or under-privileged because of his own laziness or unwillingness to accept the responsibility for providing for himself and his family. A familiar text emphasizing this point is Proverbs 6:6-11:

Go to the ant, O sluggard;
   consider her ways, and be wise.
Without having any chief,
   officer or ruler,
she prepares her food in summer,
   and gathers her sustenance in harvest.
How long will you lie there, O sluggard?
   When will you arise from your sleep?
A little sleep, a little slumber,
   a little folding of the hands to rest,
and poverty will come upon you like a vagabond,
   and want like an armed man (See also Prov. 24:30-34;
     10:4; 19:15; 20:4, 13; 26:13-16).

At the same time, the authors of Proverbs recognize that usually one is poor and needy as a result of circumstances beyond his control, and thus they admonish concern for the underprivileged and extol the practice of social justice (reference has already been made to Prov. 14:31; 15:27; and 22:2 above). These statements are characteristic:

He who mocks the poor insults his Maker;
   he who is glad at calamity will not go unpunished (17:5).

He who is kind to the poor lends to the Lord,
and he will repay him for his deed (19:17).

He who despises his neighbor is a sinner,
but happy is he who is kind to the poor (14:21).

He who closes his ear to the cry of the poor
will himself cry out and not be heard (21:13).

(See also 22:16; 23:10-11; 25:8-10; 28:27; 30:14; 31:9; etc.). In the very last paragraph of the Book of Proverbs, the author states that one quality of the good woman is that "She opens her hand to the poor, and reaches out her hands to the needy" (31:20).

The magnitude and unanimity of the teaching in the various portions of the Old Testament (the legal material, the narratives, the prophetic literature, the psalms, and the wisdom literature) on man's responsibility to his fellowman are overwhelming and incontrovertible. The matter of social justice is not peripheral in the Old Testament (or in the New, for that matter), but a vital and indispensable part of "religion." Biblically speaking, it would be unthinkable for a man who professes to love and honor God to deliberately neglect or mistreat one of his fellows. Social justice is central to biblical "religion." For a succinct summation of the Old Testament teaching on social ethics, one could hardly improve on the New Testament text, James 1:27: "The kind of religion which is without stain or fault in the sight of God our Father is this: to go to the help of orphans and widows in their distress and keep oneself untarnished by the world" (NEB).

JAMES W. THOMPSON

3

The Ethics of Jesus and the Early Church

It is doubtful if any society has ever faced a moral dilemma quite as serious as our own. On the one hand, sweeping technological and social changes are confronting us with moral questions which we have not raised before. These moral questions concern the value of human life and of those institutions which have held civilization together. On the other hand, it has been suggested that our society has never had so few resources for facing difficult moral questions. We are living in a moral interregnum where we have challenged many of our traditional sources of moral insight, but we are largely adrift in finding any source of ethical guidance.

What guidance does the New Testament provide in making these ethical decisions? We may wonder if the New Testament has any useful counsel when we try to deal with such questions as abortion and euthanasia. We have reason to ask also if the New Testament, which was written during the period of the authoritarian system of Roman rule, can give moral guidance to those who are involved in the various liberation movements. Thus we are faced with the question: To what degree can we look to the New Testament for guidance or clues for our moral behavior?

When we turn to the New Testament, we discover that it is no easy task to derive an ethic from Jesus and the early church. Indeed, the very word "ethics" is the legacy of the Greek

45

philosophers, for whom ethics was the rational inquiry about human obligations and concepts of right and wrong. Thus if we are to follow the traditional definition of ethics as "the systematic account of our judgments of right and wrong,"[1] we will find that the New Testament is not primarily a book about ethics. Although both Jesus and Paul frequently answered moral questions, they did not, as Aristotle and others had done, produce a complete code of moral behavior. The ethical teachings of Jesus and the early church are exhortations directed to specific audiences and situations. They never attempt to legislate for society at large. Nor do they ever deal with some of our most perplexing issues—political and medical ethics, environmental ethics, abortion and euthanasia.

Nevertheless, the New Testament is concerned with practical morality in everyday affairs. Paul summons his readers to a life that is "worthy of the gospel" (Phil. 1:27). Jesus' parable of the Good Samaritan and the Sermon on the Mount are looked upon as the ethical masterpieces within his moral teaching. He was addressed as "rabbi" (Mark 9:5; 11:21), and was expected to provide answers to some of the ethical questions which were in dispute. He was asked, for instance, about divorce (Mark 10:11ff) and about the propriety of paying taxes (Mark 12:13-17). Thus there is a sense in which the New Testament is a book of ethics.

The Ethical Teachings of Jesus

Many scholars, especially in the previous generation, have attempted to treat Jesus' ethical teachings with esteem while disregarding his theology, as if the ethics were the pearl which could be extracted from the outer shell of Jesus' total message. But the gospels will not permit such a distinction between Jesus' theology and ethics, for the ethical teaching of Jesus is based on his proclamation. This fact is shown when the Gospel of Mark summarizes the proclamation of Jesus (1:15): "The time is fulfilled, and the kingdom of God is at hand; repent, and believe in the gospel." Here ethics are not, as they were in the Greek world, derived from rational considerations. Nor could they be divorced from Jesus' total message. Before Jesus gave the ethical imperative ("repent"), he proclaimed the indicative of God's saving

---

[1]John Dewey and James H. Tufts, *Ethics*, quoted in Victor P. Furnish, *Theology and Ethics in Paul* (Nashville: Abingdon Press, 1968), p. 209.

action. Just as the Ten Commandments are preceded by the announcement of God's saving action ("I am the Lord your God, who brought you out of Egypt," Exod. 20:2), Jesus' ethic is based on the proclamation of God's coming reign. Ethics are thus a response to God's saving acts. God, by intervening and establishing his rule, has created the possibility of a new kind of life.

In Hebrew thought, repentance involved much more than contrition for one's past. The idea suggested a "turning around," a 180-degree turn in one's behavior. Thus Jesus, whose message was a summons to repentance (cf. Luke 13:1-3; Matt. 18:3), called for a totally new lifestyle which involved a new obedience to the will of God.

The Sermon on the Mount

The nature and shape of Jesus' demand for repentance is to be seen in the Sermon on the Mount, the collection of Jesus' ethical teachings brought together in the Gospel of Matthew. The Sermon on the Mount has always presented us with a perplexing problem about the ethical teachings of Jesus. We are amazed by the radical demands which confront us there. Jesus' counsel against anger, lust, oaths, and divorce, as well as his summons to love our enemies and live without anxiety are undoubtedly a problem. Does Jesus really expect this to be a law code for society at large? Or does he even expect his disciples to live by such a rigorous standard? The demand of the Sermon, and especially of 5:21-47 (the antitheses), has forced Christians for generations to ask, How is it possible to live by the Sermon on the Mount?

But the ethical requirement found in the Sermon on the Mount does not stand alone. Before there is the demand, there is the proclamation of the good news of the kingdom.[2] The Sermon on the Mount is, in human terms, an impossible ethic. It is the ideal for life in the kingdom of God. It is because God has intervened to establish his kingdom that Jesus summons his disciples in the Sermon on the Mount to live up to the "better righteousness" (Matt. 5:20, NEB).[3]

---

[2]See J. Jeremias, *The Sermon on the Mount* (Philadelphia: Fortress Press, 1963), pp. 25, 31f.

[3]George Eldon Ladd, *The Presence of the Future* (Grand Rapids: Eerdmans, 1974), p. 288. Ladd quotes Otto Piper ("Kerygma and Discipleship," *Princeton Seminary Bulletin* 56, p. 16): "Understood apart from the fact that God is now establishing his realm here on earth, the Sermon on the Mount would be excessive idealism or pathological, self-destructive fanaticism."

It is not accidental that the beatitudes stand at the opening of the Sermon on the Mount, for the beatitudes are declarative statements pronouncing God's blessing on those who have taken on a certain style of life. The "poor in spirit," the mourners, the meek, and those who hunger and thirst for righteousness' sake will have their misery reversed. Those who are familiar with the Jewish expectations for the new age will recognize that Jesus is announcing the coming of God's blessings in a way that is reminiscent of the prophetic hope expressed in Isaiah 61. In the new age God would bring "good tidings to the poor" (61:1) and would "comfort all who mourn" (61:2). The beatitudes are thus an announcement of the good news of salvation.

But the beatitudes are not only gospel; they are also a demand. They serve as a challenge or summons to the readers to join the ranks of the "blessed" by meeting the requirements implied in these declarations.[4] The good news is a challenge that summons the disciple to radical obedience and a new lifestyle.

This relationship of gospel and law in the beatitudes is implied throughout the Sermon. The Sermon on the Mount calls for a righteousness that "exceeds that of the scribes and the Pharisees" (5:20). To exceed the righteousness of the scribes and Pharisees was no easy task, for the Jewish faith was a religion of ethical obligations. For generations the scribes and Pharisees had struggled to preserve the Jewish identity by handing down an oral tradition (cf. Mark 7:8) that was intended to keep the demands of the written law up to date. Where the written law was not specific or where the change in circumstances rendered the legislation of the Old Testament obsolete, the oral law was used to protect God's commandment; or, in rabbinic terminology, to "put a fence around the Torah" (Pirke Aboth 1:1). This oral law is largely to be found now in the Mishnah, which was finally codified in A.D. 200.

In the Jewish oral tradition one discovers weighty discussions over such questions as, "What is meant by the 'indecency' that serves as a grounds for divorce?" (Deut. 24:1). Or, "When is an oath actually binding?"[5] The purpose of the oral tradition was to delineate all of the rules, complete with the exceptions to the rules by the detailed study of case-by-case examples.[6]

---

[4]See Robert R. Guelich, "The Matthean Beatitudes: 'Entrance Requirements' or Eschatological Blessings?", *Journal of Biblical Literature* 95 (September 1976): 415ff.

[5]See esp. the Mishnah tractates Gittin and Nedarim.

[6]According to the Jewish-Pharisaic document Pirke Aboth ("The Sayings of the

This whole oral tradition is the background for our understanding of the Sermon on the Mount, for the righteousness which exceeds the righteousness of the scribes and Pharisees is absolute and radical. It does not ask for exceptions or qualifications to the rules, for it radicalizes the existing demand. Thus each time Jesus says, "You have heard . . . but I say . . ." he is challenging the entire approach of the Jewish tradition.[7] He does not enter into the exceptions to the rules in a casuistic manner. Where the rabbis discussed the grounds for divorce, Jesus counseled against contemplating divorce. Where the rabbis asked which oaths must be kept, Jesus said, "Swear not at all" (Matt. 5:34). Where they had asked how far the neighbor-love (Lev. 19:18) must extend, Jesus said, "Love your enemies" (Matt. 5:44). The unmistakable new thing in Jesus' ethical teaching was the absoluteness of the demand which elaborated on the nature of life in the kingdom.[8]

The Sermon on the Mount is also unmistakable in the particular way Jesus radicalized the Jewish ideas of ethics. The antitheses describe an ethics of the inner life.[9] The law condemned murder; Jesus condemned anger. The law condemned adultery; Jesus condemned lust. Jesus' demand for non-retaliation and his demand for love of enemies can only be understood as part of his demand for a change of will. Over against Jewish insistence on legal obligations, Jesus said, "For from within, out of the heart of man, come evil thoughts" and other defiling offenses (Mark 7:21).

It would be unfair to suggest that Jewish writings paid no attention to the inner man, for there are excellent examples in Jewish literature of the emphasis placed on the heart (cf. Test.

Fathers"), the oral tradition was handed down at Sinai, from which it passed on to the men of the Great Synagogue.

[7]David Daube, *The New Testament and Rabbinic Judaism* (London: Athlone Press, 1956), pp. 55-62, has helped us understand the form of these antitheses. The first part of the antithesis ("You have heard") meant, "You have understood the meaning of the law to have been." In the second part ("but I say"), Jesus is giving a new interpretation of the law. See also W. D. Davies, *The Setting of the Sermon on the Mount* (Cambridge: At the University Press, 1964), p. 101.

[8]Ladd, p. 290, says that the Sermon on the Mount "portrays the ideal of the man in whose life the reign of God is absolutely realized." This righteousness "can be perfectly experienced only in the eschatological kingdom of God. It can nevertheless to a real degree be attained in the present age, insofar as the reign of God is actually experienced."

[9]Ibid., p. 292.

Gal 6:3; Test. Benj. 8:2). Nevertheless, a casual reading of the Mishnah makes it clear that the focus of rabbinic ethics was on outward activity.[10] Jesus rejected the Jewish oral tradition and called for a repentance that changed the will. The demand is predicated on God's gift, the coming of the kingdom.

As an epitome of Jesus' ethics, the Sermon on the Mount shows how radically Jesus challenged the culture of his day. The Pharisees had originated at a time when the continued existence of the Jews as a separate people was in jeopardy. In the second century B.C., a considerable segment of the Jewish people had come under the cultural domination of the Greeks and were in the process of becoming assimilated to the larger society. It was the Pharisees, with their oral tradition designed to preserve the purity of the Jewish people, who came forth with the strict laws which were aimed at preserving Jewish identity. But Jesus challenged the oral tradition that was intended to preserve Jewish purity and culture, both in the Sermon on the Mount and elsewhere (Mark 7:1-15).

Jesus As the Friend of Sinners

This challenge to Jewish culture was nowhere more evident than in Jesus' frequent table fellowship with sinners. At the heart of Jewish identity was the sense of being "holy" or separate, in accordance with the demand of Leviticus 19:18 to "be holy" as God is holy. Thus the Pharisee's oral tradition was designed to protect him from people or things that were impure. His table fellowship was to be shared only with others who were pure, for to associate with those who did not keep the law would bring impurity on oneself.[11]

Against this background, we can understand the dismay of the Pharisees when they noticed that Jesus regularly brought impurity on himself by associating with sinners. He lodged openly with them (Luke 19:5) and called them into discipleship (Mark 2:14). Indeed his regular table fellowship was so much a part of his normal pattern of behavior that his enemies were saying, "Behold a glutton and a drunkard, a friend of tax collectors and sinners" (Matt. 11:19).

---

[10]Ibid., p. 293.

[11]J. Jeremias, *New Testament Theology* (New York: Charles Scribner's Sons, 1971), p. 118.

There is no record of a Jewish rabbi who was as open in his acceptance of sinners as was Jesus.[12] But this table fellowship was more than a mere social convention. It was a part of Jesus' proclamation of the kingdom, a demonstration that God accepts sinners even before they have proven the seriousness of their repentance. The story of the prodigal son aptly describes Jesus' mission. The father in the story was eager to have a party in honor of his wayward son long before the son demonstrated his repentance. The story was thus a defense of Jesus' practice of eating with sinners. His table fellowship was at the same time an announcement of the good news of the kingdom and a summons to repentance. As Jesus said, "I came not to call the righteous, but sinners" (Mark 2:17).

The Shape of Repentance

If the coming of the kingdom brought with it the possibility of a changed life, what was the shape of this new lifestyle? What difference did Jesus and the kingdom make in the moral life? We have already noticed in the beatitudes that Jesus challenged his disciples to a lifestyle which was far removed from the culture of that day—or ours. Disciples were to be "poor in spirit," "meek," and "those who mourn." That is, it was a style of life that had no place for self-seeking and egoism. Those who are called "blessed" are not the power-hungry or the self-serving. The new life had a definite shape which challenged normal cultural values.

We can recognize this shape of discipleship in Jesus' exhortations to his disciples. As we read the Gospels, we frequently discover the disciples caught up in the world's values. They want the best positions of power (Mark 10:35ff.), and they argue over the question of greatness (Mark 9:33ff.). But Jesus confronts his disciples with a totally new direction in life. The distinctive summons of Jesus, "Follow me," was a call to a new lifestyle in which the disciples rejected common cultural values and adopted the lifestyle of the Master.[13] Jesus redefined the concept of service (*diakonia*), the word for the menial task of waiting on tables, and summoned his disciples to adopt his style of active service (Luke 22:26; Mark 10:44-45). In the Gospel of John the action of foot-

---

[12]Ibid., p. 121.

[13]Eric Osborn, *Ethical Patterns in Early Christian Thought* (Cambridge: At the University Press, 1976), pp. 21-23.

washing is given as an example of active service initiated by Jesus Christ (John 13:15, 34).[14] Thus there is a definite shape to the life of discipleship that is involved in Jesus' call to repentance. The disciple is freed from excessive self-concern. He is called to adopt the life of service which conforms to the model of Jesus.

This shape of discipleship is further to be seen in Jesus' love commandment which permeates the Gospels. Before Jesus, the rabbis had said that the law could be summarized in the command, "Thou shalt love thy neighbor as thyself" (Lev. 19:18). But Jesus was the first, so far as we know, to bring the commands to love God (Deut. 6:4, "Thou shalt love the Lord thy God . . .") and our neighbor (Lev. 19:18, "Thou shalt love thy neighbor") into an indissoluble unity. That is, there is no discipleship which consists of "the retreat of the soul into a paradise of spirituality."[15] We cannot love God without also loving those children whom He loves. No one is allowed to come to worship without being reconciled to his neighbor (Matt. 5:23ff.). The pious Pharisee who devours widows' houses stands condemned (Mark 12:40). In good prophetic tradition, Jesus summons his disciples to practice their religion by being actively involved in the needs of others.

The scribe who asked, in response to Jesus' announcement of the love commandment, "Who is my neighbor?" (Luke 10:29) asked a very appropriate question. How far did the love command of Leviticus extend? In Jewish tradition, the "neighbor" was the kinsman, in contrast to the foreigner.[16] The command to love one's neighbor was interpreted as license to hate one's enemy (cf. Matt. 5:43ff.).

What is shocking is the absolutely revolutionary interpretation Jesus gives to the love command. The neighbor of the story was a hated Samaritan who behaved as no one ever behaved. According to Jesus, the "neighbor" is not only one's fellow countryman. It is even the hated foreigner! And love is not only the uttering of pious prayers. It involves providing money, ambulance service, and one's own time and energy. Or, as in the parable of the sheep and goats, it involves caring for the hungry and thirsty, and visiting the sick and the imprisoned. The story suggests much about the disciple's lifestyle. Life under God's reign opens up the possibility for genuine love.

---

[14]Ibid., p. 21ff.

[15]G. Bornkamm, *Jesus of Nazareth* (New York: Harper & Row, 1960), p. 111.

[16]Ibid., p. 112.

This style of discipleship is also obvious in the radical reinterpretation of the love commandment found in Matthew 5:43-48. The new situation under God's reign even allows us to love our enemies. That is, as the Samaritan demonstrated, there are no limits to neighbor love. Contemporaries of Jesus were in fact calling for the hatred of foreigners.[17] But Jesus demands a discipleship with a radical new attitude.

It is important to notice, as H. D. Wendland has observed, that no question is ever asked about the value of the one who is loved.[18] We are not called to love because of the productivity or the innate goodness of the other. Love is directed even toward "the least of these my brethren" (Matt. 25:40).

The Early Church and Paul

On the surface, there seems to be a considerable difference between the ethical teaching of Jesus and that which is reflected in the literature of the early church. Issues which were central in the teaching of Jesus are no longer of paramount concern in the new situation. The missionary labors of the earliest Christians have caused new ethical problems to surface. Thus we discover in many of the Epistles in the New Testament a common pattern of ethical advice. Readers are told to "put off" old vices and to "put on" new characteristics.[19] We frequently discover ethical lists which include tables of duties for Christian converts.[20]

This common pattern of ethical advice suggests that, from the earliest days, there was something like a baptismal catechism for

---

[17]Victor P. Furnish, *The Love Command in the New Testament* (Nashville: Abingdon Press, 1972), p. 46. The most prominent example is in the Qumran scroll 1 QS 1:9-10, where the members of the community are told to "love all the sons of light, each according to his lot among the council of God, but to hate all the sons of darkness, each according to his guilt in the vengeance of God."

[18]H. D. Wendland, *Ethik des Neuen Testaments*, Das Neue Testament Deutsch Ergänzungsreihe 4 (Göttingen: Vandenhoeck & Ruprecht, 1970), p. 15.

[19]For the language of "putting off" and "putting on" see Rom. 13:12; Eph. 4:24; Col. 3:10; Col. 3:8; Eph. 4:22, 25.

[20]See O. J. F. Seitz, "Lists, Ethical," in *The Interpreter's Dictionary of the Bible*, ed. George Buttrick, 4 vols. (Nashville: Abingdon Press, 1962) 3:138. See, for instance, the "household codes," or *Haustafeln* in Col. 3:18—4:1; Eph. 5:22—6:9; I Peter 2:18—3:7. For lists of vices and virtues, see Gal. 5:19-22; I Cor. 6:9; Col. 3:5-9; Eph. 5:3-8.

new converts.[21] They were being told that Christ makes a difference in the moral life. Christianity was not like one of the mystery religions which made no moral demands on the initiate.
New Christians were taught that there was a definite shape to the
life in Jesus Christ. Baptism was the beginning of "newness of
life."

There is, nevertheless, a continuity between Jesus and the early
church that cannot be overlooked. The early church was careful to
preserve Jesus' words on important moral issues. Jesus' teachings
on divorce, chastity, and the love commandment were maintained. The newness of the ethical advice which we find in the
teachings of Paul reflects not an abrupt break from the legacy of
Jesus, but the early church's attempt to face new issues with the
moral insights which they had learned from Jesus.

While there is much that is new in the ethical teaching of Paul,
there are points of contact between Paul and Jesus. Paul follows
Jesus in not laying down legislation for the whole society. And,
like Jesus, he describes a lifestyle that is an appropriate response
to what God has done. It has often been observed that Paul's
Epistles are normally divided into two sections—the doctrinal and
the paraenetic. The paraenetic, or practical, section frequently
follows the transitional "therefore" (cf. Rom. 12:1). Thus for Paul,
as for Jesus, the ethical life is a response to the good news. As
Paul says in Romans 12:1, "I appeal to you by the mercies of
God." Indeed, Paul agrees with Jesus that the ethical life is a *new
possibility* because of the coming of the good news. God's righteousness is the power that has invaded our lives and restored us
to a right relationship with Him (Rom. 1:17; 3:21-24). But it is
more. God's righteousness enables us to become ethical beings.[22]
There is an inseparable connection between the power and the
gift, so that the Lord who calls man to serve enables him to perform the service.[23] The new life includes becoming a "servant of
righteousness" (Rom. 6:18). That is, the Christian is called on to

---

[21]This suggestion was made by Philip Carrington in *The Primitive Christian
Catechism* (Cambridge: At the University Press, 1940), and is widely accepted by
biblical scholars. The new Christian, coming from a pagan background, was made
aware of the ethical significance of his baptism and the moral nature of the new
life into which he was entering. Thus the ethical instructions listing vices to be
"put off" and virtues to "put on" would have been appropriate at baptism.

[22]Osborn, p. 17.

[23]E. Kasemann, *New Testament Questions of Today* (Philadelphia: Fortress Press,
1969), p. 174.

"become in his moral life what God has already made him through Jesus Christ.[24]

How is this "newness of life" concretely manifest in the life of the Christian? We notice, in the first place, Paul's insistence that Christ makes a difference in the moral life. Paul insists that the Christian's calling sets him in conflict with his culture. He encourages the Romans, "Do not be conformed to this world but be transformed by the renewal of your mind" (Rom. 12:2). The Christian is one who is "formed" or "shaped" by the Christian story, which gives him a critical distance from normal cultural values. The Christian's whole life becomes a "spiritual worship" in which he presents his body to the Lord as a living sacrifice (Rom. 12:1).

The Shape of the New Life

Nowhere is the Christian's distance from culture more apparent than in sexual ethics. Sex for the Greeks had been a trivial matter of the flesh, much like food (cf. I Cor. 6:13), and thus did not concern the real "self." But for Paul, it is the body which is to be presented to the Lord (Rom. 12:1). Consequently, Paul consistently calls on Christians not to allow their bodies to be controlled by their passions (Rom. 6:12ff; I Cor. 6:9ff; Gal. 5:19ff.). They are, instead, to learn to take a wife "in holiness and honor" (I Thess. 4:4). Over against the decadence of Gentile morality, which is described in Romans 1:18-32, Paul is true to his Jewish heritage in calling new Christians to recognize that the body is not irrelevant to their service to God. It is "the temple of the Holy Spirit" (I Cor. 6:19). His ethical advice to new Christians appears uniformly to contain advice about sexual conduct,[25] for it was assumed that pagans practiced no sexual discipline. The new insight of the Christian ethic was that we may "glorify God in our bodies" (I Cor. 6:20).

This new shape of Christian morality which is at variance with culture is also to be seen in the distinctive way in which Paul calls for a community ethic. Greek ethics had been largely individualistic. The Greek cardinal virtues—wisdom, temperance, courage, and justice—were directed toward individual self-improvement. But for Paul the accent has shifted to the com-

---

[24]G. Bornkamm, *Paul* (New York: Harper & Row, 1969), p. 202.

[25]See Rom. 6:12ff; Gal. 5:19 ("The works of the flesh are manifest, which are immorality, impurity, licentiousness . . ."); I Cor. 6:9; Eph. 5:3; Col. 3:5.

munity. To be a Christian is to live within the corporate body
(I Cor. 12:4ff.) A moral infection in the church can be like a little
leaven which "leavens the whole lump" (I Cor. 5:6). He calls on
believers to "mind the same thing" (Rom. 15:5; Phil. 2:2; 4:2). The
vices against which Paul warns are (with the exception of the sexual vices) antisocial in nature.[26] He encourages readers to
develop qualities that were not highly treasured in the Greek
world—"patience" (*makrothumia*) and "lowliness" (*tapeinophro-
sunē*).[27] Indeed, so strongly community-oriented is Paul's ethic
that he recommends that his readers "be wronged" rather than
insist on their own rights in a law court (I Cor. 6:7).

This emphasis on a community ethic is especially apparent in
Paul's thorough description of the life of "spiritual worship"
which is described in the ethical section of Romans (chaps. 12—15).
Paul does not call on individuals to develop virtues after the fashion of a Greek philosopher. Instead, he calls on them, as members of the corporate body "not to think more highly of
themselves than they ought to think" (Rom. 12:3; cf. Phil. 2:3).
This advice is apparently the key to the moral life as envisioned
by Paul, for he proceeds to describe a lifestyle for a community. It
involves genuine love (*agapē*, Rom. 12:9), honor towards fellow
members of the community (Rom. 12:10), responsibility for the
financial needs of others, hospitality (Rom. 12:13), and the practice of non-resistance to others (Rom. 12:17-21).

Paul's consistent emphasis on a lifestyle free from the egoism
that destroys a community is the background for understanding
his emphasis on submission. It has long been observed that subjection is an important aspect of the Pauline ethic. Paul insists
that wives be subject to their husbands (Col. 3:18), and that
women in church be subject (I Cor. 14:34). In addition, Christians
are to be subject to the ruling authorities (Rom. 13:1). This emphasis on submission is not evidence that Paul was merely being
conservative with regard to the institutions of his day. It indicates
instead that submission has become a positive value for Paul, a
lifestyle for people who are not always insisting on their own
rights. Indeed, subjection is an obligation for the entire com-

---

[26]The antisocial vices in Gal. 5:20 are enmity, strife, jealousy, anger, selfishness,
dissension, party spirit, and envy. Cf. Phil. 2:3, "Do nothing from selfishness, or
conceit. . . ."

[27]For the New Testament insistence on these qualities, see Gal. 5:22; Eph. 4:2;
Phil. 2:3; 3:12; Col. 3:12. See Furnish, *Theology and Ethics in Paul*, pp. 85-87; R.
Bultmann, *Theology of the New Testament* (London: SCM, 1955) 2:22.

munity, and not only for those who are considered inferior. As Paul says, "I urge you to be subject to such men and to every fellow worker" (I Cor. 16:16). We may compare the words of Ephesians: "Be subject to each other out of reverence for Christ" (Eph. 5:21). One does not insist on his own rights, for he has learned to consider the welfare of others.

Many people have been disturbed by the apparent onesidedness of the household codes, where subjection is demanded for wives, children, and slaves—those who were considered inferior—but not for husbands, parents, and masters. John Howard Yoder has shown, however, that the most striking aspect of the household codes is their reciprocal nature.[28] In the Greek household codes, those who were in the superior position had rights, while those who were in the inferior position had responsibilities. However, in the New Testament household codes the obligations are reciprocal. Husbands are obligated to love their wives; fathers are told not to "provoke" their children; and masters are told to recall that they have a Master in heaven. At the same time, those who were in the socially inferior position are addressed in the New Testament as responsible people. Thus we may say that everyone in the community had a responsibility for others. Such reciprocal responsibilities indicate that Paul's community ethic was capable of breaking down human barriers and creating a new social integration within the church.

This ethic of responsibility for others—or subjection—was the crucial point in Paul's doctrine of freedom. Many of Paul's original listeners apparently misunderstood his doctrine of freedom and thought of it as a freedom from restraint. Indeed, Paul's advice to slaves and women may reflect a situation where freedom was understood as the release from all controls. Over against this view, Paul calls for a new definition of freedom. Freedom is neither freedom from responsibility nor the absence of restraint. Freedom is expressed in loving service to others (Gal. 5:13). It considers not only one's rights; it is concerned also with the edification of the community (I Cor. 8:1). As Paul says, "For being free from all men, I became a slave to all" (I Cor. 9:19). Thus for Paul, even freedom is characterized by submission to others.

Paul's ethic of submission would have been considered absurd

---

[28]John Howard Yoder, *The Politics of Jesus* (Grand Rapids: Eerdmans, 1972), p. 171.

among most Greeks, for whom humility was linked with adjectives like ignoble, slavish, downcast, and low.[29] Paul's emphasis had its roots in the Christian story of the cross, for Jesus had become the great example of submission. Thus when Paul summons his readers to look to the interests of others, he recalls the one who "emptied himself" (Phil. 2:7). When Christians insist on their rights at the expense of others, Paul reminds them that the weaker brother is one "for whom Christ died" (Rom. 14:15; I Cor. 8:11). Thus the cross gave the church a new way of looking at others and a new source of moral insight. It reminded them of the concrete meaning of love and the value of human life. Every person was one "for whom Christ died."

The Relevance of New Testament Ethics

Are the ethics of Jesus and the early church helpful in providing moral insight for the decisions we face today? Indeed, although the ethical advice of the New Testament was directed to an ancient culture, it still shapes our values long before we are faced with a concrete ethical decision. The relevance of the biblical ethic is not merely to be seen as a matter of looking to the Bible for an appropriate verse for every ethical dilemma. Rather, the reading of Scripture affects what sort of persons we are. Thus it is appropriate to read not only the legal sections of the Bible for ethical insight, but the entire drama as well.[30] We may find insights about race relations from the experience of the early church as it broke down ethnic barriers to form the one community. We may find insights about world hunger when we observe the compassion of Jesus toward those who were hungry. The psalms may be a source of insight as we develop an ethic of the environment. Thus the reading of Scripture may give us, in the words of James Gustafson, a disposition, a posture and an intention that will help us in making ethical decisions.[31] This "renewal of our minds" (cf. Rom. 12:1-2) provides us with the character that allows us to make difficult decisions which may be at variance with common cultural values.

---

[29]Osborn, p. 32.

[30]See Bruce Birch and Larry Rassmussen, *Bible and Ethics in the Christian Life* (Minneapolis: Augsburg, 1976), pp. 161-94, for ways of making biblical resources available for ethics.

[31]James Gustafson, *Christ and the Moral Life* (New York: Harper & Row, 1968), pp. 238-71.

We are, for instance, faced with questions dealing with the value of human life in our dilemma over abortion, euthanasia, and genetic engineering. We are asked to determine which lives are valuable and worthy of protection. Jesus' radical interpretation of the love command and Paul's doctrine of the cross remind us that the value of human life does not depend on its function or its productivity. All human life stands under God's care—even that which is, in our terms, useless.

A society which is caught up in the egoism of a "have it your way" ethic which divides communities over conflicting rights can learn much from Paul's doctrine of freedom. Paul's doctrine of freedom, instead of separating groups from each other, will teach us to consider the interests of others, and thus bring people together.

Undoubtedly many other ethical issues will present us with new decisions which will challenge us to look for moral insight. The Bible does provide moral insight by shaping our values and forming Christian character. Those who have been shaped by the biblical story will find resources for dealing with complex issues.

PAUL B. HENRY

4

Christian Perspectives on Power Politics

There has been a great deal of attention paid to the evangelical community's renewed concern with social issues. Yet, in the midst of the social awakening of American evangelicalism, it is already becoming clear that there is a great deal of inconsistency and incoherence within the evangelical community when it comes to addressing social issues.

No doubt the very diversity of evangelicalism contributes to the kaleidoscopic character of evangelical social ethics. The "confessional" wing of evangelicalism, rooted in classical Calvinism and Lutheranism, approaches questions relative to the relationship of church and society quite differently than does the "free church" wing of evangelicalism. The unique flavor of "American fundamentalist" evangelicalism contrasts sharply with the "mainline" evangelicals to be found in denominations such as the Episcopal Church.

This diversity within evangelical Protestantism is one of its strengths—and at the same time one of its weaknesses. In seeking to establish what evangelicalism stands for theologically, one can refer to evangelicalism as a broad community of Christians concerned with maintaining theological orthodoxy in the larger Christian community. But when it comes to establishing what the relationship between that theological orthodoxy and the social concerns of contemporary civilization may be, the diversity of opinion and response from the evangelical community is so overwhelming and contradictory that it has dissipated its capacity for social influence. When a movement stands for everything, it effectively stands for nothing. Such, I believe, is the present situation of evangelicalism with respect to the great social issues of today.

While this broad generalization is true relative to evangelicalism and social ethics in general, it is particularly true when dealing with questions of politics. This failure on behalf of the evangelical community is a devastating indictment of its self-professed capacity to restore integrity and vitality to the nation's political system. It is particularly tragic given the fact that our world is one in which seemingly all questions relative to life and death have become politicized. And it calls into question the sincerity of evangelical claims to being a "world and life view" addressing the total human condition. Large segments of evangelicalism have supported the cross-breeding of the cross and the flag, thereby compromising evangelicalism's ability to offer prophetic judgment on acts of state. Other segments of evangelicalism have defined Christian discipleship so radically as to effectively remove Christian presence from affairs of state, and in the name of "radical discipleship" have fostered a new movement of withdrawal from the world in the hope of establishing model Christian communities separated from the ambiguities of moral choice which face those who seek to live within, so they may witness to, the secular world.

It is true that evangelical Protestantism's failures to deal adequately with social and political questions have protected it against other failures. The apoliticism of a large segment of evangelicalism has protected it from the errors of Protestant liberalism which too simply equated the kingdom of God with the cause of social democracy. The sectarian and institutional pluralism of evangelicalism has protected it from forming a political party seeking to engineer a "Christian politics." And the individualistic pietism of evangelicalism has protected it from seeking to link the gospel to political particulars without appreciation for the finitude and relativities of political decision-making. But the "virtues" of evangelicalism in this regard are not grounds for pride. It must simply be recognized that our sins and shortcomings have been of a different character than those of liberal Protestantism. Our job is not to determine which is the greatest of sinners, but continued repentance and renewal in the quest for mature Christian discipleship.

Political Ethics Juxtaposed to Social Ethics

Why has evangelicalism failed to deal with *political* questions adequately? One of the chief reasons, I believe, is the failure of the evangelical community to take seriously the unique feature of politics as a phenomenon to be distinguished from other social questions by its peculiar relationship to the possession and use of power. For all of the renewed concern within evangelicalism relative to questions of race, economic justice, world hunger, ecology, sex, violence, war, and other pressing social issues, there is little meaningful discussion of the moral questions facing the use of the state as the instrument by which many of these questions will be settled.

Evangelicals are prone to talk about "changing hearts to change behavior"—but what happens when hearts are not changed? Under what circumstances and conditions ought the state to use its power to seek ends which the community will not voluntarily pursue? And what means are appropriate to the use of the power of the state?

In the nineteenth century, Karl von Clausewitz defined war as "politics by other means." He might just as well have defined politics as "war by other means." For the very essence of politics is the use of power--the power to determine who in a given society gets what, how, when, and where. The political system is nothing less (although hopefully something more) than the institutionalized means a society employs to resolve questions incapable of being resolved voluntarily without the use of the sword. When Jimmy Carter spoke of a government "which is as loving as its people," he should have been reminded that government acts not as an agent of love, but as a final resort to force when love, compassion, and voluntarism have failed.

We have grown accustomed to moralizing about our government to such an extent that we forget that at the bottom line, government holds institutionally legitimatized rights to use the sword to effectively carry out its decisions. Struggles over control of the government and the policies of a government are, therefore, struggles over the right to use the power of the sword.

Such talk sounds distasteful to many Christians. It is for that reason that they seemingly do anything they can to escape facing the *political* significance of social questions. For the significance of politics is the significance of power. Paul Tillich referred to the moralizing so common in the Christian community when he wrote:

> One speaks of "power politics," and one often does so with moral indignation. But this is the consequence of mere confusion. Politics and power politics are one and the same thing. There are no politics without power, neither in a democracy nor in a dictatorship.[1]

If we fail to deal with the issue of power, we fail to distinguish between the state and other social institutions such as the family, the church, and voluntary associations. As Karl Lowenstein states:

> The basic urges that dominate man's life in society and govern the allness of human relations are threefold: love, faith, and power. . . . Of this triad of societal motivations, power, while operative in all human relations, is of paramount significance for the socio-political realm. Politics is nothing else but the struggle for power.[2]

Or again, in the words of sociologist Robert Strausz-Hupé:

> To explore the nature of politics is to encounter the enigma of power. Power is the staff of orderly government. Without the exercise of power, political order could neither be established nor maintained. Power guards society against anarchy. Yet power spawns tyranny and violence, corrupts the mighty and crushes freedom.[3]

I emphasize the power relationships in politics for the simple reason that evangelicals generally tend to shy away from facing the brutal reality that power is at the essence of the political relationship. When evangelicals speak of restoring broken relationships through renewed God-man and man-man reconciliation, they are speaking of social realities which will affect the context in which politics operates. But they are not dealing with politics. When evangelicals speak of demonstrating love and compassion to the poor, the downtrodden, and the oppressed, they are speaking of changing relationships within our society which will have a profound impact on the quality and character of our social existence. But unless and until they speak explicitly of what role the state should take in reordering and reforming relationships between white and black, rich and poor, or young and old, they are not speaking of politics proper.

---

[1]Paul Tillich, *Love, Power, and Justice* (New York: Oxford University Press, 1954), p. 8.

[2]Karl Lowenstein, *Political Power and the Governmental Process*, (Chicago: University of Chicago Press, 1957), p. 3.

[3]Robert Strausz-Hupé, *Power and Community*, (New York: Praeger, 1956), p. 3.

Politics As Allocation of Resources

The resources on our planet are limited. The people on our planet hold differing views as to how those resources should be distributed. And not surprisingly, given the fall of man, individuals are prone to support allocation of those resources in such a way that the distribution formula is personally advantageous. Hence, conflict over resources and their distribution is an integral part of human existence.

Because this situation, left alone, is anarchic and inherently unstable, societies generally find it to their advantage to designate an agent to settle disputes concerning the distribution of those resources. This agent, of course, is the state. And the interrelationships and activities surrounding the decision-making authority of the state are what politics is all about. Indeed, the most commonly accepted definition of politics used by political scientists is the following: *"Politics is the authoritative allocation of values and resources for all society."*[4]

Implied in that definition are several concepts which must be looked at carefully if we are going to discuss meaningful Christian concerns relative to the political order. First, let us note that politics is an "allocative" activity. It is engaged in the process of decision-making which rewards and penalizes members of society through the distribution of a society's fixed resources. There is no such thing as a political decision which affects all members of a society equally. Some decisions will be of benefit to the masses at the expense of the few. Other decisions will be of benefit to the few at the expense of the masses. Still other decisions may well be of benefit to everybody, but they will benefit some people relatively more than others. There is no such thing as a political decision which makes all members of society equally happy—for every political decision re-allocates the fixed resources of a society among its members.

Recognition of this fact means that when Christians address political questions, they must be extremely careful to acknowledge that while they may seek to help some through political decision-making, they necessarily implicate themselves

---

[4]This definition, or variants thereof, is derived from David Easton's *The Political System* (New York: Alfred A. Knopf, 1953). Easton was one of the first political scientists to introduce systems theory to the discipline of political science.

in hurting others. It also indicates that all political questions are at least in some way economic questions. Politics necessarily becomes involved in questions of "distributive justice." (This must be noted since several prominent evangelical spokesmen, articulating conservative political philosophy, have suggested that the state should limit its concerns to questions of "retributive justice"—that is, should be solely concerned with protecting order and the execution of freely negotiated contracts. While I would not wish to question the concept of limited government which such a position seeks to protect, I would point out that such a policy does affect distributive justice simply because it seeks to protect the rules which have sustained the present allocation of resources in a society. Hence, it by default assumes that present patterns of distributive justice are consistent with Christian concerns.)

Politics As Allocation of Values

Second, let us note that our definition of politics points out that political decision-making allocates not only resources, but "values." What is meant here is that the distribution of resources reflects value judgments concerning what is or is not a "just" allocative formula within a society. In other words, political decision-making is never "value-free."

A "conservative" who opposes a certain change in government policy operates on the assumption that change would be for the worse. A "liberal" who supports change in government policy operates on the assumption that change would be for the better. Of course, what must be remembered is that the points of view taken by the conservative or the liberal are strongly influenced by the relative effect given policies have on his or her own well-being. In other words, we must recognize that what appears to be good or bad, in terms of political decision-making, is strongly influenced by our own calculations of self-interest.

This is not to say that individuals are incapable of transcending their own self-interest for the well-being of the community at large. Were this the case, politics would be nothing more than a struggle between competing private interests. It would reduce itself to a power struggle in which people sought power and influence simply and solely on the basis of private greed.

Though mankind is prone to maximize his self-interest at the expense of others, he also has the capacity to transcend self-interest for the good of the community. Mankind is driven not only by selfish egoism, but by his inherent nature as a social animal which mitigates and questions his predisposition to seek only personal well-being. Thus, while mankind has a prediliction toward favoring his self-interest, he has an abiding capacity for altruistic concern of his neighbor's interest.

Politics thus operates amid the conflicts of self-interest and the conflicts within individuals and groups relative to private interest versus public interest. Thus, politics is always a struggle over moral decision-making which affects the allocation of resources in a society. The distribution of resources reflects moral assumptions inherent in the political choices being made.

Further, these moral choices are made in the context of mankind's acknowledgment that he is a being with moral responsibility. The entire concept of constitutionalism (or limited government) implies acknowledgment that government itself operates under moral constraint.

One of the chief opportunities for Christian witness in the political order is the constant call to recognize the moral implications of political decision-making. Since all political decisions allocating the fixed resources of a society rest upon value judgments of what is "in the best interest of all" or "in the interest of certain groups or individuals" (always at the expense of other interests), the clear articulation of Christian principles affects the context out of which final political decisions are made.

Thus, when the Christian community speaks forcefully about concerns relative to racism, sexism, world hunger, environmental limitations, war, and so forth, it is effecting a political role—insofar as it shapes the civic culture and the public philosophy which informs the moral assumptions of public policy. The Christian community, through its recognition of God's call to justice in society, affects the social context from which political decisions are made.

While this is an extremely important role for the church in any given society, it must be emphasized that it is not a complete political strategy. While the values of a society underlie and influence political choice and decision-making, and while politics is therefore never morally neutral or amoral, this role does not completely fulfill the church's political responsibility.

To simply acknowledge that resource allocation (the final political decision) reflects value allocation (the moral assumptions which underlie and sustain resource allocation) is not enough. For it is those very resource allocations which define in substance the values to which we subscribe. Conscience, in matters of state, necessarily involves very difficult "weighing of moral choices" in which values compete and in which complex choices concerning the prudential application of values must be made. To say that the church must call the state to be conscious of world hunger is not enough. For if we simply insist that America's surplus wheat should be shipped to starving nations (rather than dumped in the ocean as it was in the 1950s to keep domestic prices high and give the farmer an equitable return on his investment), we risk destroying the economies of those nations which are dependent on grain exports for their own economic (and political) stability.

Let me elaborate on this example for purposes of discussion. If the United States would encourage maximum wheat production by raising price-support guarantees for wheat farmers, removing lands presently reserved from production by means of "soil bank" programs, etc., and then ship our "surplus" grains to China, the USSR, and third world countries, we would seriously disrupt the Canadian economy, which relies on its grain exports. The disruption of the Canadian economy would seriously disrupt our export of industrial goods to Canada (our largest trading partner) which in turn could cause severe unemployment in our own country. The loss of government revenues through decreased economic output and increased welfare benefits would create not only serious domestic political unrest, but would threaten the government's ability to "guarantee" price supports for the grain producers. Hence, the moral-sounding appeal to develop a government food policy to feed the world's hungry, if not properly designed in particulars, may have devastating moral effects which outweigh the well-intended policies advocated by those concerned with world hunger.

The situation is more complicated when we recall that during the 1970s, the United States shipped enough food to the famine-struck countries of Ethiopia and Bangladesh to completely absolve the hunger in those countries. But the receiving countries themselves were so corrupt and inept in their distribution of the food that substantial famine relief did not take place. Thus, questions must be raised as to whether we should seek to administer such programs directly (neo-colonialism?), and whether we should continue to "waste" foodstuffs through price supports which encourage "excess" production—using tax resources which could otherwise be applied to other social needs.

The point to be remembered is that every resource allocation must be morally evaluated in relation to other resource allocations. It must further be evaluated in relation to the possible unintended consequences which may result from possible decisions. Abstract calls to "feed the hungry" and the simple sensitization of the populace through raising Christian concern are not enough in themselves to bring about policy decisions which are morally adequate.

Politics As Authoritative Use of Power

Third, our definition of politics states that allocation of values and resources is *authoritative*. One of the unique features of politics is its association with the use of the sword to establish compliance with the allocative decisions being made in the name of the state. The state, therefore, cannot be an instrument of "love." For love must be an act of personal volition, whereas the very nature of things political is that they ultimately rely on the power of the sword to accomplish their ends. It is true that states rely on the consent of the governed (either explicitly, as in contemporary democratic governments, or implicitly, as in traditional autocratic governments) as a source of moral legitimatization which enables the state to act "authoritatively." It is also true that states seek to exploit public opinion and support for their policies in order to legitimatize their actions (either through monopolisitic control of opinion formation, as in modern totalitarian states, or through exploitation of the deference normally shown to political leaders in traditional and democratic societies). But in the final instance, decisions of state are enforced with sanctions which render compliance therewith as something short of being voluntary. While it is less than voluntary, however, we nonetheless acknowledge that the state is "authoritative" in the sense that it possesses a sense of legitimacy.

Hence, if a coalition of minority groups would engage in guerilla activities which effectively "taxed the rich to aid the poor," we would have to maintain that however noble the cause, the action of such a guerilla band would be illegitimate. We would designate their activities as robbery and stealing. But when the state seeks the same goal through an established system of taxation, it is no longer stealing or robbery, but an act of authority which (however misguided the policy may be in the eyes of some) possesses a particular character of moral legitimacy.

The state's use of force is called forth in just those situations where there is not voluntary compliance with social goals. Hence, when Christian spokesmen suggest that we would not have to pass laws on racism, sexism, or welfare rights, if our nation would but repent, humble itself, and conform to the teachings of Christ, they are absolutely correct. But, they must realize they are speaking of an *alternative* to politics, not merely a Christian political style. The fact of the matter is that peoples are not prone toward complying with the demands of justice, and for that very reason states have always served to seek the demands of justice through the power of the sword. Granted, Christian voluntarism would have a tremendous affect on the social structures of our society and upon the political demands with which government has to deal. And granted, a "Christianizing" of the public philosophy would have a tremendous affect on the value system informing allocative decisions which government must make. But this obviously is not a satisfactory solution to the total political question.

The state establishes and protects economic and social systems which render goods and resources in a society. Hence, Christians must deal critically with the *systemic* character of policies and institutions rooted in the power of the state which reflect moral decision-making. And as modern society becomes increasingly interdependent, the state as "economic manager and co-ordinator" has become increasingly involved in regulating the nature of those interrelationships. And we, as Christians, are increasingly implicated in the decisions of the state. Every dollar we earn we have earned within a system which is upheld by the power of the state. Every dollar we are taxed is used for different purposes—the building of neutron bombs, subsidies for the trucking industry through interstate highways, subsidies for the mariner unions through cargo-preference legislation, the exportation of tobacco products as "food for peace," or aid to dependent children.

Thus, while we correctly believe that the state is not the soteriological answer to the moral dilemma of man as sinner, we must nonetheless recognize its practical necessity in a fallen world where force is necessary as a means to insure a modicum of justice. We must likewise recognize that the force which states use to insure compliance with their policies is a force which can be used for relative good or relative evil. As we have pointed out above, all decisions of state are value-related. Hence, to abandon concern about affairs of state through simple dismissal with slogans such as "The state can't save us!" is to abandon concern in a significant area of moral decision-making. And to denigrate the state as an instrument of force—"The state's way is evil compared with the love ethic taught by Christ!"—is to denigrate concern for the relative justice which the state seeks to insure through its deployment of power.

Finally, to repudiate involvement in affairs of state in the name of Christian love implicates us in sins of omission for not having done what we might have done to affect public policies for the good. I shall concede that involvement in affairs of state implicates us in sins of commission, and that the policies of state fall short of absolute justice and the demands of Christian love. But to avoid involvement in the struggle for justice under the power of the state is to bear responsibility for the unspoken word, the unfulfilled deed, and the withdrawal from the decision-making process which removes Christian witness from the political struggle. And how can one claim fidelity to the norms of love and righteousness at the top of the moral ladder if he is unwilling to serve also the norm of political justice with all of its relativities at the lower rung of the moral ladder?

The Universal Scope of Politics

Fourth, our definition of politics stresses the fact that political decisions are made for *all of society*. Political decisions are involuntary not only insofar as they are enforced by the sword, but involuntary insofar as their scope includes all people in a society regardless of whether they desire to be so included. All other associations in society are voluntary, and all other associations in society are limited in scope. One joins all other associations through direct or indirect consent. But where the state is concerned, one is bound by fact of birth into the existing political system. All other associations make decisions governing only segments of the society at large, and those decisions are not backed by the power of the sword to force compliance. The state, on the other hand, governs all peoples within a society and enforces its decisions with the sword.

The ecumenical inclusiveness of the state thus requires that the values and norms governing its actions be sufficiently inclusive and latitudinarian. It must not serve the value preferences of one set of particular individuals in a society to the exclusion of others. This principle creates an environment of moral ambiguity and moral inconsistency which is difficult for many evangelical Christians to accept and operate within.

Righteousness and Justice in Political Ethics

The evangelical Christian accepts the lordship of Jesus Christ and the Scriptures which bear witness to him as the standard by which all human endeavor is to be evaluated and judged. It is understandable, therefore, that evangelicals are prone to suggest that their understandings of right should serve as norms of national righteousness in political life. The difficulties of this for politics are manifold, however.

First, it must be remembered that Christians themselves disagree substantially on the meaning and interpretation of Scriptures. The Bible is not self-interpreting. Calvinists and Lutherans disagree over the Scriptural teaching concerning the Lord's Day observances. Evangelical Christians with strong ethnic ties to continental Europe feel quite differently about the appropriateness of alcohol and tobacco in private and public life than do many Christians with Anglo-Saxon evangelical traditions. To put the matter simply: if evangelical Christians have difficulty coming to agreement on substantive theological questions relative to eucharist, the second coming of Jesus Christ, and matters of church governance to which the Bible speaks directly, how can they presume to establish coherent and unitary positions on matters of social and political ethics to which the Bible speaks only indirectly?

Second, it must be remembered that substantial portions of the population adhere to varying Christian, non-Christian, and agnostic religious traditions which must be respected in the political arena. Even if evangelical Protestants could come to common understanding concerning the particulars of public policy based on Christian teaching, they would still have to take into account the necessity of respecting the civil rights of those who disagree with their positions on public policy. While all political decisions reflect moral decision-making and value choices, it is nonetheless true that it is bad public policy to root political decisions strictly and solely on the basis of a particular sectarian goal.

The reasons for this are several. It must be remembered that the means a state employs to secure its ends affect the ends themselves. A nation cannot seek to curtail civil rights as a means of securing civil rights. Thus, means of the state which are always rooted in force and involuntarism cannot be used to secure Christian standards of love in society. A father may beat his child into compliance with parental standards. But such acquiescence of behavior by the child reflects not a relationship of love, respect, and voluntarism but simply a relationship of force. To use the sword of the state to enforce standards to which a broad spectrum of society does not agree undermines the broad consensual foundations of legitimacy upon which the state's authority must rest. And to use the sword of the state in the name of Christian love is contradictory—for the compliance to Christian norms would result not in voluntarily returned love but merely in a passive acceptance of superior physical force.

What, then, is a Christian to do when he has learned all his life that "righteousness exalts a nation, but sin is a reproach to any people"? Is not the use of the sword appropriate in the quest for righteousness for the well-being of a people even if they are not able to recognize that it is for their own good?

Several distinctions must be made here. First, let us remember that the Old Testament prophets were speaking in particular to a covenant people existing as a nation-state—a nation-state uniquely used in the providence of God to usher in his salvation to the world. Thus, the standards of national righteousness established for Israel cannot apply in the same manner to the New Testament era unless one assumes that nation-states today are direct inheritors of the promises made to Israel. While the Christian community and the confessing church may be the "new Israel," the nation-states of the twentieth century are not. (The Constantinian Church and Calvin's Geneva are examples where the attempt to wed the state to the Christian church were made, and attempts at applying explicitly Christian standards of righteousness to national politics were deemed appropriate applications of Old Testament principles to New Testament situations. The results were so disastrous both politically and religiously that few evangelicals would covet an attempted return.)

Thus, we must be willing to admit that there is a gap between what may be a just, as distinct from a righteous, political policy. It may be said that any injustice violates the will of God and hence may be considered unrighteous. It does not hold, however, that

any effort to arrive at public righteousness is necessarily just.
Let me give an example. When people are discriminated
against because of their race by virtue of social structures and
public policy, we may say that such an injustice is unrighteous.
However, not all attempts at resolving the problem are
necessarily righteous or just. Should, as in the case of South
Africa, the Bantu natives gain political power and systematically
apply discriminatory policies against their former white oppressors, the outcome of such a practice is simply a return of evil
for evil without a substantial movement toward justice in that
society. However, should a policy of non-discrimination and
equal opportunity genuinely evolve, the outcome is a move
toward justice and thus also a step toward righteousness. In this
case, justice serves the cause of righteousness.

But to suggest that the cause of righteousness necessarily
serves the cause of justice is another matter. God's standards of
righteousness exceed justice and demand that justice be crowned
by a moral motivation which complements the moral act. But the
motivations which inspire mankind to action are beyond the control of the state. The state, through force, can compel the external
behavior of individuals to conform to the demands of justice. But
the state cannot measure or control the motivations which inform
external behavior. Indeed, since the element of force or coercion
is always implicit in policies of state, to compel "righteousness"
would be to force love.

In other words, while injustice is always unrighteous, justice
falls short of righteousness. Further, the use of the state to compel righteousness, as opposed to justice, may in and of itself be
unjust. Not only would the state have to exceed the demands of
justice and seek to "compel love," but it would have to disregard
the limits which govern our concepts of civil liberties and constitutional limitations on the state's proper use of power. An example might be when a state seeks to enforce Sabbath observance
through public law for sectarian purposes. God does call us to
honor the Sabbath by setting it aside as a day of rest. More
particularly, he desires that the day of rest be one in which the
saints gather together to worship him and sing songs of praise to
him. If the state would seek to enforce church attendance because
church attendance is righteous, the state would obviously violate
justice in the search of righteousness. If the state would seek to
enforce Sunday "blue laws" for the sake of honoring the Sabbath
(as opposed to secular criteria which might conclude prag-

matically that it is to the well-being of all to have established times of relief from commercial activity), the state would violate the limitations of just government because it would exceed the demands of justice *per se.*

Our considerations thus far have dealt mainly with theoretical considerations and distinctions which must be made if evangelicals are to think clearly about the nature of politics. But in the last analysis, politics is not a theoretical activity so much as it is a practical activity. Politics is not simply the distinguishing of principles, but the application of those principles in particular circumstances. While political scientists may define politics as "the authoritative allocation of values and resources for all society," political practitioners would much prefer the popular definition, "Politics is the art of the possible."

I shall, accordingly, shift my discussion from some of the theoretical questions with which evangelicals must deal in regard to politics to matters of practical concern. These must be considered in relation to the potential for evangelical political influence on society.

The Social Context of Evangelicalism

First, we must remember that evangelical Protestantism represents a very distinct segment of the American polity. It is not representative of the multifaceted and diverse character of American society. Evangelicalism is largely composed of white, Anglo-Saxonized, middle to upper-middle class, suburban Americans. Thus, the issues which possess political saliance for American evangelicalism are not necessarily representative of the broad interests of American society, nor are they necessarily the critical issues facing the country as a whole.

Recalling our earlier discussion of the propensity of groups and individuals to maximize their own self-interest at the expense of the whole, we should remember that evangelical Christians are no exception. Political issues are perceived largely through the context of those socio-economic variables which describe the evangelical community. Hence, it has a tendency toward political and economic conservatism since such positions generally best reflect its own self-interest. Often evangelical moralizing about politics is little more than theological rationalization for positions derived independently of genuine Christian reflection.

Thus, evangelicals moved by the significant ministries of organizations such as World Vision International may be sensitized to the needs of the world's hungry. But they are less often sensitized to the hungry of their own communities. Evangelicals may, however belatedly, have become sensitized to the needs of racial minorities. But when the Department of Health, Education, and Welfare issues guidelines for minority participation in the governance of their own religious and educational enterprises, they react indignantly about excessive government interference, oblivious to the fact that the churches themselves are now the most segregated social institutions in American life. Evangelicals have a tendency toward taking a "hard line" on matters of criminal justice, forgetting that their own community has seldom been at the receiving end of the criminal justice system. Evangelicals can rally around welfare abuse much more readily than can the United States Catholic Conference, for example, because evangelicals are more likely to represent the socially advantaged than is the Catholic community with its large concentration of Latinos and other ethnic groups. Evangelical Christianity should include a substantial portion of America's black community. But the fact of the matter is that sociologically speaking, white evangelicalism has cut itself off from the black evangelical, the rural white fundamentalist, and even the inner-city ministries of the Salvation Army.

Thus, the socio-economic predispositions of evangelicalism have tended to interfere with thoughtful reflection of Christian standards of justice as they apply to the value and resource allocation of the political process. The political behavior of the evangelical Christian can be predicted more precisely through standard sociological analysis of income, education, ethnic identity, and geography than anything relating to the confession of Jesus Christ as Savior and Lord. Evangelical Christians have an obligation to rethink the political implications of their faith for political responsibility so that it transcends the simple reflection of socio-economic interests. And they must be particularly careful, in the meantime, not to engage in crusades which simply baptize political positions reflecting those interests as somehow possessing particular moral authenticity.

The Structural Context of Evangelicalism

We must remember that there are some very practical consequences of evangelical Protestantism's very loose organizational structure. While estimates of the number of evangelical Protestants in the United States frequently range up to the forty million figure, there is no umbrella organization or common institutional tie where evangelicalism can unite for the purposes of unitary social and political impact.

First of all, the very Protestant character of evangelicalism tends to stress the priesthood of the believer at the expense of the organized church's authority over the life of the individual believer. Further, it must be remembered that a great number of evangelical churches are governed on the principle of congregationalist polity which diminishes institutional relationships between church bodies. The situation is taken to the absurd, organizationally, by the extremely sectarian nature of much of evangelical Protestantism. Hence, leadership in evangelicalism takes place in terms of identifying with personalities and movements which sweep through it and cut across the multiplicity of organizational structures. The Catholic tradition, on the other hand, places more emphasis on the organizational integrity of the church. The latter is much more effective in terms of potential for political impact—it is clear who speaks for the Catholic church, and there are in existence ready lines of internal communication of the church's posture on social and political issues.

This situation has both its strong points and its weak points. We have alluded to the strength of this loose organizational structure when pointing out that the organizational diversity of evangelicalism protects it against simplistic organizational commitments to secular causes in the name of the kingdom of God. (It must be remembered, however, that there is nonetheless an evangelical subculture which does indeed create predispositions toward informally linking certain public policies with Christian standards of virtue.) The weakness of this arrangement is that it substantially prohibits the leadership of the church from acting prophetically on those social and political issues where the church most severely needs direction.

An example of this weakness can be found in racial patterns in the church. During the 1960s, for example, the Catholic churches of the South were able to play a substantially more active and crucial role in the civil rights movement in states such as Louisiana (where Catholicism is strong) because the hierarchical character of the church's organizational structure protected the leadership of the church from cavalier dismissal or repudiation due to its aggressive posture on civil rights. When contrasted with the congregationalist structure of the Baptist tradition, as illustrated in the well-publicized events leading to the dismissal of the pastor at Plains Baptist Church in Plains, Georgia, the comparison becomes obvious.

It must be further remembered that while there may be some forty million "evangelicals" in the American society, most of that number do not consistently and self-consciously identify with evangelicalism as a religious movement. The leadership of the Southern Baptist Convention, for example, which accounts for the largest segment of evangelical Protestantism (broadly defined) has stated at several times that it does *not* consider itself to be properly so classified. If one talks with leaders of the Southern Presbyterian church, one is surprised to find that they little understand the informal and parachurch organizations by which the communication of evangelical Protestantism's character is transmitted in the North.

Even if we turn to the North, we must remember that the self-professed National Association of Evangelicals which spearheaded the leadership of modern evangelicalism accounts for only roughly 5 percent of the forty million evangelicals. (There are probably more evangelicals in the United Methodist Church alone than in the entire NAE fellowship.)

It is also interesting to note that estimates of evangelicalism tend to dismiss the black community's extensive ties to conservative Protestantism. Further, there has been little effort to establish working ties with the Roman Catholic and Orthodox communities even though conservative Protestants probably hold more in common with these groups than with liberal Protestantism.

Evangelicalism, as the term is increasingly being used, is not an organized, self-conscious movement within the church or American society. It is really a very general term designating an eclectic group of Christians from differing Christian traditions who resist the theological humanism which has captured much of establishment Christianity. It has no organizational superstructure. It has no self-conscious posture as a movement. And thus, it can hope to accomplish little by way of direct political action. This, I hasten to add, is not necessarily a bad situation. But it is an important consideration when examining the potential strategies which evangelicalism may adopt relative to social and political issues.

The Cultural Isolation of Evangelicalism

Finally, it must be remembered that the disparate character of evangelicalism is nonetheless marked by a degree of cultural isolation from the major purveyors of influence in our society. There are few journals of evangelical opinion which speak widely enough to attract the following of a broad section of evangelicalism, and those which do tend to be largely concerned with matters internal to evangelicalism itself as opposed to directed witness and challenge to secular culture.

Evangelicalism is poorly positioned for expressing its points of view in the national media. It seldom reaches heights of artistic expression in the cultural life of the nation. This is due not only to the organizational weakness of evangelicalism, but also to a tendency of the community toward otherworldliness. Fundamentalism has been defined by some as "orthodoxy gone militant." The fundamentalist movement, the forerunner of contemporary evangelicalism, was basically reactive in temper. It was reacting against secularism, scientism, humanism, the rejection of theism, and so forth. Accordingly, the psychological environment of contemporary evangelicalism is still tempered by tendencies toward social withdrawal and rejection of the world's concerns.

Sociologists have studied the social involvements of church members and have found, for example, that members of conservative, evangelical churches tend to devote their time and energies disproportionately to their churches as opposed to their communities at large.[5] The church becomes a primary association to the exclusion of other associational activities. Even when evangelical churchmen join secondary associations, they tend to be parachurch groups. Instead of the Kiwanis Club, evangelical leaders are prone to join "Christian Businessmen's Fellowship." While this accounts for many of the strengths in evangelicalism, it also fosters many of its weaknesses. It cuts its influence off from the general social structure outside of the church, and prevents its concerns from being affected by questions the world is asking. As others have stated, "How can evangelicalism say that Christ is the answer when it is deaf to the questions being asked?"

If evangelical Protestantism is serious about social and political

---

[5]See, for example, Lowell Streiker and Gerald Strober, *Religion and the New Majority*, (New York: Association Press, 1972).

witness, it must develop strategies of cultural penetration and social involvement with which it is presently unfamiliar. If I might speculate for a moment, I would suggest that there is tremendous potential for evangelical Christianity to vitally impact our culture if it would be willing to consider linkages with the black religious community and the conservative elements of American Catholicism (both Roman and Orthodox). This addresses itself immediately to problems of race, problems between Anglo-Saxon dominance in our society *vis-à-vis* the ethnic groups in the Catholic churches; it offers the potential for a massive movement of resistance to the secularistic rejection of the Judeo-Christian traditions upon which our social structures and political system have been built. But the organizational fragmentation of evangelical Christianity, its cultural isolation, and its inability to distinguish major issues from parochial concerns have all kept evangelical Christianity at the periphery of our social and political order, despite the numbers of individuals who share the basic tenets of evangelical Christian faith.

I am proud of my evangelical Christian faith. But I am embarrassed by its sectarian temper, its cultural isolation, and its "bourgeois captivity." I believe that God calls us to more noble discipleship. However much I value the diversity of social and institutional structures within evangelicalism, I believe we stand in judgment for allowing these structures to dissipate opportunities for witnessing to our world. Although I recognize that this world is not my home, I believe that God created, sustains, and gave his Son to save this world. Obsession with the world's concerns in the name of Jesus Christ is no sin. And however "bourgeois" I may be as a white, middle-class, midwestern male, I believe the captivity of American evangelicalism to such interests is just as devastating to the integrity of the church as the Babylonian Captivity was to the church of the Middle Ages.

Evangelical Christianity must do some serious thinking about the theoretical problems I have outlined above, of relating the Christian faith to the political order. But it must also put its own house in order. Otherwise the cause of evangelical Christianity, while achieving political effectiveness, may foster a movement which it will live to regret.

RICHARD V. PIERARD

5

One Nation Under God: Judgment or Jingoism?

The civil religion controversy, an object of considerable scholarly attention in recent years, has encouraged people to look more closely at the complex relationships between church and state that are such a significant part of the fabric of American history. In its simplest terms, civil religion is the use of commonly-accepted religious sentiments, concepts, and symbols by the state for its own purposes. This action may be unconscious, but it does constitute a blurring of religion and patriotism and of religious values with national values. In the American context it is a rather elaborate matrix of beliefs and practices born of the nation's historic experience, and for millions of citizens it is the only real religion. To be sure, civil religion in the United States superficially resembles Christianity and makes copious use of its symbols and terminology, but it does not identify with any particular church, denomination, or faith and serves primarily as an extra-ecclesiastical religion enlisted in the patriotic cause of illuminating the national identity.[1]

---

[1] On defining civil religion see Robert N. Bellah, "Civil Religion in America," *Daedalus* 96 (Winter 1967): 1-21; Russell E. Richey and Donald G. Jones, ed., *American Civil Religion* (New York: Harper & Row, 1974); and Robert D. Linder and Richard V. Pierard, *Twilight of the Saints; Biblical Christianity and Civil Religion in America* (Downers Grove, IL: InterVarsity Press, 1978). The latter two works direct the reader to the voluminous literature that the topic has generated.

Detractors of the American civil faith usually argue it has become a substitute religion, one that supplants historic Christianity in an idolatrous fashion and sanctifies the existing political order. Its proponents contend that it holds the social order together and stands in transcendent judgment over the state and its officials. In order to shed light on the vexing problem of civil religion and its impact on American public life, this essay will concentrate on some of the more obvious manifestations of civil religiosity during the 1950s.

The Eisenhower Years

With the breakdown of the Protestant consensus that dominated the nineteenth-century scene in the United States, a Judeo-Christian religion-in-general gradually took shape as the "social glue" binding Americans together. Although this transformation was clearly evident by the time of World War II, its period of greatest flowering was in the 1950s, particularly under the benevolent hand of President Dwight D. Eisenhower, the quintessential patron of American civil religion.[2] Of humble origins, he was reared in a devout, pietistic home in Kansas that inculcated in him such virtues as integrity, courage, hard work, self-reliance, and confidence in the Holy Scriptures, which he read and memorized. Eisenhower had little concern for formal religion and only became a church member in 1953, but he had internalized the Bible and made it a vital part of his expression. He seemed to feel that denominationalism and ritualism were merely outward manifestations, whereas true religion lay in the mind and heart. This explains how he could make such widely quoted comments as: "I am the most intensely religious man I know," and "Our form of government has no sense unless it is founded in a deeply religious faith—and I don't care what it is."[3]

The presidential inauguration excellently reflected Eisenhower's

---

[2]William Lee Miller, *Piety Along the Potomac: Notes on Politics and Morals in the Fifties* (Boston: Houghton Mifflin, 1964); Merlin Gustafson, "The Religion of a President," *Christian Century* 86 (April 30, 1969): 610-12; idem, "The Religious Role of the President," *Midwest Journal of Political Science* 14 (November 1970): 708-22. These are useful treatments of official religiosity in the Eisenhower years and I have drawn upon them for background materials.

[3]For a discussion of Eisenhower's religious faith and activity in greater detail see my *Twilight of the Saints*, chap. 3.

religiosity and in fact set the tone for his administration. On the morning of January 20, 1953, the president-elect, cabinet members, and their families attended a special worship service at National Presbyterian Church where he "sought strength in prayer and the Word of God for his overwhelming new responsibilities."[4] After taking the oath of office at the Capitol, he offered a "little private prayer" which he had composed in his hotel room that morning, an action unprecedented in the annals of presidential inaugurations, and his address called for spiritual rededication and moral renewal on the part of the American people. Included in the inaugural parade which followed was a monstrosity known as "God's Float," one that was dominated by a central edifice denoting a place of worship and pictures of churches and scenes of worship on the sides, and supposedly it was a symbolic representation of the idea that America was a nation whose people believed in God.[5]

According to his pastor, Edward L. R. Elson, Eisenhower "brought in a new moral tone and spiritual vitality into American life" and in a very real sense was "the focal point of a moral resurgence and spiritual awakening of national proportions."[6] This development was reflected in various actions on the part of the president. He was baptized, joined National Presbyterian Church, gave a talk about the power and meaning of prayer at the first Presidential Prayer Breakfast, initiated the practice of opening cabinet and other important White House meetings with prayer, and frequently spoke to ecclesiastical bodies and delegations about the moral and religious basis of American freedom. He also appointed a staff assistant, Congregationalist minister Frederic E. Fox, to coordinate his religious activities and serve as a liaison between himself and religious interest groups and the public at large on such concerns. Eisenhower attended his newly-found church home with regularity, circulated Dr. Elson's sermons among his staff, and lent his prestige to a fund

---

[4]This is the view expressed by the minister who officiated, the Rev. Edward L. R. Elson, *America's Spiritual Recovery* (Westwood, N.J.: Revell, 1954), p. 53.

[5]*New York Times*, January 19, 1953, p. 16.

[6]Elson, *America's Spiritual Recovery*, p. 57. William Lee Miller alleges that the Republican National Committee even said Eisenhower "is not only the political leader, but the spiritual leader of our times." *Piety Along the Potomac*, p. 48. Billy Graham writes that Eisenhower told him personally five days before the inauguration: "America has to have a religious revival if we are to be saved." Graham, "A Christian America," *American Mercury* 80 (March 1955): 71.

drive which raised twenty million dollars for a new church building.

Of course, Eisenhower was not acting in a spiritual vacuum, as the national mood was congenial to such an outpouring of religiosity. Such preachers as Norman Vincent Peale, Fulton J. Sheen, and Billy Graham gained enormous followings in the early 1950s and church membership levels increased significantly during these years. Moreover, the indefatigable Abram Vereide, head of International Christian Leadership, had for some time been promoting the "prayer breakfast" idea among the leaders of government and business, and in 1953 his efforts were crowned with success with the first Presidential (now National) Prayer Breakfast.

President Harry S. Truman had already channeled civil religion into the Cold War struggle, arguing that "our religious faith gives us the answer to the false beliefs of Communism" and it was America's duty "to defend the spiritual values—the moral code—against the vast forces of evil that seek to destroy them."[7] It goes without saying that "godless, atheistic communism" was denounced with regularity from the pulpits of the land. To help show the country's spiritual colors, the 82nd Congress passed a resolution in April, 1952 mandating the president once a year to "set aside and proclaim" a National Day of Prayer in which the citizenry "may turn to God in prayer and meditation at churches in groups, and as individuals," and every chief executive since then has dutifully carried out this charge.[8] The American Legion at its Miami convention in 1951 decided to sponsor an annual "Back to God" observance which commemorated the heroic deaths of the "Four Chaplains," two Protestants, a Catholic priest, and a Jewish rabbi, who, when the troop transport *Dorchester* was torpedoed in the North Atlantic in February, 1943, gave away their life jackets to men who had none. The Legion hoped to increase the awareness of God in people's lives by urging them to seek divine guidance in their everyday activities and to engage in regular church attendance, daily family prayer, and the religious training of youth.[9]

---

[7]*Public Papers of the Presidents of the United States, Harry S. Truman, 1951.* (Washington: U.S. Government Printing Office, 1965), pp. 212-13.

[8]Frederic Fox, "The National Day of Prayer," *Theology Today* 30 (July 1973): 258-80; Pub. L. 324, chap. 216, *Statutes at Large* 66 (1952): 64.

[9]*New York Times*, February 8, 1954, p. 11.

A "prayer for peace" movement set in motion by a prominent American Legionnaire and State Department employee, Herve J. L'Heureaux, swept the country in the early 1950s. Eisenhower himself elevated it to a global level when in a speech before the Evanston Assembly of the World Council of Churches on August 19, 1954 he invited every person in the world who believed in the power of a Supreme Being to pray for peace. A government official later interpreted the president's speech to mean that this action would reveal the true spiritual foundation of the American government and society, in contrast to that of the Russians.[10] Even the post office canceled stamps with the slogan "Pray for peace" thanks to the efforts of Michigan Congressman Louis C. Rabaut, sponsor of a measure which passed in 1955. His rationale was that because of the ever-increasing attacks upon the United States "by the forces of godlessness and atheism, it is well indeed that we be reminded of our dependence upon God and our faith in His support."[11]

The president also gave his support to the Foundation for Religious Action in the Social and Civil Order, a venture launched in the mid-1950s by Edward Elson and a number of luminaries from the three major faiths. Their purpose was to "unite all people who believed in a Supreme Being" in a "spiritual and ideological counteroffensive" which would "shatter the militant self-confidence of international Communism and put it on the defense." Through use of the mass media the group hoped to communicate the values of democracy and evils of communism and dramatize the strength of a religiously-based view of life, but the endeavor amounted to little.[12]

Similarly unsuccessful was the Christian Amendment Movement which had been trying for nearly a century to secure the insertion of a reference in the Constitution acknowledging the country's allegiance to Jesus Christ. In 1951 Senator Ralph E. Flanders of Vermont submitted an amendment which stated: "This nation devoutly recognizes the authority and law of Jesus Christ, Saviour and Ruler of Nations through whom are

---

[10]Memo by Abbott Washburn, Deputy Director of the U. S. Information Agency, Nov. 2, 1954, OF 144-H, Dwight D. Eisenhower Library, Abilene, Kan. *Public Papers of the Presidents of the United States. Dwight D. Eisenhower, 1954.* (Washington: U. S. Government Printing Office, 1960), pp. 739-40.

[11]*Congressional Record* 101 (June 2, 1955): 7533.

[12]Program Proposal in GF 188 (1954), Eisenhower Library.

bestowed the blessings of Almighty God." Additional sections included a disclaimer that this statement contradicated the Bill of Rights and a procedure for exempting those citizens whose religious scruples would prevent them from giving unqualified allegiance to the Constitution as so amended.[13] Flanders (along with Congressman Robert D. Harrison of Nebraska) again introduced the amendment in 1953, and a subcommittee of the Senate Judiciary Committee conducted a hearing on it in May 1954. Jewish and civil rights organizations heavily criticized the measure for being vague and divisive—for example, who would decide what the law of Christ was when scores of denominations could not agree on the matter, and how could a secular authority resolve such differences anyway—and as a result it was never reported out of committee.[14] Nearly every year in the 1950s one or more Christian Amendment resolutions were dropped into the hopper, including eight in 1959, but they were regularly killed in committee.

In 1954 Congress voted to establish "a room with facilities for prayer and meditation" for the individual use of its members, and a small room on the west side of the Capitol rotunda was set aside for this purpose. The legislation provided that it should contain the "appropriate symbols of religious unity and freedom of worship," and currently found in the room are two kneeling benches and ten chairs, a simple altar with an open Bible flanked by two seven-branched candlesticks and an American flag, and a stained glass window portraying George Washington kneeling in prayer at Valley Forge beneath the phrase, "One nation under God."[15]

However, by far the most significant acts of official religiosity during the Eisenhower years were the addition of the words "un-

---

[13]Leo Pfeffer, *Church, State, and Freedom* (Boston: Beacon Press, 1967), pp. 241-42; *Congressional Record* 97 (February 5, 1951): 910; 83rd Cong., 2nd Sess., Senate Committee on the Judiciary. *Christian Amendment*, Subcommittee hearing, May 13-17, 1954, p. 1.

[14]Ibid., pp. 70-92; *Congressional Record* 99 (June 11, 1953): 6380; May 19, 1954, A3696-97.

[15]*Congressional Record* 100 (May 4, 1954): 5929. A photograph and description of the Prayer Room is contained in Benjamin Weiss, *God in American History: Religious Heritage*, rev. ed. (South Pasadena, CA: National Educators Fellowship, 1975), pp. 224-25. Paul F. Boller, *George Washington and Religion* (Dallas: Southern Methodist University Press, 1963), demonstrates convincingly that the popular belief Washington had been seen kneeling in prayer at Valley Forge in 1777 is historically incorrect.

der God" to the Pledge of Allegiance in 1954 and the adoption of "In God We Trust" as the national motto in 1956. A closer examination of these two matters will provide the basis for drawing some meaningful conclusions about the implications of civil religion for American Christians.

The Establishment of the Pledge

The Pledge of Allegiance was composed in 1892 by Francis Bellamy (1855-1931), a one-time Baptist minister who was employed in the Boston office of *The Youth's Companion*, a magazine which at the time was promoting rededication to Americanism. He was also chairman of the executive committee for the National Public School Celebration, a nationwide observance that was to take place in conjunction with the dedication of the World Columbian Exposition grounds in Chicago on October 12, 1892, the four-hundredth anniversary of the European discovery of America. Included in the program was a flag-raising ceremony, and Bellamy composed a simple salute for the children to use. His pledge of allegiance to the flag quickly gained public acceptance, and within a few years it came to occupy a revered place in the canon of patriotic rituals.[16] In 1923 and 1924 the first phrase of the salute was modified slightly (from "I pledge allegiance to my *flag* . . ." to "I pledge allegiance to *the flag of the United States of America* and to the republic for which it stands, one nation indivisible, with liberty and justice for all"), and in June 1942 it was included in the codification of existing rules and customs pertaining to the use and display of the flag.[17] Only in legislation signed on December 28, 1945 did Congress at long last recognize it as the official Pledge of Allegiance.[18]

---

[16]*Congressional Record* 100 (May 5, 1954): 6077; June 22, 1954, 8618; Margarette S. Miller, *I Pledge Allegiance* (Boston: The Christopher Publishing House, 1946). Four years later Bellamy left the magazine for a career in the advertising field and the remainder of his life was spent in obscurity. Margarette Miller was responsible for uncovering the story of his achievement and her findings provide the basis for the historical accounts which have appeared frequently in the popular press since the early 1950s.

[17]Pub. L. 623, chap. 435, Sec. 7, *Statutes at Large* 56 (1942): 380. The pledge was to be rendered by standing with the right hand over the heart and then extending it, palm upward, toward the flag at the words "to the flag," and holding this position until the end, when the hand would drop to the side. Because of this obvious similarity to the Nazi salute, the procedure was changed on December 22, 1942 so that the entire pledge would be rendered with the right hand over the heart. Pub. L. 829, chap. 806, *Statutes at Large* 56 (1942): 1077.

[18]Pub. L. 287, chap. 607, *Statutes at Large*, 59 (1945): 688.

There was growing sentiment in the ensuing years for the inclusion of a reference to the Deity in the pledge. As early as 1951 the Knights of Columbus began adding the phrase "under God" to the pledge when they used it in meetings, and during the next two years various national gatherings of the Roman Catholic fraternal order urged Congress to implement this change.[19] Stimulated by a letter from a man in Brooklyn, New York, Congressman Louis C. Rabaut introduced on April 30, 1953 a joint resolution to insert the phrase "under God" between "one nation" and "indivisible," but it was promptly buried in the House Judiciary Committee.[20]

Suddenly, however, a Lincoln Day Sermon delivered by Rev. George M. Docherty on February 7, 1954 at Washington's New York Avenue Presbyterian Church (known as the church where Abraham Lincoln had worshiped) brought the issue out into the open. Eisenhower was present at the service on that day, seated in the Lincoln pew. He heard Docherty point out that the expression "under God" was in the Gettysburg Address and that it needed to be in the Pledge of Allegiance as well. Belief in God was the "definitive factor in the American way of life" and without that phrase the pledge could be utilized by any republic. In melodramatic terms the pastor described how "Muscovite" children could just as easily recite it, since the Soviet Union claimed to be indivisible and to stand for liberty and justice for all.[21]

At once Congress was stirred to action. Senator Homer Ferguson of Michigan introduced a resolution on February 10 proposing that the two words be placed after "one nation indivisible" and two days later Rabaut gave an impassioned speech on behalf of his pigeon-holed measure.[22] Within a short time no less than fifteen more congressmen submitted "under God" bills for House consideration. During the spring the Hearst

[19]Article in the July 1954 issue of *Columbia*, reprinted in the *Congressional Record* 100 (July 13, 1954): A5037; *Newsweek* 43 (June 21, 1954): 2, 6.

[20]*Congressional Record* 100 (July 13, 1954): A5038.

[21]Text of the sermon published in the *Congressional Record* 100 (March 8, 1954): A1794-95.

[22]*Congressional Record* 100 (February 10, 1954): 1600; February 12, 1954, 1700. A concise and useful account of the action is Gerard Kaye and Ferenc M. Szasz, "Adding 'Under God' to the Pledge of Allegiance," *Encounter* 34 (1973): 52-56.

newspaper chain and various veterans and patriotic organizations spearheaded a campaign to rally public enthusiasm, and the result was a deluge of mail at the White House and congressional offices.

The proponents argued that America "is a God-fearing country and every person in this land of opportunity believes in God".[23] Thus, in the words of Congressman Rabaut, "the consciousness of the American people will be more alerted to the true meaning of our country and its form of government."[24] What could be better, Senator Alexander Wiley of Wisconsin suggested, than that the youth of the nation would reassert in the pledge their own belief and that of their forefathers "in the all-present, all-knowing, all-seeing, all-powerful Creator?"[25] A woman in New York wrote to President Eisenhower: "We owe a flag to a great nation but we owe a great nation to a supreme being, God its creator." Methodist minister and Senate Chaplain Frederick Brown Harris commented in a sermon: "To put the words 'under God' on millions of lips is like running up the believer's flag as the witness of a great nation's faith."[26] In other words, the change was simply an affirmation of America's spiritual heritage and thus did not constitute any real kind of spiritual innovation.

Another line of argumentation was that this recognition of the divine presence would help to insure the nation's prosperity and survival in the struggle against communism. As one person put it: "Surely the daily declaration of our dedication as a nation under God will be most pleasing to Him and will bring forth His blessings upon our endeavors."[27] Senator Thomas A. Burke of Ohio regarded the modified pledge as "a formal declaration of our duty to serve God and our firm reliance, now as in 1776, on the protection of divine providence."[28] Senator Ferguson maintained that "spiritual values are every bit as important to the defense and safety of our Nation as are military and economic values. . . .

---

[23]Resolution of the Chelsea, Mass., Board of Aldermen, May 10, 1954, GF 1-D 1954, Eisenhower Library.

[24]*Congressional Record* 100 (May 5, 1954): 6078.

[25]Ibid., May 4, 1954, 5915.

[26]Jean Marie Bullock, Binghamton, N. Y. to Dwight D. Eisenhower, June 11, 1954, GF 1-D 1954, Eisenhower Library; *Congressional Record* 100 (June 22, 1954): 8617.

[27]Evelyn T. Mechler, New York, N. Y. to Dwight D. Eisenhower, June 16, 1954, GF 1-D 1954, Eisenhower Library.

[28]*Congressional Record* 100 (June 22, 1954): 8563.

We have an infinite lead over the Communists in terms of our spiritual and moral values because of our firm belief in God, and because of the spiritual bankruptcy of the Communists."[29] Congressman Rabaut stated flatly: "The fundamental issue which is the unbridgable gap between America and Communist Russia is a belief in Almighty God."[30] The *Milwaukee Sentinel* (a Hearst paper) editorialized: "In times like these when Godless communism is the greatest peril this nation faces, it becomes more necessary than ever to avow our faith in God and to affirm the recognition that the core of our strength comes from Him."[31]

However, the movement to insert "under God" in the pledge was not going very well because, as evangelist Billy Graham put it: "We are directing the Ship of State, unassisted by God, past the reefs and through the storms of time. We have dropped our pilot, the Lord Jesus Christ, and are sailing blindly on without divine chart or compass, hoping somehow to find our desired haven."[32] Most supporters of the change, however, did not go so far as to bring in Christ; they were content merely to affirm the rather vague deity of civil religion. Their sentiments were accurately mirrored by an Ohio businessman who declared: "If we are to survive as a free nation against the threats of atheistic Communism, we must maintain and manifest our belief in God."[33]

Opposition to the move was minimal, but a few critics did feel that it conflicted with the First Amendment guarantee of religious freedom.[34] One person suggested that since the pledge was used

---

[29]Ibid., Feb. 10, 1954, 1600-1.

[30]Ibid., Feb. 12, 1954, 1700.

[31]Reprinted in the *Congressional Record* 100 (May 4, 1954): 5915. The paper's readers were urged to clip the editorial and mail it to their congressmen.

[32]Quoted by Rep. Homer D. Angel in the *Congressional Record* 100 (May 20, 1954): 6919. This sermon was actually preached on February 17, 1952, the final day of his Washington crusade, and was earlier inserted in the *Congressional Record* 98 (Feb. 18, 1952): A910-11.

[33]T. E. Maher, Dayton, Ohio to Dwight D. Eisenhower, May 3, 1954, GF 1-D 1954, Eisenhower Library.

[34]A lower court decision in 1957 held that the use of the words "under God" in the pledge does not violate the Constitution when the recitation of the pledge is voluntary. John P. McGrath, ed., *Church and State in American Law: Cases and Materials* (Milwaukee: Bruce, 1962), p. 236. Since the Supreme Court ruled in *West Virginia State Board of Education* v. *Barnette* (319 U. S. 624 [1943]) that the authorities may not compel the flag salute and Pledge of Allegiance, the fear that the change infringes upon the principles of church-state separation does not seem to have much substance.

in the public schools, they would be assuming the task of religious instruction.[35] A Bostonian questioned whether non-believers might be suspected of disloyalty if they refused to take a pledge acknowledging God's dominion over the nation, and a New Yorker remarked that now everyone who wished to declare allegiance to the flag had to believe in God.[36] In an address before the American Unitarian Association in Boston, Mrs. Agnes E. Meyer implied that this was an example of "the frenzy to legislate Christianity into people's consciousness by spurious methods." But, she said, the Christian religion would in the long run be harmed more by the pledge than by the persecution it was now suffering at the hands of the communists.[37] The *Christian Century* concluded that no member of Congress would dare vote against this any more than against a resolution approving motherhood, but the editor said he would "be more excited if schools and civic associations were to direct their attention toward putting real meaning into the last six words" of the Pledge of Allegiance.[38]

As the public enthusiasm for the change mounted, a most curious turn of events took place. The Ferguson bill cleared the Judiciary Committee, was passed by the Senate on May 11, and sent to the House where it was referred to its Judiciary Committee for consideration along with the other sixteen bills. On June 7 only Rabaut's measure was reported out of committee, but Paul Cunningham of Iowa moved to substitute the Ferguson motion so it would be possible to have the new pledge signed into law on Flag Day, which was only one week away. Rabaut objected, insisting that "my resolution was the granddaddy of them all, and I see no reason why we should not pass the House resolution."[39] The only difference in the two after the committee actions was a comma, (the Senate version was "one nation, under God, indivisible"), but Rabaut seemed to prefer no resolution at all to that of the Senate, and the House measure was finally adopted. This was a serious breach of protocol, but on the next day Ferguson persuaded his Senate colleagues to overlook what

[35]Kenneth H. Bonnell, Los Angeles, to Dwight D. Eisenhower, June 11, 1954, GF 1-D 1954, Eisenhower Library.

[36]William F. Porter, Boston, to Dwight D. Eisenhower, June 14, 1954, Ibid; Martin W. Abel, letter to the editor, *New York Times*, June 18, 1954, p. 22.

[37]*New York Times*, May 23, 1954, p. 30.

[38]*Christian Century* 71 (May 26, 1954): 629.

[39]*Congressional Record* 100 (June 7, 1954): 7757-58.

had transpired, pass the House resolution, and send it on to President Eisenhower for his signature.[40]

The American Legion arranged for the ceremony inaugurating the new pledge on June 14, 1954, the 175th anniversary of the official adoption of the Stars and Stripes by the Continental Congress. An honor guard from the Legion brought a flag to the Capitol which Vice President Richard Nixon had recently presented to the veterans group, and it was raised in the presence of the Congressional leadership who had gathered on the steps of the building. Then Rabaut and Ferguson together recited the pledge, thereby smoothing over the controversy about authorship, and a bugler played "Onward Christian Soldiers."[41] At the White House President Eisenhower signed the measure, expressing his pleasure that:

> From this day forward, the millions of our school children will daily proclaim in every city and town, every village and rural schoolhouse, the dedication of our Nation and our people to the Almighty. To anyone who truly loves America, nothing could be more inspiring than to contemplate this rededication of our youth, on each school morning, to our country's true meaning. . . . In this way we are reaffirming the transcendence of religious faith in America's heritage and future; in this way we shall constantly strengthen those spiritual weapons which forever will be our country's most powerful resource, in peace or in war.[42]

The modified Pledge of Allegiance gave recognition to the Deity but it was the God of civil religion, not historic Christianity. This deity was equally acceptable to Christians and Jews and was a valuable ally in the struggle against communism. He was the author of American liberty and guarded the nation through the vicissitudes of its history, but he was something other than the God whom Christians believed made possible the reconciliation of mankind through the atoning death and glorious resurrection of Jesus Christ.

Coins, Stamps, and Mottos

Now that the American nation had acknowledged its position

---

[40]*Congressional Record* 100 (June 8, 1954): 7833-34; Kaye and Szasz, "Adding 'Under God'," p. 53; Pub. L. 396, chap. 297, *Statutes at Large* 68 (1954): 249.

[41]*Congressional Record* 100 (June 22, 1954): 8617.

[42]*Public Papers of the Presidents of the United States, Dwight D. Eisenhower, 1954*, p. 563.

before the Almighty, the next logical action was a formal declaration of faith, and this was accomplished by the adoption of "In God We Trust" as the national motto. The phrase found its origin in American patriotic hymnody, in the same manner as so many other pious expressions in contemporary civil religion, as for example: "God bless America" from Irving Berlin's song of that title; "let freedom ring," "our fathers' God," "Author of liberty", and "great God, our King," from Samuel F. Smith's "America"; "America, God shed His grace on thee" and "crown thy good with brotherhood" from Katherine Lee Bates' "America the Beautiful"; and "As He died to make men holy, let us die to make men free" from the last stanza of "The Battle Hymn of the Republic" by Julia Ward Howe. In the fourth verse of "The Star-Spangled Banner" which Francis Scott Key scribbled down after witnessing the British bombardment of Fort McHenry, Maryland in 1814 (and since March 3, 1931 the official national anthem of the United States[43]) are found the following lines:

> Then conquer we must, when our cause it is just,
> And this be our motto,—"In God is our trust";

Early in the Civil War some officials of the federal government recognized the value of mobilizing popular religious sentiments in the Union cause, and Secretary of the Treasury Salmon P. Chase wrote on November 30, 1861 to the Director of the Mint in Philadelphia: "No nation can be strong except in the strength of God, or safe except in His defense. The trust of our people in God should be declared on our national coins." He then instructed the director to prepare as quickly as possible a motto expressing this national recognition. Various suggestions were considered and two years later designs for some new small coins were submitted which contained the mottoes: "Our country; our God" and "God our trust." Chase recommended on December 9,

---

[43]Pub. L. 823, chap. 436, *Statutes at Large* 46 (1931): 1508. The tune was a popular English drinking song, *To Anacreon in Heaven*, written about 1775. The song had semiofficial status since 1916 when President Wilson authorized the army and navy to use it on ceremonial occasions. On the history and development of the composition see Joseph Muller, *The Star Spangled Banner: Words and Music Issued Between 1814-1864* (New York: Da Capo, 1973). The lines quoted above are those in the first edition published in 1814, and reproduced on page 51 of Muller. Some more recent versions of the song replace "when" with the more jingoistic word "for" in the first line, thus making it: "Then conquer we must, for our cause it is just."

1863 that they be changed to "Our God and our country" and "In God We Trust."[44]

Legislation passed in 1864 authorized the issuance of this coinage and permitted the two above officials to determine their design, and in that year appeared the first United States coin with the inscription "In God We Trust," a bronze two-cent piece. An act of March 3, 1865 went one step further and stipulated that it would be lawful for the Director of the Mint, with the approval of the Secretary of the Treasury, to place the motto on such gold and silver coins as would admit of the inscription.[45] The Coinage Act of 1873 also contained the proviso that the Secretary of the Treasury might authorize the inscription of "In God We Trust" in the same manner as the 1865 measure.[46]

Some years later President Theodore Roosevelt commissioned the eminent sculptor Augustus Saint-Gaudens to design new gold pieces which would be artistically superior to the ones currently in circulation, and after some wrangling with the mint the President in 1907 succeeded in having the coins introduced. When church groups discovered that the motto had been omitted from the new gold dollars, they protested vigorously. Roosevelt defended his action in a letter to a clergyman where he insisted that the motto "not only does no good but does positive harm, and is in effect irreverence which comes dangerously close to sacrilege." He felt the motto's presence on coins cheapened it, and he had never heard anyone use it reverently. To the contrary, it had been a source of ridicule during the recent free silver controversy when quips like "in God we trust for the other eight cents," were commonly heard, and therefore "a use of the phrase which invites constant levity of this type is most undesirable."[47] Congress, however, indignantly reacted to the removal of the

---

[44]84th Cong. 1st Sess., House of Representatives, report no. 622, from the Committee on Banking and Currency, May 26, 1955. *Providing That All United States Currency and Coins Shall Bear the Inscription "In God We Trust,"* pp. 2-3; Anson Phelps Stokes and Leo Pfeffer, *Church and State in the United States*, rev. ed. (New York: Harper & Row, 1964), p. 568.

[45]House Report No. 622, May 26, 1955, p. 3; Public Acts of the 38th Cong., 2nd Sess., chap. 100, March 3, 1865, *Statutes at Large*, 13:518. The motto was not placed on the one-, five-, and ten-cent coins, and the $1.00 and $2.50 gold pieces.

[46]Public Acts of the 42nd Cong., 3rd Sess., chap. 131, February 12, 1873, *Statutes at Large*, 17:427.

[47]Joseph Bucklin Bishop, *Theodore Roosevelt and His Time: Shown in His Own Letters* (New York: Charles Scribner's Sons, 1920) 1:358-61; 2: 72-73.

now sacrosanct motto from the gold pieces and passed a law signed on May 18, 1908 which mandated placing the inscription on those gold and silver coins as had been the practice heretofore.[48]

Two opponents of the bill in the House criticized it in terms that not only were prophetic for the times but also looked accurately into the future. Gustav Küstermann of Wisconsin condemned the measure for the way it fostered "advertising" the country's religious faith, and he asserted that if those who favored the motto on coins of higher denomination actually believed this would improve the people and make them better Christians, then why not put it on the small coins, "so as to extend the helpful influence of Christianity to the poor newsboy, the boot-black, and to all those who do not possess the larger coins." And for that matter why not place it on the paper currency as well? (He also suggested, tongue-in-cheek, that the legend "Honesty is the best policy" should be embossed on the thousand-dollar bills.) In a sarcastic vein George N. Gordon of Tennessee told the august lawmakers that they should inscribe the motto above the Speaker's chair in the House chamber so that every member "can daily see and read it," and thereby receive the benefit of its inspiration.[49] Within a few decades the American people were to see both of these expressions of public piety implemented by the Congress.

The matter lay dormant until the 1950s when an effort was mounted first to place the phrase on postage stamps and currency and then to recognize it as the official national motto. The words were utilized on a two-cent stamp portraying Washington kneeling in prayer which was issued in 1928 in observance of the sesquicentennial of the winter encampment at Valley Forge, but this was only a commemorative issue. In 1952 Ernest A. Kehr, stamp news editor of the *New York Herald Tribune*, initiated a one-man campaign to have a regular stamp put into use with the motto so that people at home and abroad would be reminded that the United States was still a "nation under God." The American Legion rallied to his cause and in 1954 an eight-cent, red, white,

---

[48]Pub. L. 120, chap. 173, *Statutes at Large*, 35 (1908): 164. The new design of the one-cent in 1909 and the dime in 1916 included the motto but it was not placed on the nickel until 1938.

[49]*Congressional Record*, 42 (March 16, 1908), 3386, 3389-91. The vote in the House on the measure was 259 to 5 with 124 answering "present" or not voting.

and blue stamp containing the Statue of Liberty and the words "In God We Trust" was released.[50] The *Washington Star* praised this for bringing the postal paper "in line ideologically" with the coinage and for being "definitely an expression of the whole American people." The stamp spoke "of our national goals and purposes in world-wide terms" as it carried mail abroad.[51]

In 1953 Congressman Rabaut had drafted a resolution which never got out of committee, calling for the use of the motto as a mail cancellation mark. In any event, pressures for putting it on stamps intensified in 1954-55. A three-cent stamp was issued with the phrase, and Frank Carlson of Kansas proposed a bill in the senate that would place it on all new stamps. This was buried in the Committee on Post Office and Civil Service, and although there was some support for it (the Catholic War Veterans adopted a resolution at their annual convention favoring this), the post office argued convincingly that the present "In God We Trust" stamps were adequate.[52]

While the motto was being extended to the postage, Congressman Charles E. Bennett of Florida in January, 1955 introduced a bill to have it included on all United States currency within six months after enactment of the measure. He apparently was stimulated by some of his constituents to look into the matter and found that the treasury was reluctant to make such a change without congressional authorization. He defended the bill by arguing:

> In these days when imperialistic and materialistic communism seeks to attack and to destroy freedom, it is proper for us to seek continuously for ways to strengthen the foundations of our freedom. At the base of our freedom is our faith in God and the desire of Americans to live by His will and by His guidance. As long as this country trusts in God, it will prevail. To remind all of us of this self-evident truth, it is proper that our currency should carry these inspiring words, coming down to us through our history: "In God We Trust."[53]

---

[50]*Christopher News Notes*, no. 59, May 1954, p. 2.

[51]Editorial of April 11, 1954, reprinted in the *Congressional Record* 100 (April 14, 1954): A2805-6.

[52]*Congressional Record* 101 (January 6, 1955): 102; June 29, 1955, 9448; *Christian Century* 72 (September 7, 1955): 1014. A *Christian Century* reporter mentioned the postal officials had raised the point that misunderstandings could occur if stamps were issued bearing presidential figures and at the same time containing the motto. *Christian Century* 72 (July 20, 1955): 837.

[53]*Congressional Record* 101 (April 13, 1955): 4384. Bennett used almost the identical language in a House speech on June 7 supporting the legislation. Ibid., p. 7796.

President Eisenhower more or less concurred with Bennett's sentiments in a rather revealing memorandum: "While my convictions on the matter of placing the motto "In God We Trust" on paper currency are not too sturdy, my general feeling is that it would be rather nice to have this done. . . . I am not conducting a crusade in this matter—merely expressing a rather moderate view."[54]

There was also some hesitation because of the costs that would be involved in redesigning the plates used to print currency, but then officials in the Bureau of Engraving and Printing reported they were planning to make some technological improvements shortly that would necessitate the preparation of new plates, and there apparently would be no problem in adding the motto at that time. When Eisenhower was apprised of this, he instructed the Secretary of the Treasury to add the motto, and the president himself selected the design to be used.[55] After consulting with the treasury secretary, the House Banking and Currency Committee amended Bennett's bill to remove the six-month deadline for the changeover, and the measure now read:

> That at such time as new dies for the printing of currency are adopted in connection with the current program of the Treasury Department to increase the capacity of presses utilized by the Bureau of Engraving and Printing, the dies shall bear, at such place or places thereon as the Secretary of the Treasury may determine to be appropriate, the inscription "In God We Trust," and thereafter this inscription shall appear on all United States currency and coins.[56]

The bill passed in the House and Senate with no difficulty and was signed by President Eisenhower on July 11, 1955.[57]

During his research for the currency measure, Congressman Bennett had discovered that no motto, not even the widely-used "e pluribus unum," had been established as the national motto of

---

[54]Dwight D. Eisenhower memorandum for Nelson Rockefeller, Special Assistant to the President, March 5, 1955. Papers of Dwight D. Eisenhower as President of the U. S., Administration Series, Box 33, Eisenhower Library.

[55]Dwight D. Eisenhower memorandum for the Secretary of the Treasury, April 26, 1955, Ibid.

[56]House Report No. 622, May 26, 1955, pp. 1, 4; *Congressional Record* 101 (June 7, 1955): 7796. Because the previous legislation did not specifically state the motto was to be on all coins, the wording of his measure was such that both coins and currency would be included under the statutory requirement.

[57]Pub. L. 140, chap. 303, *Statutes at Large* 69 (1955): 290.

the United States. Bennett thus introduced a bill on July 21, 1955 to cover this historical oversight with "In God We Trust."[58] The House Judiciary Committee agreed with Bennett that the custom of placing it on coins and new currency as well as its position in "The Star Spangled Banner" constituted sufficient precedent for adopting it, and the report declared it would "be of great spiritual and psychological value to our country to have a clearly designated national motto of inspirational quality in plain, popularly accepted English."[59] The measure easily sailed through both houses of Congress and was signed into law on July 30, 1956.[60]

Six years later the House of Representatives decided to inscribe the national motto in gold above the Speaker's chair. Representative Fred Marshall of Minnesota, author of the resolution, argued the phrase would serve as "a reminder to all of us and would reaffirm our faith in God." Speaker John McCormack acknowledged it symbolized "the journey that our country has always taken since its origins." William J. Randall of Missouri added that the presence of the motto would inform the entire world that: "We are not an atheistic country or a godless Nation like our enemies behind the Iron Curtain; that we cast our lot on the side of the Almighty and reposing faith in His guidance we will ultimately win all of our struggles."[61]

Perhaps yet another sentiment besides public piety or even the Cold War was in the back of the minds of those legislators who endorsed placing the national motto in the House chamber. Congressman Randall explained that one of the by-products of this action was that he and his colleagues had given "in a not so subtle way" their response "to the recent decision of the U. S. Supreme Court banning the regents prayer from the New York State schools." In his view this would go "a long way to reaffirm the faith of every Member in our Heavenly Father by the constant reminder of our national motto, 'In God We Trust.' "[62] The motto became, in effect, a weapon that could be utilized to help overturn the Supreme Court decisions in the school prayer and

---

[58]*Congressional Record* 101 (July 21, 1955): 11193; Oral history interview, Charles E. Bennett, M. C., December 17, 1970, OH-129, Eisenhower Library.

[59]84th Cong. 2nd Sess., House of Representatives, Report No. 1959, from the Committee on the Judiciary, March 28, 1956, *National Motto.*, pp. 1-2.

[60]Pub. L. 851, chap. 795, *Statutes at Large* 70 (1956): 732.

[61]Debate on House Resolution 740, *Congressional Record* 108 (September 27, 1962): 21100-2.

[62]Ibid., 21102.

Bible reading cases (*Engel* v. *Vitale*, 370 U. S. 421 [1962]), and *Abington School District* v. *Schempp*, 374 U. S. 203 [1963]) which were the focal points of so much contention in the 1960s.

An excellent illustration of this possible usage was provided in the House Judiciary Committee hearing on the so-called "Prayer Amendment" in 1964. Speaking before the committee in favor of the amendment on April 30 was the popular Roman Catholic Bishop Fulton J. Sheen. Congressman Peter Rodino, one of the cosponsors of the 1954 measure adding "under God" to the Pledge of Allegiance, asked Bishop Sheen whether Congress would have the authority to formulate the prayer that would be presented in public bodies. His response was: "I would suggest that the prayer to be said in all of the schools of this country be the prayer that every Member of Congress is already carrying with him in his pocket, 'In God We Trust.' [This prayer] is the answer to the problem of pluralism [in America. It] is already in our tradition and it is a perfect prayer."[63] Testifying before the committee later that day, Governor George C. Wallace of Alabama referred to the motto to help back up his contention that America is a religious nation,[64] and numerous other witnesses during the six-week-long hearing did likewise. A nation that trusted in God obviously must permit the devotional reading of the Bible and the recitation of prayers by public school children or it could no longer claim to be the object of divine favor.

America Under God?

The implications of the popular conception that America is a nation "under God" and one that trusts in him are far-reaching. For one thing it fosters the wrong-headed assumption that the United States is a "Christian nation," when in fact no country has the right to make such a pretentious claim. Political entities by their very nature fall outside the definition of Christian, for they govern a mixed population of believers and non-believers. Only the church of Jesus Christ, the body of believers everywhere in the world, can be a Christian nation, as I Peter 2:9, 10 and Romans 9 so unequivocally express. It is one thing to acknowledge the historical reality that Christian values and convictions shaped the

---

[63]88th Cong., 2nd Sess., House of Representatives, Committee on the Judiciary. *Proposed Amendments to the Constitution Relating to Prayers and Bible Reading in the Public Schools*, hearing, April 22—June 3, 1964, p. 829.

[64]Ibid., p. 848.

development of American political, social, and cultural life but something far different to conclude that these produced a Christian nation.

Such civil religion rituals as the Pledge of Allegiance contribute to this confusion of God and country. One insightful study shows that school children up to about the age of ten have the tendency to interpret the pledge as a prayer—a request either to God or to some unidentified but infinite power for aid and protection. After the fifth grade, children began seeing the flag salute as an expression of loyalty to country and solidarity with other citizens, and the religious effect is gradually displaced upon the political object. The religious sentiment is subtly transferred to the bond with the political community, but yet the initial and early intermingling of the religious with the political has created a tie difficult to dissolve.[65] These feelings are readily linked to the nation-state and thereby serve as a potent energizing force for American nationalism. That hardly is an appropriate role for a faith like Christianity, whose founders were harassed and slaughtered by a Roman empire which demanded just this sort of ultimate allegiance from them.

Another danger of the widespread appeal to God is a defensive religiosity that numbs public sensitivity to the country's actual role in history. A messianic consciousness has pervaded the American experience from the earliest days of its history, and this conception of the United States as the darling of divine Providence resulted in a doctrine of national mission that can only be regarded as a mixture of both good and ill.[66] From one side the country may be viewed as the light of the nations, a city

---

[65]David Easton and Robert D. Hess, "The Child's Political World," *Midwest Journal of Political Science* 6 (August 1962): 238-39.

[66]The literature on national mission is extremely vast in scope. Some useful titles include: Reinhold Niebuhr, *The Irony of American History* (New York: Scribners, 1952); Edward M. Burns, *The American Idea of Mission* (New Brunswick, N. J.: Rutgers University Press, 1957); John E. Smylie, "Protestant Clergymen and America's World Role, 1865-1900," (Ph.D.Diss., Princeton Theological Seminary, 1959); Frederick R. Merk, *Manifest Destiny and Mission in American History* (New York: Knopf, 1963); Ernest L. Tuveson, *Redeemer Nation: The Idea of America's Millennial Role* (Chicago: University of Chicago Press, 1968); Winthrop S. Hudson, *Nationalism and Religion in America: Concepts of American Identity and Mission* (New York: Harper & Row, 1970); Conrad Cherry, *God's New Israel: Religious Interpretations of American Destiny* (Englewood Cliffs, N. J.: Prentice-Hall, 1971); Robert T. Handy, *A Christian America: Protestant Hopes and Historical Realities* (New York: Oxford University Press, 1971); and Paul C. Nagel, *This Sacred Trust: American Nationality, 1789-1898* (New York: Oxford University Press, 1972).

58416

on a hill, ordained to demonstrate to the world the marvelous benefits of free institutions and popular sovereignty. From another perspective may be seen the more seamy side of America—the "manifest destiny" of expansionism, the policeman making the world safe for democracy, and the denial of justice to minority groups.

A growing public resentment of social criticism and continuing referral to America's shortcomings helped to fuel the explosion of civil religiosity in the 1950s and even more so in the 1960s. As "Americanism" came to be allied with conservatism and the national faith was increasingly invoked in the struggle against "godless" communism, Americans looked askance at any attempt to assess critically the nation's values and world role. The problem was further exacerbated by the onset of the Vietnam War, as the country's leaders sought to justify the conflict as necessary and right and argued that the peace they hoped to obtain would be one with "honor." The nation was glorified in religious terms that ranged in scope from the following crude comments of the militant anticommunist evangelist Billy James Hargis:

> The only thing I will assume is, one, that America is right and, second that God is right. . . . America is the greatest country in the world and . . . Jesus Christ is everything he said he was and from there I will go. . . . Now I'm not going to argue about America; I'm not going to argue about Christ.[67]

to the pious sentiments of Gerald R. Ford:

> Ours is—and will remain—the healthiest society, mentally and physically, and more importantly, spiritually, the world has ever known. . . . This is a strong country, a good country, and it is overflowing with honest, decent people who try to lead honest, decent lives.[68]

But as historian Sydney E. Ahlstrom cogently points out, Americans must come to terms with the irony of the phrase "un-

---

[67]Statement made in an interview with Dale Leathers, March 11, 1965. Quoted in Leathers, "The Thrust of the Radical Right," in *Preaching in American History*, ed. Dewitte Holland (Nashville: Abingdon Press, 1969), pp. 322-23.

[68]Vice President Gerald R. Ford, speech before the Congressional Prayer Breakfast of the National Religious Broadcasters, excerpts published in *Christian Crusade Weekly* 14 (February 14, 1974): 1.

der God." Although it was added to the Pledge of Allegiance in
the halcyon days of President Eisenhower when people so
blithely assumed that "God was for us and we were for God,"
the primary meaning of that affirmation is really "under judgment."[69] In other words, God stands for such things as righteousness, justice, and love, and a nation that is truly under
God will be judged according to how it measures up to these
divine standards. The only way a nation can ever claim in any
legitimate fashion to be under God is to make a thorough and
continuous effort to be obedient to his will. Churchman Dean M.
Kelley clearly captures the significance of this profound truth when
he serves notice that:

> If we are still the same old self-seeking, greedy, ruthless, envious,
> gluttonous, malicious animals we were before, then taking on the
> phrase "under God" is indeed "taking the Lord's name in vain," the
> essence of profanity indulged in on a national scale.[70]

The idea of a nation trusting in God is trivialized and vul-
garized when such pious words are embossed upon the money
and scattered through the public addresses and papers of politi-
cians. Yet, the element of judgment still inheres there, as Richard
M. Nixon so prophetically acknowledged in his second inaugural
address: "We shall answer to God, to history, and to our conscience for the way in which we use these years."[71] This sentiment was reiterated in the presence of Mr. Nixon by one of his
staunch supporters, Congressman William Hudnut of Indiana, a
scant nine months before his fall: "We need the concept 'this nation under God' to keep us from becoming a government of men
instead of a government of laws, and in the long run, from
becoming a divine right of kings type of autocracy."[72]

Because Americans so often tend to idolize the democratic

---

[69]Sydney E. Ahlstrom, "Requiem for Patriotic Piety," *Worldview* 18 (August 1972):
11.

[70]Dean M. Kelley, "What Is a 'Nation under God'?" in *Preaching on National
Holidays*, ed. Alton M. Motter (Philadelphia: Fortress, 1976), pp. 57-58. At the time he
made these remarks Kelley was the executive director of the Department of Civil and
Religious Liberty, National Council of Churches.

[71]*Public Papers of the Presidents of the United States. Richard Nixon, 1973.* (Washington: U.S. Government Printing Office, 1975), p. 15.

[72]Sermon preached in the White House on October 14, 1973, printed in the *Congressional Record* 119 (October 15, 1973): 34188.

process and their political institutions and to overlook their own need for redemption, it is well to recall the pithy observation of the eminent Christian historian Kenneth Scott Latourette that Jesus Christ was crucified by "representatives of as high a religion and as good a government as men had thus far known. Thus God at once passed judgment on men's best achievement and sought to save the world which had committed the crime."[73]

Lutheran theologian Richard J. Neuhaus' response to the question of whether one nation under God is an indication of jingoism or judgment is forthright and unequivocal: "The idea of America being 'under God' does not imply some special privileged position, but immediately places the American experiment into a network of global accountability."[74] If the United States is a "nation whose God is the Lord" (Ps. 33:12)—the virtually unanimous view of the exponents of civil religiosity dealt with in the preceding pages—then it must walk in his ways. God loves justice (Isa. 61:8) and he requires a person "to do justice, and to love kindness, and to walk humbly with your God" (Mic. 6:8). To follow the Lord is to practice the way of peace, not trust in arms, and it involves extending the benefits of freedom, opportunity, and justice to all members of the society, irrespective of their social class, race, sex, or political and religious beliefs.

Obviously, American performance has fallen far short of these lofty standards, and the only way Americans can aspire to be "under God" in any genuinely Christian sense is to seek a renewal of the national moral fiber and purpose. To bring this about would require first of all a renewal of the spiritual strength and purity of the individuals making up the American nation, and without that the references to God in the civic rituals and public statements of political leaders are as a noisy gong or a clanging cymbal (I Cor. 13:1). The recognition that the Lord reigns over this nation (as well as all nations) will have no practical meaning until he first reigns in the hearts of the individuals who comprise it, and their lives and values are brought into total submission to the standards and principles he has laid down in the Scriptures.

Perhaps most Americans find it easier simply to express their public religious feelings through pious phraseology, but the God whom they address in this manner demands far more of them.

---

[73]Kenneth Scott Latourette, *A History of Christianity* (New York: Harper, 1953), p. 1472.

[74]Richard J. Neuhaus, *Time Toward Home: The American Experiment as Revelation* (New York: Seabury, 1975), p. 184.

6

Changing Family Patterns

"I'm seeing it all in a new light. The man I marry is just as responsible to fit into *my* world as I am to fit into *his* world! It's mind-blowing!" The speaker was a college senior contemplating a change in career plans. As Judy shared her thoughts with my husband and me, she was a mixture of enthusiasm tempered with a touch of apprehension. What would it all mean? The idea of an equal-partner, dual-career marriage was so different from the traditional views of family life she had heard since childhood. The traditional way was for the woman to do all the fitting into the man's world. The wife, not the husband, was required to do the adjusting and sacrificing in marriage. His interests, not hers, were considered the more important.

Today such thinking is being challenged. But Judy's fiance wanted no part of it. He wanted a traditional wife and a traditional life—one that would ensure masculine privilege, power, and comforts. "I'm finding my affection for Mike is beginning to cool," Judy wrote during her first year of graduate school. "I've tried to talk these matters over with him, but he says he can't see it this way at all. I'm convinced he doesn't really want what's best for me, and I can't love a man like that." Trust was broken, and—by mutual agreement—so was the engagement.

But let's take another example. Craig and Diane have been married four years and have one child. Diane is pressing for a second child, and Craig reports they have more disagreements over this topic than any other. "Diane has really changed since marriage," Craig complains. "She used to be so different—so active in all sorts of projects, student body president in high school, a campus leader in college (until she quit to marry me). I'm not sure what it is about marriage, but it's as though she feels she has to fit into some sort of prearranged mold or pattern. She seems so much more helpless and dependent, centers her whole life around little Cindy and me, and nags me constantly for more time and attention. When I dated her she was so vivacious and interesting—always had so many fascinating things to talk about and keep busy with. From her viewpoint, she is fulfilling the role of Christian wife exactly as it should be filled—exactly the way the books and speakers say. But I find myself wanting something more. I wish she'd realize her own identity, her self-worth. I'd like to see her go back to school and develop her career potential. In fact, you may find this hard to believe, but I wouldn't mind if she even became the chief breadwinner someday and I'd stay home as the househusband. Honestly! It might even give me a chance to try my hand at writing novels, something I've always wanted to do."

These opening stories are true. Only the names and a few identifying facts have been changed. They serve to illustrate some of the most basic areas of change in modern society. Traditional expectations for male and female roles are being altered and seem to be associated with a wide range of other changes: participation of women in the labor force, family size, the allocation of power in the husband-wife relationship, household division of labor, decisions about when (and even whether) to marry, decisions about continuing or breaking up relationships, and much more.

For many Christians, such news is alarming. However, instead of wringing our hands, perhaps we should be trying to see what changing family patterns may be telling us about ourselves and our society. In other words, what can we, as people of Christ, learn from census findings and other behavioral science research that can make us aware of emerging trends? Might not compassion be a more appropriate response than condemnation in many cases? In fact, we may even find cause to rejoice in certain trends! Still other findings present a *challenge* to Christians, both with regard to rethinking some important issues and also in channeling our ministry to others.

We as Christians need to be aware of such facts as these from recent census reports:[1] (1) Both men and women are waiting longer to

---

[1] Unless otherwise indicated, all census statistics are taken from the U.S. Bureau

marry. (2) The percentage of persons electing to remain single is increasing. (3) More and more women are entering the labor force. (4) The incidence of divorce has been growing dramatically in recent years. (5) Families are smaller than they used to be and some couples are choosing to have no children at all. (6) "Nonfamily" households (those households in which persons either live alone or with persons not related to them) have increased by 40 percent since 1970. (7) The number of persons living in two-person households made up of unrelated adults of the opposite sex has doubled since 1970. (8) The percentage of one-parent families has been growing. Let us examine each of these facts.

Later Age at Marriage

In 1960, the median age at which men married was 23 years, but sixteen years later, the median age was 24 years. For women during that same period of time, the median age for marriage increased from 20 to 21 years. In other words, persons of both sexes are now waiting one full year longer before marrying. This is certainly no cause for despair, since it has clearly been established that the younger persons are when they marry, the greater is the likelihood of divorce. Marriages entered during the teen years are particularly unstable in our society. [2] And contrary to popular belief, young persons may be indicating by their postponement of marriage that they are taking marriage *more* seriously rather than less so. Many say they want time to know and develop themselves, to try different educational, occupational, and travel experiences, and to enjoy the challenge and adventure of being entirely on their own before settling down to undertake what they realize are serious responsibilities in marriage and possible parenthood. They want to be ready for marriage and not just drift into it unthinkingly.

Shouldn't Christians view this in a positive light? By taking time to develop various aspects of their unique personhood and God-given gifts, many young men and women will find they have much more to bring to the marriage than could otherwise be the case. Chances are they will have greater skills at interpersonal

---

of the Census, "Marital Status and Living Arrangements: March, 1976," series P-20, no. 306, *Current Population Reports* (Washington, D.C.: U. S. Government Printing Office, 1977).

[2] See Letha and John Scanzoni, *Men, Women, and Change: A Sociology of Marriage and Family* (New York: McGraw-Hill, 1976), pp. 134-35, 460-63.

communication which can help equip them to handle the negotiating and conflict management that are inevitable parts of living
together in a marriage relationship. Particularly encouraging are the
signs that *women* are waiting longer to marry and instead are taking
advantage of opportunities for education, employment, and service
for Christ in ministries that might be impossible if they were married
and had small children.

Traditionally, Christians have done all too little to encourage girls
and women to develop and utilize their talents, including
leadership talents. Instead, churches (along with parents, peers,
schools, and the media) have given both direct and indirect
messages that no sound is sweeter than wedding bells, no sight
more beautiful than a bridal gown, no role more important than
being someone's wife. The pressures may be subtle, though often
they are not ("When are you going to get married?"); and rather
than risk failure in attaining what she has been told is woman's true
calling, many a Christian young woman has accepted the first
chance for marriage that came along. Often that decision has been
unwise if not disastrous, and it has meant a stifling of what she could
have been and a halt to the contributions she could have made.
There are times, of course, when this isn't the case at all; and two
young persons in an early marriage are able to affirm and encourage
one another's full potential in such a way that both they and the
world they touch are enriched *because* they have come together and
have grown together. But the reverse happens often enough to alert
us to the merits and wisdom of willingness to delay marriage. (Actually, this pattern is not something radically new. In 1890, the median
age at which men married was 26; women, 22.)

Singleness Increasing

Somewhat related to the matter of postponing marriage are certain indications that, for a growing number of persons, a single
lifestyle may be viewed as desirable for a longer period of time—for
some, perhaps throughout the entire life span. The percentage of
never-married women and men under age 35 increased between
1960 and 1976, although at the same time there has been a slight
decrease in singleness among persons over 35 during that same
period.

We can detect a possible trend in the United States Bureau of the
Census' statistics of the age group in which most first marriages
have traditionally taken place, the 20-to-24-year-old category. In

1960, slightly more than half the men in this group were single; by the mid-1970s two-thirds of men aged 20 to 24 have never married. Among women in this age group in 1960, only 28 percent were still single. Now 43 percent of 20-to-24-year-old women are single. Exactly what this signifies for the future is not known.

However, there is no reason for Christians to view the singleness phenomenon with disapproval. Singleness is treated with high respect in the New Testament. But for too long, the Christian community has made single persons feel like second-class citizens. For example, what is more insulting to the never-married (not to mention the divorced or widowed) than to be assigned to a class called "Pairs and Spares"—which leaves no doubt about who the "spares" are. We've been suspicious of single persons ("I wonder what's wrong with that person that he/she never married?") and haven't known quite what to do with them in our nuclear-family-oriented church life. We simply haven't valued highly enough the contributions of single persons to the body of Christ. Perhaps their growing numbers will shake us into an awareness of their presence and potential among us.

Both Jesus (Matt. 19:10-12) and Paul (I Cor. 7:7-9) taught that the ability to live a single life is a special gift given to some persons, just as the ability to live in a marriage relationship is a gift given to others. Of course, there is no denying that some single persons are persuaded they don't have the "gift of singleness," just as some married persons may discover they don't have the "gift of marriage"—and some parents don't have the "gift of parenting." People may find themselves in any of these categories by force of circumstance rather than by choice or a sense of God's call. Therefore, they may need our special love, encouragement, and understanding.

Yet it is important to keep in mind that Jesus and Paul demonstrated by their own examples how positive, dynamic, and beneficial to the world a dedicated single life can be. As far as we know, Mary, Martha, and Lazarus were also unmarried, as undoubtedly were many others of those close to Jesus. And of course, there was John the Baptist. To the apostle Paul, one of the greatest benefits of the single life was the freedom it provided to serve Christ without the distracting pull of family obligations (I Cor. 7:32-35). The range of ministries open to the single person may be quite different from that which is open to the married person, including ministries that require various risks, greater geographical mobility, availability at all hours, and so on. Thus, the trend toward increasing singleness is nothing for Christians to view with alarm. Rather, these statistics can call us back to a Scriptural position which emphasizes that persons are *not* halves waiting to be made whole through marriage. Rather, each person—whether female or male—is a complete person made in God's image and called to live for the glory of God and the benefit of his or her sister and brother human beings.

More Women in the Work Force

It does not seem too far afield to suggest that being created in God's image includes the ability to reflect those qualities God reveals about Himself in the first two chapters of Genesis: the ability to create and the ability to relate. Traditionally, the ability to create has been stressed for men, while the emphasis for women has been on the ability to relate. Therefore, women have been trained to consider men as the *doers* in life and to consider themselves as the *supporters* of the doers ("Behind every great man is a woman"). As a result, women's interests and talents have often been set aside to make sure that life's best opportunities go to males. If family budgets are tight, it is more likely that sons and not daughters will be the ones to go to college. After marriage, the traditional expectation has been that women will put aside their own interests and give top priority to the needs and interests of their husbands and children. To question this arrangement is likely to bring charges of selfishness and give rise to guilt feelings.

One of the biggest changes occurring today is the rethinking women are doing in this area. And that includes Christian women. The Christian woman looks at Genesis 1:26-28 and discovers that the "creation mandate" was given equally to both sexes. *Both* women and men were told by God to be fruitful and multiply (that is, to have responsibility for home and family). And *both* women and men were told by God to have dominion over the earth. "Thou has given humanity (man, generic; not man, male) dominion over the works of Thy hands" is the message of Psalm 8:6.

If males have a need to reflect God's image through working, cultivating, building, making, controlling, discovering, inventing, and achieving; so do women have a need to express the "creation" side as well as the "relation" side of the image of God. If men are given a *variety* of talents and abilities suiting them for all kinds of work, so too are women. Some women are immensely talented as creative homemakers and are gifted in caring for children. Other women have no interests or talents along these lines. For them to be forced into a full-time homemaker role on the assumption that this is woman's *only* work would be as foolish as forcing all men to be farmers or mechanics or physicians—or insisting that all men are to make their husband/father role their full-time career. Historically, males have been encouraged to discover their interests and talents and choose their occupations on that basis. Should it be any different for females?

Many Christian women today are taking a new look at the notion of calling or vocation or career. Many are taking a serious look at their own lives in order to discover talents and abilities. And many of us see this as a matter of God-given responsibility, a matter of stewardship. Jesus had something to say about hiding lights under bushels or burying talents in napkins!

In discussing changing family patterns, we cannot ignore the matter of paid employment for women; some of the biggest changes of all are related to this growing trend. As the option to work outside the home began to open to women, economic dependence on men began to decrease. It became possible for a woman to be free to develop her own career interests rather than to feel she must settle into a marriage to which she was not suited. It was no longer necessary to have a man support her for the sake of survival; the opening up of job opportunities as well as higher education for women meant that she could support herself. Thus, a trend that began in the last century continues today. Women have been entering the labor force in record numbers. Nearly half of all women over sixteen years of age are now employed. Or to look at it another way, four out of every ten persons in the United States labor force are women. Among married women whose husbands are present, 44 percent are employed. This figure may be compared to 1950 when only one-fourth of married women were employed, or 1900 when only 6 percent of married women were in the labor force.[3]

Women are working for varied reasons: economic need, added benefits for their families (such as making possible the purchase of a new house or college for their children), a desire to utilize

[3]Howard N. Fullerton, Jr. and Paul O. Flaim, "New Labor Force Projections to 1990," *Monthly Labor Review* (December, 1976), pp. 9-10; U. S. Bureau of the Census, "A Statistical Portrait of Women in the United States," series P-23, no. 58, *Current Population Reports* (Washington, D.C.: U. S. Government Printing Office, 1976); Scanzoni and Scanzoni, *Men, Women, and Change*, p. 214.

skills, a desire to make a contribution to the world and help others through their knowledge and talents, self-fulfillment, a sense of accomplishment. Sociologist Jean Lipman-Blumen has pointed out that traditionally women have been taught to expect only "vicarious achievement" in life—to live through the achievements of others, particularly the significant males in their lives (fathers, husbands, sons, the executive one assists as secretary, the physician with whom one is associated as nurse, and so on). Now that is changing, and more and more women want the rewards of *direct* achievement rather than vicarious achievment.[4]

The phenomenon of growing labor force participation among women may be expected to be noticed increasingly among those women in church congregations as well as those outside. As Christian women are taking a new look at and emulating biblical role models, we may expect to find more and more Lydias (Acts 16) who are just as at home in the marketplace as they are in a prayer meeting. Interestingly, the ideal wife described in Proverbs 31:10-31, whose activities are so highly praised, is a woman whose activities include such financial ventures as investing in real estate, planting a vineyard, and operating a garment manufacturing business!

Changing attitudes toward gender roles and work are affecting men as well as women. Author Warren Farrell points out that just as women no longer want to be treated as "sex objects," many men today no longer want to be regarded as "success objects."[5] The competitiveness of the "rat race," the concern about measuring up to all that is expected of the masculine image, the way self-esteem is tied to how many rungs a man has climbed on the ladder of success—all this and more is being questioned by many men. While work can be something positive and can be related to the "creation aspect" of God's image, work can also be perverted into something that drives and enslaves a person so that other riches of life are bypassed. Thus, many fathers work day and night to give their families a good living, only to find that "good living" might mean something altogether different than they thought. Jesus said, "A man's life does not consist in the

---

[4]Jean Lipman-Bluemen, "The Vicarious Achievement Ethic and Non-Traditional Roles for Women," (Paper presented at the Eastern Sociological Society, annual meeting, New York City, April 1973).

[5]Warren Farrell, *The Liberated Man* (New York: Random House, 1975).

abundance of his possessions" (Luke 12:15). Some men discover this too late, after their children are grown and gone, and they realize they never really got to know them. It was always, "Daddy's busy now, honey. I'll talk to you some other time," or "I'll play with you later." And later never came. Many young men today, having seen that attitude in their fathers, are determining to have a different set of priorities.

Some men are seeing that by having been assigned the bread-winner role by society, with laws to back it up, they have been strapped into a role without regard to their own feelings or individual abilities just as much as women have been strapped into roles assigned them by others. Thus, while women have been cheated by being kept from employment opportunities under traditional ideas about "a woman's place," men have been cheated in the opposite direction. If "a woman's place" was in the home, "a man's area" was the marketplace. If women were told, "You can't be free to work," men were told, "You can't be free *not* to work." Even now, work for women is a choice; work for men is a duty.

Some couples today are choosing to reduce the husband's burden of bearing full responsibility for supporting the family by becoming coproviders. Such husbands and wives are following the biblical example of Priscilla and Aquila who not only shared the joys of married life, but also shared the breadwinning role (both were tentmakers) and served together in evangelistic work and church planting (Acts 18; Rom. 16:3-5). Such couples are discovering that the true message of Ephesians 5:21-33 is a far cry from a dominance-subordination model. Rather, it is a picture of love on the part of both husband and wife that is self-expending rather than self-expanding (to borrow from theologian Arthur McGill's choice wording).[6] The model is one of *mutual* submissiveness and *mutual* affirmation—serving, supporting, encouraging, building one another up, and cheering one another on in the use of God-given talents.[7]

Some dual-career couples are calling for changes in society's work arrangements. One example is the possibility of part-time

---

[6]Arthur C. McGill, *Suffering: A Test of Theological Method* (Philadelphia: Geneva Press, 1968), pp. 51-53.

[7]For an excellent discussion of mutual submissiveness and mutual affirmation, see Virginia Ramey Mollenkott, *Women, Men, and the Bible* (Nashville: Abingdon Press, 1977). See also Letha Scanzoni and Nancy Hardesty, *All We're Meant to Be: A Biblical Approach to Women's Liberation* (Waco, Texas: Word, 1974); Richard and

work so that both parents can take turns being with the children during the half-day not at work. Some men and women are pressing for child-care arrangements at the place of employment so that one or the other parent is nearby all day long—a plan that was put into effect during World War II and has been used in other countries. Just as some women take maternity leaves and go back to their place of employment later, some men are asking for paternity leaves and in a few cases are getting them, thus enabling them to be with their wives and new babies for a time. Business and industry seem to be giving some indication that they are beginning to listen, and certain experiments are starting to be made, with more flexible work hours and other innovations that will make it easier for both husbands and wives in their career aspirations at the same time that they are concerned about time for relating to one another and to their children.

Another job-related concern of some couples today is the two-persons-fill-one-career situation in which the husband's occupation requires not only *his* total devotion but also the devotion, support, and help of his wife. Traditional examples would be the case of the minister's wife who is expected by the church to act as a kind of assistant pastor, but without title or paycheck; or the politician's wife who is expected to campaign for him, putting her own interests aside; or the wife of a man hoping to rise in corporate management who is expected to aid his climb by keeping a certain kind of home and lifestyle, being ready to entertain important clients, and so on. Just as the old English Common Law decreed that the husband and wife are one and that one is the husband, many careers have had the built-in assumption that there should be only one occupation to a marriage and that occupation should be the husband's. Now that many women are saying *no* to this arrangement and insisting that vicarious achievement is not enough for them, there may be many more adjustments necessary within many careers and much more negotiation necessary in husband-wife relationships.

Business magazines in recent years have expressed some worries over the changes. For example, wives with careers of their own are not so willing to drop everything and move to the branch

Joyce Boldrey, *Chauvinist or Feminist?: Paul's View of Women* (Grand Rapids: Baker, 1976); Paul K. Jewett, *Man as Male and Female* (Grand Rapids: Eerdmans, 1975); and John Scanzoni, *Love and Negotiate: Creative Conflict in Marriage* (Waco, Texas: Word, 1979).

office where the company wants to send the husband. Increasingly, even wives who in the past appeared willing to serve as adjuncts to their husbands' careers (because they had been taught that was their role and mission in life) are coming forth to express discontent with the unfairness of the arrangement. Christians who chide women for such discontent and call it "selfishness" are not taking seriously the biblical concept of justice. A husband who really loves his wife as his own flesh will want to treat her as he himself would wish to be treated.

One last area relating to the matter of women's labor force participation has to do with the decision of some husbands to be househusbands. These are men who are glad for the wife's willingness to assume the breadwinner role in order that they can be free to stay home and look after the house and children. There are some delightfully happy couples who find the arrangement works very well for them. In one case, the wife is a career officer in the U.S. Army while the husband cares for the children and is trying free-lance writing—something he had always hoped to do but never had a chance because of the time demands on a conventional job. In another case, the wife is pursuing graduate studies, teaching at a university part-time, and supporting the family through an assistantship while her husband cares for the children and is attempting to start a house church in their home. Those Christians who find such arrangements upsetting and "unmanly" may be surprised to learn that Jesus and the disciples were financially supported by women (Luke 8:2-3).

The Rise in Divorces

Of all the changing family patterns that most alarm Christians, this perhaps tops the list. In 1960, there were 35 divorced persons for every 1,000 persons in an intact marriage. By 1976, that figure had jumped to 75 divorced persons per 1,000 married persons. Many concerned Christians are shaking their heads and asking, "What is happening to marriage?" Many things are happening to marriage, chief of which seem to be higher expectations than ever before and less willingness to remain in a situation that is unrewarding, unfulfilling, or in some way punishing. People quite simply demand more from marriage than was once the case. Evidently, they are not really giving up on the institution itself, however, because according to current statistics four out of five divorced persons marry again.

More than a million divorces in a one-year period took place for the first time in 1975. Furthermore, the latest census projections are that if the present pattern continues, about one-third of recent marriages are likely to end in divorce. And although the rate at which divorces have been increasing is now slowing down and may be heading toward a plateau, the divorce rate (5 divorces per 1,000 population) is still higher than ever before in our country's history. (During the 1950s and early 1960s, the divorce rate had been just slightly over 2 per 1,000; but that plateau ended in 1963 and began the climb that continued into the 1970s.)[8]

What do these facts say to us as Christians? For one, they are challenging us to take a more realistic look at divorce and to search anew for biblical principles to guide us. Among many Christians, the stigma attached to divorce has meant that a divorced person was somehow considered unworthy to serve Christ in various capacities. Somehow Christ's redemptive love and power to uplift are considered insufficient in the case of the divorced person. I remember one young woman telling me of her deep unhappiness in her marriage while at the same time struggling with whether divorce might be permissible for a follower of Jesus Christ. "Is God going to hold me accountable all my life for one mistake I made when I was only eighteen years old? Doesn't God give any second chances in this one area of life?" she asked. As more and more churches are being faced with divorced persons and remarried-after-divorce couples, Christian leaders are being forced to face up to this young woman's question.

In his excellent and Scripture-based book, *The Right to Remarry*, Dwight Small sums up the issue when he asks: "How can one feel right about proclaiming the free and full pardon of *all* sin and failure, while insisting that one failure alone—marital failure—must be forever penalized? Is divorce following the death of marriage really socially unpardonable and unrestorable to the extent that all divorced persons cannot again contract a normal marriage, never enjoy another life-partner, never live normally in the intimate society called the family, never again hold office, or serve significantly in the Church of our gracious Redeemer?"[9]

---

[8]U. S. Department of Health, Education, and Welfare, "Births, Marriages, Divorces, and Deaths for 1976," vol. 25, no. 12, *Monthly Vital Statistics Report*, (Washington, D.C.: DHEW, 1977). See also Scanzoni and Scanzoni, *Men, Women, and Change*, p. 457.

[9]Dwight Hervey Small, *The Right to Remarry* (Old Tappan, N.J.: Revell, 1975), p. 18.

And echoing the reasoning of the great writer John Milton who asked in his seventeenth-century essays on divorce if we could conclude that God is less merciful under the gospel than under the Mosaic dispensation, Dwight Small ends his book with these words: "As the divorce law in the Old Testament was a concession to human weakness and failure, so New Testament grace allows for the same. It is never God's pure intention that marriage be dissolved, but it is never God's intention that some marriages be formed and continue as they are, either."[10]

Yet there is no denying that divorce is painful. Nor can it be treated casually. Furthermore, it must be seen as a process that begins long before the divorce decree is granted and continues for some time afterward. Divorced persons need the nurture, love, and supportiveness of a community of Christians who really care about them—and who care also about their children, who especially need love and understanding at this time. It is also important to nurture those new family units that come into being upon the remarriage of divorced and widowed persons with children from previous marriages—what one sociologist calls "reconstituted families."[11]

What else do current divorce statistics have to say to us? For one thing, they call us as God's people to renewed efforts toward social justice for those segments of the population that are economically and educationally deprived. Along with the young, it is the poor who have the least stable marriages. Racial discrimination also enters the picture, because studies indicate that by denying black people equal access to educational and occupational opportunities, a white-dominated society contributes to marital disruption among blacks.

We as Christians also need to raise fundamental questions about love and justice within the institution of marriage itself, particularly the matter of justice for women. Increasing numbers of women are becoming aware that both law and custom have treated them unfairly. As we saw earlier, English Common Law declared that a husband and wife were one, and that *one* was the husband. His rights, concerns, interests, needs, wishes were what mattered; the wife was an appendage (even if, in better marriages, a *loved* appendage), and her needs and interests were

---

[10]Ibid., pp. 186-87.

[11]Lucile Duberman, *The Reconstituted Family: A Study of Remarried Couples and Their Children* (Chicago: Nelson-Hall, 1975).

considered secondary if they were considered at all. Seeing such an arrangement as unfair, many women are negotiating for change; and if change is not forthcoming, they are willing to end a marriage. Such factors entered into the divorce of Jane Spock and the noted pediatrician Dr. Benjamin Spock after forty-eight years of marriage. In a *New York Times* interview (March 19, 1976), Jane Spock told of coauthoring the best-selling book, *Baby and Child Care*, with her husband and then suffering in silent pain for thirty years when he failed to give her credit. "I don't think he could stand it, sharing the spotlight," she said. "He saw me only as a wife and mother. I was expected to have a good dinner ready when he came home. I don't think he realized what he was doing to me."

In another case, a minister's wife returned to her teaching career after twenty years of marriage. The husband was so threatened by his wife's success and by no longer having her "at his constant beck and call" that he had an emotional breakdown and was hospitalized. That marriage, too, ended in divorce. From one standpoint, as Dr. Gordon Allport has pointed out, it may seem easier for a woman who lives with a man who considers her inferior to try to act as though she agrees with him.[12] But of course this is a denial of the biblical principle of *justice* and all that it means to be *one in Christ* (Gal. 3:28), mutually submitting to one another and mutually affirming one another's God-given gifts.

Perhaps one of the biggest challenges presented to us by the divorce statistics is the need to train young men and women for marriages that can mean personal growth for both individuals, with each encouraging the other to be all she or he can be, and with each working together to make the *relationship* all that it can possibly be for the glory of God. Likewise, we need to help couples learn communication and negotiation skills so that they can handle and resolve problems and conflicts without feeling the only solution is to break up the marriage.

One other point needs to be made. If, as historian William O'Neill suggests,[13] there may be a connection between the rise in divorce rates and the rise in employment rates among married women, beginning in the last century, let us not rush to blame

---

[12]Quoted by Jill Ruckelshaus in a speech before the National Press Club, Washington, D. C., September 12, 1975.

[13]William O'Neill, *Divorce in the Progressive Era* (New Haven, Conn.: Yale University Press, 1967).

the working woman. Rather, let us ask what injustices in the structure of marriage in our society have caused many women to be eager to leave the institution when other alternatives open up and economic dependence on a man is no longer necessary.

Smaller Families

In a discussion of changing family patterns, we cannot overlook the matter of children. For one thing, families are choosing to have fewer children.[14] In 1967, when American wives between the ages of 18 and 39 were asked how many children they expected to have during their lifetime, the average was 3.1. In 1976, the average was down to 2.4. And when census interviewers asked young women not yet married (ages 18 to 24 years old in 1976) how many children they expected to have over their lifetime, the average was 1.9.

Christians should also be aware of the pattern of voluntary childlessness. About one out of twenty married couples is choosing not to have any children at all, and a few Christian leaders (both Catholic and Protestant) are asking if this might not be a positive good—to be compared with individuals who choose celibacy in order to be more free (in terms of time, geographical mobility, and so on) to serve Christ. If so, such couples need our supportiveness rather than condemnation and accusations of selfishness—especially in a world that is already concerned with problems related to population, hunger, energy depletion, and the like. We should also be realistic enough to know that some persons are not well suited to parenthood and may choose to be voluntarily childless for that reason alone. It is far better that children not be born that than they suffer the scars of being unwanted or battered, and it is far better for couples to have no children at all than to have children born for no reason other than that the couple conformed to social pressures and expectations.

However, 95 percent of married couples *do* plan to have children; and both women and men are taking a new look at what parenthood really means. For example, contrary to popular belief, many women in the women's movement appreciate children more than ever. By having a positive view of themselves and of

---

[14]Scanzoni and Scanzoni, *Men, Woman, and Change,* chap. 9; U. S. Bureau of the Census, "Population Characteristics," series P-20, no. 300, *Current Population Reports* (Washington, D. C.: U. S. Government Printing Office, 1976).

womanhood (having moved away from old ideas about women's "inferiority"), women are taking great joy in the processes of pregnancy, birth, breastfeeding, and training their children. This is true whether or not they are pursuing careers in addition to motherhood. Many women are finding that by having learned to love themselves, they are more free to love their husbands and children (Matt. 22:39). No longer *living through* their husbands and children, they are less apt to drain them or "smother love" them; rather, they are finding they have more to give out of their own fulfilled lives. Women are also taking delight in the challenge of what sociologists call the "socialization process," training children to take their place in society. Many women today are especially working hard to train their daughters and sons in ways that will help them avoid the limitations of gender-role stereotypes.

Similarly, men are taking a new look at parenthood. In the past, it was common for men to assume that the care of the children was the wife's domain, and if they participated at all it was "to help the wife." Today, more and more men not only see the injustice of letting the wife bear full responsibility for children; they also see they have been cheating themselves as well. Men want to get more involved. It is not a matter of "helping" with the children or the house but of "sharing" something that concerns both partners in a marriage. Many husbands are joining their wives in natural childbirth classes, are present at the deliveries of their babies, are sharing in infant care, are even taking paternity leaves. One father who took a paternity leave wrote a newspaper article on exciting ways fathers can teach preschoolers in the home.

The biblical models are there. The Book of Proverbs emphasizes a father's involvement with his children, and the apostle Paul talked about that, too. Child care is not women's work or men's work, but parents' work. We need to ponder the high regard Jesus had for children and how he made sure he took time for them, even though the disciples seemed to think that more important matters should occupy a man's time and interest. Jesus showed that nothing was more important. In answer to the question, "Who is the greatest in the kingdom of heaven?" Jesus called a little child to him (Matt. 18).

One of the changes many men want to make today is to take more time to know and relate to their children. This includes forming close bonds with daughters and appreciating their worth just as much as sons. Too often, female children have been devalued. (In one extreme case, I heard a father say he had been "shortchanged" when his baby daughter was born.) Again things are changing. One example is a factory worker who in a men's consciousness-raising group told of having made a decision with his wife to have only two children. When his second daughter was born, he was greatly disappointed. He asked himself why he felt as he did: "Why did I want a son so badly? It's because boys grow up and do important, interesting things. Girls just get married." Then he thought some more and exclaimed, "I realize it's all different now. Girls can do just as exciting things with their lives!" Recently, there has been a growing number of father-daughter family businesses. We are accustomed to seeing shop signs or lettering on trucks announcing "John Jones and Sons." It is likely that we shall increasingly be seeing signs saying "John Jones and Daughters"—or maybe even "Mary Jones and Daughters" or "Mary Jones and Sons"!

The Growth in "Nonfamily" Households

Church programs and Sunday school materials are usually built around the assumption that most people live in "typical" or "conventional" families of husbands and wives and their children. However, many persons live alone or else in arrangements which may redefine or expand the meaning of the word "family."

According to census reports, the number of households maintained by persons either living alone or with persons not related to them increased by about 40 percent between 1970 and 1976. A person considered "head" or representative of such a household is called a "primary individual" by the Census Bureau. Primary individuals may be persons who have never married or who have been divorced or widowed. At present, 89 percent of primary individual households are made up of persons living alone. Another 9 percent live with an unrelated person who may be of the same sex or the opposite sex, and the remaining 2 percent live in households of three or more.

The last two categories mentioned suggest the possibility of forming the functional equivalent of a family—a shared life together in the maintaining of a household (splitting up both chores and expenses) and providing household members with a sense of emotional belonging and supportiveness. In other words, a sense of *home*. Not all two-or-more "primary individual households," of course, provide emotional gratifications and family-like warmth for household members; and some have no intention of doing so (households with boarders, resident employees, etc.). But the possibility of building up kin-like relationships does exist, as many persons living in "intentional community" arrangements will enthusiastically testify. Sometimes it will be two or three close friends who share a house or apartment. Sometimes the situation is one in which a larger number of persons live together in an urban or rural commune setting. Yet either of these "substitute kin" living arrangements can provide close feelings of family—the security of knowing one is not alone and that others really *care*, even if the world at large may often seem cold and impersonal.

Anthropologist Robert Brain, in a fine cross-cultural study of friendship, writes: "To me, it is the strangest thing that in Western Christian society, founded on the love of God and the fellowship of mankind, loneliness has become one of the hall-marks. We are the only people who have had drummed into them from childhood the impossible commandment to love our neighbors like ourselves and yet so many of us eke out an existence as loveless and unloved atoms—free individuals in an open society, condemned to form part of the great, grey sub-culture of the lonely."[15]

Theologian Herbert Richardson has pointed out that one of the greatest benefits of marriage is the continuity it provides persons in a change-oriented society—a way of sharing a past and planning a future "with at least one intimate friend throughout all the geographical and vocational relocations and removals that a rapidly changing society requires." In this way, says Richardson, a person is helped to construct a "symbolic identity" in which all of one's life is bound together as a continuous story.[16] Could it be that not only marriage but also deep friendship is a possible means of providing such "symbolic identity" so that one could see oneself in an ongoing "story" where one's past, present, and future are in some way shared and valued? Such a sense of continuity could be especially meaningful in the lives of single, divorced, and widowed persons; in some cases, it could mean actually sharing a home together.

---

[15]Robert Brain, *Friends and Lovers* (London: Hart-Davis, MacGibbon, 1976), pp. 259-60.

[16]Herbert Richardson, "The Symbol of Virginity," in *The Religious Situation: 1969*, ed. Donald R. Cutler (Boston: Beacon Press, 1969), pp. 794-95.

The Bible contains a number of examples in which friends "adopted" each other to form a kind of family. Ruth and Naomi are a prime example of such a commitment to each other: "Where you go, I will go, and where you lodge, I will lodge" (Ruth 1:16). David and Jonathan were similarly bound together in a friendship pledged to go even beyond death by the survivor's remembering the other's offspring. Thus, many years after Jonathan was killed in battle, his crippled son and young grandson were invited to live with David "and to eat at the king's table always" (II Sam. 4:4; 9:1-13). And because of Jesus' words from the cross, "Behold, thy mother" and "Behold, thy son," Mary and the apostle John became informally adopted relatives to one another (John 19:26-27).

Sharing life together helps persons to see how much human beings are alike and need each other. It can be a way of learning to get along with others and to enrich one another intellectually and spiritually. Deep friendship also helps us learn to handle problems and conflict. In short, it helps us learn about life—because in a very real sense, relating to others *is* life. This kind of sharing can be life at its very best for many persons who are willing to take the risk of building such friendships. Warm, caring relationships can help us live up to our full potential; they can prevent us from stopping short of our best. Sharing life with others can help us keep from being discouraged and giving up or being afraid to risk new ventures. There is a sense of "We're in this together! We're with you all the way!" that can make all the difference in joyful, creative living. Furthermore, as Robert Brain emphasizes, "Friendship need not derive from an unconscious sexual drive but a cultural imperative to exchange ideas, sentiments, and goods."[17] Of course, friendship can be just as real and deep in non-living-together arrangements, too; but for some friends, there is no denying that sharing a common household is a wonderful lifestyle option—one that Christians need to take seriously and view with more support and less suspicion. That brings us to the next topic.

Cohabitation

The growing phenomenon of two unrelated adults of the op-

---

[17]Brain, *Friends and Lovers*, p. 223.

posite sex sharing a household together has stirred up considerable concern among many Christians, mainly because of the assumed sexual relationship in such cases. Not surprisingly, the Census Bureau's finding that 1 percent of all households consist of two unrelated adults of the opposite sex sharing living quarters together has been sensationalized by both the Christian press and the general mass media. However, we must keep biblical principles of honesty in mind. With few exceptions, the media have tended to ignore the Census Bureau's own caveat: "Data users who make inferences about the nature of the relationships between unrelated adults of the opposite sex who share the same living quarters should be made aware that the data on this subject are aggregates which are distributed over a spectrum of categories including partners, resident employees, and roomers."[18]

For example, Mrs. Murphy is a 65-year-old widow who rents one of her extra bedrooms to a 20-year-old male college student who also shares the kitchen with her. A few doors down the street lives Charlie Wilson, an elderly heart patient who has hired a middle-aged woman as a live-in cook, housekeeper, and companion. Mrs. Murphy and her roomer, and Charlie Wilson and his housekeeper, would be surprised (possibly amused) to learn that worried preachers and writers are misusing statistics to imply that they are "cohabiting couples" right alongside Judy and Ken in a nearby apartment who really do live as unmarried partners. At the same time, there *are* the Kens and Judys of the world—no denying that. And this fact, of course, troubles Christians who are rightfully concerned about God's design for marriage.

There is no doubt in my mind that according to God's ideal, full sexual sharing should come after the couple have entered into the permanent, committed relationship of marriage rather than before. Jesus' emphasis in Matthew 19:3-12 is that marriage involves "leaving" (a change in social status and usually place of residence), "cleaving" (the establishment of a new relationship, a new social unit based on a unique bond), and *then* becoming "one flesh" (which of course includes more than sex; but the union of bodies provides apt symbolism of the overall oneness which I believe was the Creator's intent for marriage from the beginning).[19]

[18]*Current Population Reports*, series P-20, no. 306, p. 5.

[19]See Letha Scanzoni, *Why Wait? A Christian View of Premarital Sex* (Grand Rapids: Baker reprint, 1975. Originally published as *Sex and the Single Eye*, Zondervan, 1968) and *Sex Is a Parent Affair* (Glendale, CA: Regal Books, 1973).

At the same time, in examining the phenomenon of cohabitation, we must be honest enough to admit that it is not necessarily related to promiscuity (sex relations with a variety of persons) or even fornication (premarital sex) *in the traditional sense of the term*, at least insofar as the couple themselves are concerned. What we seem to have here is a quasi-marriage or mini-marriage or "trial marriage" rather than necessarily a repudiation of the ideals of marriage. Sociologically speaking, marriage consists of economic sharing, sexual sharing, and a public recognition of a couple's commitment. Many cohabiting men and women are persuaded that by openly declaring their relationship, they have already fulfilled all the requirements of marriage—except the licensing and formal ceremony that are part of the *legal* recognition of the union. A considerable number of such couples later go on to be formally, legally married. One campus minister recently officiated at a beautifully written marriage ceremony, prepared by the bride and groom themselves after they had been living together for eleven years! I mention such facts, not necessarily to condone the practice, but to emphasize that we as Christians must be very careful about the types of judgments we pronounce. An editorial in one evangelical periodical, for example, made the claim that "couples who live together without the commitment of marriage are compromising their humanity and reducing themselves to a level of pleasure-seeking (or perhaps convenience-seeking) animals."[20] Such a generalization not only doesn't fit the facts in many, many cases; its condemnatory tone can have the effect of driving thoughtful people away from a consideration of the Christian faith.

Just as is true of many other changes in marriage and family patterns reported by the Census Bureau, we need to ask ourselves some tough questions about cohabitation and see what we as Christians can learn. For one thing, marriage is still viewed as ideally a lifetime commitment, and the word *marriage* is reserved for such a commitment. When cohabiting couples move on to a formalization of their union through marriage, they say they are taking this step to prove to the world and each other that they are genuinely committed to a life together. Why they didn't take such a step in the first place seems to be related to a desire for assurance that there is a way out if the relationship does not

---

[20]"Without Benefit of Clergy—or Commitment," *Christianity Today* 21 (March 4, 1977): 640.

work out, yet without the trouble of formal divorce. However, couples who have gone to court over "who gets the waterbed"or larger aspects of a shared economic life have found that breaking up a cohabitation relationship can be just as much a hassle as actual divorce (emotionally, also).

Still, we must recognize that the "cohabitation route" is one attempt by some people to approach marriage rationally rather than thinking in unrealistic romantic terms of helplessly "falling in love" under some mysterious spell of moonbeams, totally apart from a consideration of what the everyday requirements of marriage really are. The idea of persons getting to know one another well and seeing one another in the myriad of circumstances of daily living can be commendable. Of course, such a rational approach to marriage need not include sex or even living together for the Christian couple. But the idea of knowing each other well and being absolutely sure before taking the step of marriage should be taken seriously.

We also need to take a new look at traditional gender roles in marriage which many cohabiting couples say they want to avoid in order simply to relate as whole persons rather than as roles. They fear that marriage changes that, because it has insisted on prescribed patterns (a "wife" does this, a "husband" does this, and so on). We need to rethink the rights and duties of marriage and get away from possessiveness concepts that prevent the growth of individuals and the enrichment of the overall relationship. (One lawyer reported that a man had begun to beat his wife frequently and severely. When asked why he had never laid a hand on her during their long period of cohabitation before marriage, the man replied, "Why, I didn't have the *right* to hit her then!")

Another matter that needs to be recognized in connection with this topic has to do with those tax laws that have made it more beneficial for people to live together unmarried than married. Christians concerned about the institution of marriage will welcome changes in social security laws that have denied payments to widows upon remarriage, thereby causing some older couples to choose cohabitation as the only way open to them.

Growth in One-Parent Families

Census reports provide many other challenges for Christians as they awaken us to all that is going on in this area of changing family patterns. The growth in one-parent families is a case in point. In 1976, 15 percent of all white children in the United States lived with only one parent. But because of the problems created by racism and its impact on many families forced to live in poverty, half of all black children live with one parent only, usually the mother (as is also true with white children in one-parent families). According to the United States Department of Labor, between 1940 and 1975, there was a doubling in numbers of American families headed by women alone, so that currently one out of every eight families falls into that category.[21] In what way are our churches taking that fact into account in planning their programs?

Further, according to Labor Department statistics, one out of three of these families headed by women only is a family living at or below the government's definition of the poverty level. Again, this calls for Christian compassion and involvement. What are we doing about the financial burdens, the need for training in skills that would fit these women for better jobs, the need for good day-care facilities, the need for emotional support? Many Christians speak out loudly against abortion and for the right to life, but to what extent are they showing concern for children who are already here?

Whereas many one-parent families result from divorce, separation, or widowhood, there are also many cases of single women rearing children born out of wedlock. Again, the question is, How can we as Christians minister to these women and their children in a way that demonstrates the love of Jesus Christ, who told us to receive the little child in his name as an act toward Christ himself (Matt. 18:5)? Also, Christians concerned about the suffering caused by the high rates of teenage pregnancy need to take an active role in seeing that school, community, church, and home sex education programs are put into action, and that contraceptive knowledge is disseminated. For Christians to oppose such efforts and yet at the same time to oppose abortion is both unrealistic and unloving.

Conclusion

We must never forget that Christian responsibility to grapple with social issues must include taking an honest look at how *family*

---

[21]Beverly Johnson McEaddy, "Women Who Head Families: A Socioeconomic Analysis," *Monthly Labor Review* 99 (June, 1976): 3.

life is changing, for it affects so many other areas as well. But there is no need for dismay. Changes need not threaten us as God's people; rather they can challenge us to face up to the questions, the hurts, and the aspirations of the people to whom we want to minister. Equipped with such knowledge, we can share God's love with understanding and compassion. We must keep in mind that God can work *through* change and can give us security in the midst of it. "When the earth totters, and all its inhabitants, it is I who keep steady its pillars" (Ps. 75:3).

7

Christian Sex Ethics

The current obsession with sex—who's doing what, how often, with whom, what for, how fast, which way—is an inevitable release from the pressure cooker of centuries of silence and misinformation. Alfred Kinsey and a squad of sex researchers freed us from Victorianism's moral prison. But the "sex revolution" has produced an unhappy group of sexual have-nots, for under the new conformity we sin by omission. We know that once is not enough, but we don't know when more has become too much. We are in one of those painful periods when people redefine themselves, as they tend to do every couple of centuries, by reaching to the depths of their emotions and asserting a new vision of what it means to be human. The sex revolution is one facet of the revolution of rising aspirations, the spiraling search for personal fulfillment.

The pill, penicillin, and the ever-present automobile and apartment have created different social possibilities we are not yet prepared to deal with. Traditional standards of sexual morality, maintained by fear of conception, infection, and detection seem obsolete to many. Although the pill has probably increased the frequency of premarital and extramarital sexual intercourse, strangely enough the percentage of illegitimate births to all live births has jumped from 1.7 percent in 1958 to over 5 percent in 1978. Likely causes include promiscuity, ignorance, or simply irresponsible romantic notions. Rollo May suggests that girls may yearn to procreate to "break up the arid desert of feelingless existence, to destroy for once if not for all the repetitive pattern of sex-to-avoid-the-emptiness of despair."[1]

Less significant, but still a factor, is the role of antibiotics in the cure of infectious venereal disease. Yet, sections of the United States have experienced venereal disease at near epidemic proportions within the last five years. Spiraling rates of abortion, illegitimate births, and rampant venereal disease indicates that a great deal of desperate and/or casual "love" is being made in America.

Affluent urban sprawls help lovers of all ages find secrecy with little fear of detection from their community. And though we talk of loving the freedom of anonymity, sex seems to be a way of saying to ourselves and to at least one other person "Hey, here I am."

We live and will continue to live in a society of rapidly changing sexual norms. Vast urban complexes, high rates of social mobility, and the appeal of the mass media have broken the power of what used to be called the *mores*—those accepted standards of right and wrong which represented the accumulated experience of the village elders, who were respected and looked upon as the models of correct behavior. Now, strangely enough, the enormously powerful models are the less wise and sometimes less responsible members of the community—the actors and actresses, the pop singers and the entertainers.

In the seventeenth and eighteenth centuries, freedom was part of a whole articulated framework of moral and religious values. Freedom meant freedom to do the good, and it was always equivalent to virtue. Under the rising criticism of utilitarianism (the useful is the good) freedom came to mean freedom to pursue self-interest, later defined as "freedom to do your own thing." Individual freedom is the last remaining element of the original American value system. Self-interest has replaced both virtue and conscience in our moral vocabulary.

Pleasure-Seeking and Myth-Making

Secular American man is often characterized by alienation-separation. Some call him schizoid, meaning out-of-touch, fearful of close relationships, and unable to feel. The apostle Paul

---

[1]Rollo May, *Love and Will* (New York: W. W. Norton, 1969), p. 71.

used similar language to describe man as sinner (Rom. 1:29-31). Because men live with much uncertainty and disillusionment concerning "belonging," sex is often divorced from commitment—love. We celebrate sex but are cynical about love. Thus sex often becomes a substitute or a compensation for lack of love, acceptance, and identity. It becomes the orgasmic trip, the trip away, or even the trip that stops all time, all drudgery. Deified sexual experiences cry out to us, "You shall have orgasm or you will be banished to nothingness." Physiological technique offers the sensuous man or sensuous woman possibilities of physical intimacy, though the "lovers" may know little about the tenderness that goes with spiritual nakedness. It may be that we are more wary of psychological and spiritual nakedness than we are of the physical nakedness in sexual intimacy.

American pleasure-seeking, which advocates the gratification of lustful desires without limit, is on the one hand a form of consistent selfishness, the purpose of which may be to display power, enhance prestige, or experience a little more happiness. But sometimes lustful behavior is not so much an advertisement of the ego's pride as it is a frantic effort to escape from the self. The element of sin in the experience is not due to the fact that sex is in any sense sinful *per se*. But once human relationships are disturbed by man's subtle rebellion against God, the instincts of sex can be either a vehicle of the primal sin of self-worship or the expression of a despair that seeks to escape from the self by the worship of another. The worship of the other is almost a literal description of many romantic sentiments. Attributes of perfection are assigned to the partner of love beyond the capacities of any human being to bear, and are therefore the cause of inevitable disillusionment.[2]

The secular romance myths offer a way of escape from the self by the worship of the lover. This commercialized mythological system, resting on the twin pillars of "falling in love" and the "one and only," systematizes the erotic and subjective elements in love, making the law of love the only criterion. The logic of the myth says, "If young people fall in love, they marry. Unless they fall in love, they should not marry. If having married, they should cease to be in love, the union should be dissolved."

If I were to define "being in love" it would include the feeling

---

[2]Reinhold Niebuhr, *The Nature and Destiny of Man* (New York: Charles Scribner's Sons, 1964), p. 237.

of "strong emotional rapport with erotic overtones." Yet, we do not want it defined, for a defined idea loses all powers. "Falling in love" love is an intoxicated state of mind. We frequently love the awareness that we are loving far more than we love the loved one. I am not speaking against romantic feelings, but I am opposed to the idolization of romantic love, the feeling of worship and the worship of the feeling of being carried along, a sense of being transported. It is literally bathed in. It is *the* addiction of the age. It takes no moral or spiritual energy—that is part of its attraction. It takes only the right stimulant—the man or woman who can send you the highest. The myth breeds a dishonest, superficial dating game. Only those people with a special cool or sexy charisma are acknowledged; all others are disregarded at a glance.

Being in love excuses all. It helps some Christian women become the ludicrous combination of St. Theresa and the Happy Hooker. Love addiction is the license to live in direct violation of our own sexual code of ethics. It is as if the Cosmic Cupid gives us an automatic pardon for all sins committed while intoxicated.

Biblical Theology and Interpretation

Unfortunately, sex remains the unmentionable in many American pulpits. And church members continue living with inordinate amounts of anxiety and guilt. Now, they feel more guilt about frigidity than adultery; they feel more anxiety regarding their lack of sex appeal than regarding any sexual temptation. If we are to say anything to this sex-satiated, sex-frustrated and sex-confused society we must get our own house in order. We begin with examination of sex within our own biblical tradition.

Biblical teaching on human sexuality must include an awareness of the historical and theological context from which the specific words are spoken. For example, Paul's discussion of sex in marriage in I Corinthians 7 is colored by his sense of the imminence of Christ's return. We should know that these words were spoken in about A.D. 55 and are affected more by expectation of the end than are his words in Ephesians 5:25ff (A.D. 60–62) where he more systematically describes the meaning of "becoming one flesh." Simply stated, the words of any single New Testament author or book must be placed within the entire historical and theological context of the New Testament.

Yet, they must also be understood in the light of the theology of the Old Testament context, including passages such as Proverbs 7, the Song of Solomon and the Book of Hosea. At this point we follow the lead of the New Testament writers who generally assumed as normative the Old Testament's understanding of the role of sex (I Thess. 4:1ff). If the two covenants are allowed to engage in dialogue with one another, two faulty moves are avoided. We avoid absolutizing Pauline teaching for Christian ethics in every age, making it the only word of the Lord and speaking this word with no reference to the Bible's historical and theological context. This faulty approach contributed to the antisexual bias of the early and medieval church, a bias that used I Corinthians 7 as the cornerstone for the medieval doctrine of priestly celibacy.

The second faulty move dismisses the Pauline teaching as a distorted and time-conditioned human judgment. This approach ignores the eschatological (end-time) basis of Paul's statements, their close similarity to the words of Jesus, and their abiding relevance to us in "these last days." Because it does not presuppose the Old Testament and Jesus as Paul's background and beginning place, it does not take I Corinthians 7 seriously as a part of the Bible's theological context.

By insisting on the place of I Corinthians 7 within the biblical tradition, and yet subjecting it to the criticism and balance of the other witnesses, another theological alternative is opened up for the serious handling of Scripture in the life of the Church. The following discussion reflects an implicit if not explicit awareness of the theology of the entire canon of scripture.[3]

Creation

The truth in the search for sexual meaning is anchored in creation. "Male and female he created them, and he blessed them and named them Man when they were created" (Gen. 5:2). There is so much to learn here. The Bible invites us again and again to discover the meaning of creaturehood. Karl Barth says, "Limitation, this is the first thing which characterizes the encounter between man and woman. Man and wife in sexual union do not attain to divinity."[4]

---

[3]Brevard Childs, *Biblical Theology in Crisis* (Philadelphia: Westminster Press, 1970), pp. 184-201.

[4]Karl Barth, *The Church Dogmatics*, (Edinburgh: T and T Clark, 1961). 3/4:125.

The creation accounts do not picture God putting a heavenly spirit into an evil body. Man was created from the first as a body-soul unity. Man is dust animated by the Lord God's breath which constitutes him a living being, a psycho-physical self (Gen. 2:7; Ps. 104:29-30; Job 34:14-15). It is important to remember that from the time of the earliest patriarchs the practice of infant circumcision was prominent throughout biblical history. Far from being considered an obscenity, the male organ with its cut foreskin became a distinguishing mark ordained by God. The idea of flesh as a principle in opposition to God and as a seat of sin is foreign to the Old Testament. In a prominent New Testament passage Paul gives the term flesh (*sarx*) the connotation of man alienated from God. But even here Paul is not singling out physical sexuality, for ten of the fifteen marks of unregenerate man constitute what we today would describe as sins of the mind (Gal. 5:19-21). Biblically speaking, it is no less a sin to call good things evil than it is to call evil things good.

The polarity of the sexes is a part of God's intention (Gen. 1:27). The fact that God has created us male or female points to the relational aspect of sexuality. Male and female exist for community, not isolation. She is made from man, who celebrates his kinship to her, crying out with rapturous joy "This at last is bone of my bones and flesh of my flesh" (Gen. 2:23). By contrast, homosexuality is identified with idolatry and the confused sexual identity of those who reject God and his created order (Rom. 1:24ff).

Concerning marriage, we can agree with Emil Brunner that it is an order of creation in the sense that it is a social structure given by God as a means of maintaining human life in community (Gen. 2:24).[5] Coitus needs the structure of marriage, reinforced by fidelity, in order for two people to share with each other their total life experience. Marriage needs sexual expression to give greater intimacy and quality to its covenant.

The Bible describes several purposes of sexual relations in marriage:

(a) Union in "one flesh" is mentioned in Genesis 2:24. Genesis 1 and 2 clearly teach that sexual union is an expression of a more profound union involving every fiber of our being. In both I Corinthians 6:16 and Ephesians 5:31 we have a quotation from

---

[5]Emil Brunner, *The Divine Imperative*, trans. Olive Wyon (Philadelphia: Westminster Press, 1947), p. 336.

Genesis 2:24, "The two shall become one flesh (*sarx*)." In both cases, we are undoubtedly to think of physical union. In the Corinthian text, indeed, Paul expressly uses the phrase "He which is joined to a harlot is one body (*soma*)." And of course Ephesians 5:28 also alludes to "being one body" in marriage. While flesh and body incontestably include the physical, they go much further and denote the whole man as a psycho-physical being which is established, animated, and sustained by the spirit. And if two human beings become one flesh or body, while this does express their physical union, beyond this it denotes the union of their total being to total and indissoluble fellowship. In the apparently partial nature of this event man and woman are totally engaged and also become totally what they formally were not—one flesh. Notice the analogy (Eph. 5:29ff) of the supreme mystery of Christ and the church under which this event, the love of husband and wife is classified. All this is understandable if the sexual consummation is not a partial event but the expression of total union of man and woman. The same view is implicit in I Corinthians 6:16 where it is again a question of sexual union, not this time in marriage but in fornication.[6]

(b) The Old Testament sees procreation as a blessing (Gen. 1:28). This is procreation, creation on behalf of God, the Creator. The fact that procreation is the purpose of intercourse does not exclude the responsible use of contraceptives. Indeed, the use of contraceptives is a means by which man can exercise dominion and control over nature (Gen. 1:28).

(c) Pleasure is a sometimes-overlooked purpose of sexual love. The Song of Songs is a hymn to the pleasures of love. In Proverbs the writer counsels, "Rejoice in the wife of your youth. . . . Let her affection fill you at all times with delight" (Prov. 5:18-19).

(d) Because the Bible uses the Hebrew *yada* ("to know") to describe sexual intercourse, communication is an obvious purpose of sexual intercourse (Gen. 4:1). More than a fusing of genitals, it is literally an intercourse, a flowing of personalities that affords a deep knowledge of the uninhibited self.

The essence of man's response to the indicative of God's creative activity is faithful stewardship. This stewardship, as described above, can be expressed through grateful praise to God, acceptance of self as a sexual being and respect for others as sexual beings.

---

[6]Barth, *Church Dogmatics*, p. 134.

Judgment

The Bible speaks very candidly of the tragedy of sin and its disruption of the oneness of a man and woman. The biblical account of the Fall reveals an alienation (separation) resulting from man's self-assertion and his usurpation of God's sovereignty (Gen. 3). The primal sin was not sexual in nature. One misses the point of the story if the record is used to prove the vulgarity of a naked body. The point is that sin affects all relationships, including the male-female relationship. Shame, guilt, and distrust mar the God-given goodness of intimate sexual love. No longer is the human couple completely open to one another in innocence.

Rebel man, under judgment, experiences estrangement from God in the affliction of hardship and skimpiness of livelihood. Woman is afflicted with the hardship of pregnancy and a profound desire for the man in whom she does not find fulfillment and rest, but rather humiliating domination (3:16). The brokenness of the man-woman relationship is further evidenced in the Old Testament by polygamy, prostitution, and adultery (Gen. 4:19-24, Judg. 16:1-21, II Sam. 11:2-5). All these facts indicate the real situation of male-female sexuality in a rebellious, confused, and alienated world: a frail thing, constantly threatened, and far removed from its original ideal.

Liberation

In the Book of Hosea God's activity as Liberator, one who lovingly restores and delivers his alientated people, becomes the model for the marital relationship. Human love can be damaged by jealousy and betrayal (Hos. 2:2), but just as God remains faithful to Israel, so must men and women practice his faithful, creative, forgiving love. No other fact is more apparent at the end of the Old Testament than the truth that the man-woman relationship is inextricably bound up with the salvation history of God with us as Lord and Liberator. Though many of our questions are asked and glimmers of hope do appear in the Hebrew prophets, the Old Testament period ends in the silence of yet-unfulfilled promises. The possibility of man's liberation depends entirely upon the coming of one who can breathe new life into the dry bones of Israel (Ezek. 37:4).

For his fulfillment as a sexual person, man does not need weaker sexual drives or more marriage laws. What he needs is the power of the new creation in his body-soul self. Then he can begin to relearn what it means to know (*yada*) a woman, to desire erotically, to caress and to care.

At the beginning of his account of the public ministry of Jesus, the evangelist Mark summarizes Jesus' preaching in these words: "The time is fulfilled, and the Kingdom (reign) of God is at hand. Repent, and believe the good news" (Mark 1:15). In Jesus, God acts to deliver his alienated people from sin and death (Mark 2:5-17). Jesus understood his kingship as a suffering servant to the sick, the lost, and the outcast (Luke 4:16-21; 15:1ff). Jesus' association with women must be included in his reaching out to the outcasts. In the time of Jesus, women were humiliated, cramped by a long tradition of organized inferiority. Though in Jesus' day no respectable rabbi had open social intercourse with a woman, Jesus' disciples marveled that he talked with women (John 4). The ministry of Jesus from beginning to end is a record of woman's liberation from her own sin and the sin of inhuman male domination (Mark 5:25-34; Luke 7:24-50; John 11:32-37; Luke 13:10-17).

In Paul's table of household duties (Eph. 5:21-32; Col. 3:18-4:1) husband and wife are characterized by their being "in the Lord." Here the degrading hierarchical values of society no longer determine the role of the wife. The nature of the wife's role comes rather from the order of creation and redemption, which brings her into the freedom of those who receive equal grace. Correspondingly, the husband's role is not determined by his prestige in the social order, and therefore his relationship to the wife is not determined by domination but by Christ's sacrificial care for his church (Eph. 5:25).

Because women possess equal dignity and value in the kingdom of God, adultery is no longer understood as the violation of another man's property. It is a violation of the God-man-woman love covenant (Matt. 19:1-9). Jesus' teachings on divorce, based on His liberation of women from sinful humiliation, destroy the double-standard divorce customs (Mark 10:1-9).

It is against the background of the male humiliation of women that one must observe Jesus' rebuke of those who look at a woman lustfully (Matt. 5:27-28). We commonly rob the passage of its full significance as though it were concerned only with the passions of man. But to look at a woman lustfully is to regard her impersonally, a thing to serve man's sensual desire, not a person but a physical instrument of transient pleasure. Study of the word translated "lust" (*epithymia*) reveals that it refers not to desire but to evil desire (Gal. 5:17; I Cor. 10:6; James 4:2). In Matthew 5:27-28 Jesus is talking about evil sexual desire. Inwardly it is the very opposite of love, and socially it is the root of woman's many and long-continued indignities.

In the new age of Christ, celibacy is a gift of God, as is marriage (Matt. 19:11ff; I Cor. 7:7). Offspring are no longer required to carry on the male's name and line (Matt. 12:46-50). Christian liberation means that one can marry not out of necessity (due to the order of creation), nor to prevent sin (due to the order of judgment), but in response to the Liberator who calls him to live a life of love (in the order of Liberation). God's Holy Spirit gives the power of self-control (Gal. 5:22-23). He calls us to consider family and fidelity, home and community, persons and covenants in making decisions about sexual temptations.

Living "in Christ" by the power of the new age which has come, and in anticipation of the consummation of all things in Christ, man finds powerful personal identity. As liberated man experiences the faithful forgiveness of God he learns to love himself and others. The self-giving love of God exposes the shallowness of the romantic love cult which motivates so many sexual entanglements. The bridal theology of Ephesians 5:25ff suggests that if a sexual relationship is to give that genuine community which a man and woman seek, it must be characterized by the same kind of fidelity that is demonstrated in God's faithfulness to his covenant people. Indeed, faithfulness is at the heart of the liberation of sexuality.[7]

Through the community of love and hope, men find demonstration of forgiveness of sexual sins and responsible control of sexuality (I Cor. 6, 7). In the community of hope we come to realize not only that sexuality is only a part of life but also that sexual behavior involves families and societies as well as individuals (I Cor. 13). A couple who live in isolation from the *koinonia* is not able to bring to sexual love the shared life which makes it an act of completeness and fulfillment. It is necessary that the marvelous diversity of the world find its place in the home and that the dialogue of the married couple be open to others.

The Christian contribution to the world's understanding of sexuality consists in its insistence that human sexuality is properly

---

[7]Harry Hollis, Jr., "Toward a Theological Understanding of Sexuality," *Review and Expositor* (Spring 71): 165.

understood only in the light of what God is doing as Creator, Judge, and Liberator.

Eros and Agape

If we take God seriously as Creator as well as Liberator we will not fall into the antisexual distortions of the Christian tradition. The tragedies of the castrated Origin, the enforced priestly celibacy of medieval Catholicism, and modern Victorianism serve to warn us of the ungodliness of such "righteousness." If we celebrate the creation of our physical selves, we can acknowledge the presence of many good loves in human experience. For example, *eros*, the urge toward union and toward higher forms of being, is detrimental only to the extent it cloaks a self-worship or it exploits persons, causing the self to make all other values subservient to its own concerns. Only the promiscuous idolization and dehumanizing of sexual impulses are condemned in Scripture (Rom. 1:24-27; Matt. 5:27-28). Thus we must not identify lust with sexual desire, but with loveless sexual desires. Neither is lust simply sexual fantasy. The Song of Solomon reminds us that sexual fantasy can constitute a call to increasing marital oneness, not a call to adultery. God's love (*agape*), his compassionate self-giving concern for us in us, preserves eros (the urge toward relationship) from the possibilities of radical selfishness. Agape does not destroy eros but rather introduces it to friendship (*philia*) and responsibility. In a world full of sex worship and sex hatred we are called to spiritually discern the very character of our man-woman relationships.

Is not marital love a combination of agape and eros? Could not someone desire his loved one and yet be able at the same time to give of himself? And, on the other hand, is not a person who gives of himself also permitted to desire the lover? When we separate the desire for oneness (intimacy), the sexual drive, (*libido*) and the unselfish giving of self (*agape*), do we not tear at the very fabric of the marital relationship? When we condemn eros and libido have we not said no in opposition to God's yes? Remember, the singer of Israel could unashamedly exclaim, "Upon my bed at night I sought him whom my soul loves" (3:1). The Word who became flesh is the Word who made male and female. The Word who loves (*agape*) us is the Word who created the sexual drive (*libido*) as one expression of *eros* (the desire for personal intimacy).

Sex as Marital Re-Creation

The biblical canon, including Genesis 1 and 2, the Song of Solomon, and Ephesians 5:25ff., invites us to re-creative sexuality. Sexual intimacy, with its possibilities for extensive emotional and physical touching, can express and help renew the vitality of marital union. Whether we are playful or romantic we can enjoy making love in ways that will feed our love for one another. Satisfaction of the personality hungers of one's mate, particularly his or her's sexual ego-needs, constitutes obedience to the biblical injunction "Love thy neighbor as thyself." Each partner should test his behavior in marriage in terms of how well he uses opportunities to help his mate *feel* more adequate, attractive, and lovable as a male or female. To say, "You made last night heavenly" helps one prize his God-given sexuality, which makes it easier to be loving, passionate, and giving next time (e.g. Song of Sol. 4:10ff).

Re-creative sexuality constitutes one expression of an already existing intimacy. The enthronement of sex as savior in an otherwise neglected relationship serves to keep sexual love-making from finding its full flowering. Because of other possible re-creative sharings in marriage, astute observers of contemporary marriage conclude that a marriage can be good even when the partners don't find uninterrupted heaven in bed.

Sex as Procreation

Responsible Christians cannot forget the unique procreative powers of sexual intercourse. Human sexual relations, from Genesis to Ephesians, are expressive of the human couple's commitment to the caretaking of human life. Until very recent times men and women, living in a survival-oriented society, were preoccupied with the reproductive powers of sex. Today's hedonistic thrill-seeking society, with its pill and penicillin, has not only moved away from a preoccupation with reproduction, it is moving away from any profound procreative awareness. The adolescents of today seldom think of procreative responsibility when they fantasize of sexual gratification. Pregnancy is no longer considered an awesome experience. Yet, if the fetus is life (and it is), then we must interject a couple of questions into our sexual fantasies: "Are we ready to parent a child? Are we taking adequate means of birth control?" Sexual intercourse remains fully human only when it is integrated into the total encounter of man and woman and when it expresses the couple's *mutual* commitment to God's created life. Reflection on the reproductive powers of sex tends to breed a sobering self-discipline and a responsible use of contraceptives. Reflection on orgasmic highs, with no other concerns, tends to breed "uncontrollable happenings."

Christian Marriage and the Pleasure Bond

Masters and Johnson's recent book, *The Pleasure Bond*, can enter into very interesting dialogue with biblical themes already discussed. The book, written by the leading sex researchers of our time, sounds many chords that Christians should enjoy hearing. For instance, Masters and Johnson believe not only that marriage shows some signs of improvement but also that its future may be much better if it involves an increase in genuine voluntary commitment, which is an act of faith and an acceptance of vulnerability.[8] Only in vulnerable commitment can there be a "free flow of verbal and non-verbal communication between cooperating sexual partners . . ." and such communication "is the cornerstone of effective sexual functioning" and also of becoming committed over time in a marriage relationship.[9] Sexual functioning itself is not sufficient in itself to establish enduring friendships. Masters and Johnson have no sympathy for sex as merely physical no matter how competent the techniques.

During the process of evolving a marriage commitment, Masters and Johnson see as equally important the principles of neutrality and mutuality. According to the former, neither partner assumes that past sexual failures will necessarily dominate the present and future. "Each, in brief, credits the other with good intentions and the will to implement those intentions."[10] For Christians, unconditional acceptance constitutes a more dynamic principle for marriage than does neutrality. Yet both neutrality and forgiveness (acceptance) do serve to rob the past of its hideous power to condemn the present.

Mutuality means two people united in an effort to discover what is best for both. Negotiation which states in effect "I will do my best to do X because I know you will do your best to do Y"

---

[8]William Masters and Virginia Johnson, *The Pleasure Bond* (New York: Bantam Books, 1975), p. 278.

[9]Ibid.

[10]Ibid., p. 52.

expresses a real mutuality.[11] The purpose of negotiation is con-
ciliation which means to "bring together, unite." This process involves honesty (no fake orgasms by the woman, for instance) and
the admission of disappointment. Masters and Johnson claim that
it is the effort itself that means so much, even when success is not
immediately achieved. In fact the struggle to do what is obviously
difficult is often more impressive evidence of emotional commitment than the actual achievement.[12]

Masters and Johnson contend that the process of sexual negotiation hinges to a considerable degree on how failure is handled.
What a man and woman need from each other is the security that
comes from knowing that occasional failures will not be used
against them—they will not be ridiculed, scolded, or punished. If
we take our own Christian doctrine seriously, we will know that
at best we are marrying a saved sinner. We will expect to fail at
times but we will also expect to commit ourselves to working
through any childish disillusionment with our loved one. We
agree that a successful approach is a creative act and the credit
belongs to both partners. Conversely, any failure would be a joint
failure.[13] This approach corresponds to the responsible "one
flesh" mutuality of biblical faith.

To expect or want or need something of another person, and to
let that person know this truth, is to be open to disappointment
or denial. But Masters and Johnson claim that as long as the disappointment or denial is not a deliberate act on the part of the
trusted person, as long as it can be seen as a reflection of such
things as forgetfulness, impatience, lethargy, or unhappiness, the
hurt can be accepted or at least put in perspective.[14] I would contend that Christ's forgiveness accepts the loved one even with his
willful abuses and his subtle hostilities. I am aware that without
mutual commitment there is no sexual union but I am also
enough aware of sin to know that willful hurt can at times be inflicted by committed lovers. I agree with Masters and Johnson that
when forgiveness is verbally asked for, and given, sharing has
taken place. Trust has been reaffirmed; openness to each other
has been maintained; and the ongoing process of sexual accom-
modation can continue. As a Christian man, I can unqualifiedly
agree with Masters and Johnson's contention that working at sex

[11]Ibid., p. 53.
[12]Ibid., p. 57.
[13]Ibid., p. 58.
[14]Ibid., p. 61.

does not improve its quality but rather improvement of its quality emerges from communication, caring, and commitment.

Though Virginia Johnson's description of pleasure as "the authentic abiding satisfaction that makes us feel like complete human beings" is richer, and considering the rest of the book, more responsible than I have previously seen, pleasure is not the ultimate bond of Christian marriage. Christian marriage is bonded by the liberating Father who brings us to and remains the binding force in our love covenant. This transcendent point of reference, this God of mercy and judgment covenanting with us, gives us the power to vulnerably commit ourselves to persons and in marriage to one person. I think I hear in Virginia Johnson's description of pleasure as "that which *makes* us feel like *complete* human beings" an inappropriate emphasis on marital intimacy as that which completes all things. Sexual satisfaction is always powerless to *make* me feel like a complete person. Possessing a reasonably healthy "I am," satisfying sex can *help* me feel more complete as God's person. And finally, I must ask, "Should we *ever* expect marriage alone to make us feel like complete human beings?"

Premarital Sex

After discussing sex in marriage we now have a perspective from which to discuss premarital sex. While an episode of sexual encounter may produce a sensation of adventure, there is no evidence that young people who have such experiences are enjoying life any more than those who do not. It is apparent that though virginity may have lost much of its magic for young people, fidelity and commitment have not. They talk a great deal about both. However, the concepts of fidelity and commitment are difficult to integrate with sexual freedom as it is now understood.

While many educators and parents still stress "don't frustrate," our policy should be, "Don't keep children at an infantile level but rather help them learn to deal with frustration." For economic reasons, the mass media promotes discontented infantilism; yet at the same time we want to cherish our national memories of pilgrims and plenty, including the sexual code of the Massachusetts Bay Colony. Exposed to all the stimulants to which married people are exposed, young people are forbidden the socially acceptable form of fulfillment. Remember also that dating, encouraged by parents, now reaches back to the sixth grade. For men under thirty *Playboy* is the most popular magazine in America. Because Hefner generally ignores married life, *Playboy* suffers a drastic drop in popularity among the married men over thirty. The Playboy, after he has "had sex" while avoiding lovemaking, usually has a difficult time understanding what Romeo and Juliet and Abelard and Heloise were all about.

"What I'm looking for is a girl who will give me a beautiful sexual experience. I don't want only relief of my sexual tension." A college junior blurted out these words in a question-and-answer period before a college audience. The speaker, Dr. Peter Bertocci asked the young man, "What is standing in your way if you and your consenting partner have no sexual hangups?" After a moment he conjectured: "Oh, it must be because they all want to be serious. But I don't see why I can't go to bed with a girl and have a really beautiful experience, even though I have no intention of taking her seriously in any other way." Bertocci then asked, "What makes you think beauty is easy to come by? Why do you think that you, on your terms—no commitments!—can find what you call a beautiful sexual experience?"[15]

The real sexual revolution will spring from the realization that quality in sexual experience is rooted in what we have known for ages, that persons never live by technology and technique alone. *They live by meanings and values.* There cannot be quality in sexual experience when we try to close it off from the rest of the meanings and values that we as persons prize. Recently a college sophomore wrote: "We came as freshmen, with our pills—some of us just in case we should want them, some of us out of principle—to be free to experiment. Well, here I am. I've had my orgasms. So what?" Why neglect in the sexual area what we know to be true in other areas of our lives? We breed hostility and aggression, we undermine self-confidence, when we say to each other: "I don't want to be responsible for you, but I want you to respond to my needs. I want you to act so that my comfort and pleasure will be assured, but don't expect me to care for you beyond this transaction." Are we willing to grant that it is good policy for persons to condone even a "more genteel form of prostitution—the art of making one's body responsive to another's need but nothing else"?[16]

[15]Peter Bertocci, "Keeping Quality in Sexual Experience," *The Christian Century*, vol. 93, no. 40 (December 8, 1976): 1096.

[16]Ibid., p. 1097.

If our words on behalf of premarital virginity are to be heard they must (1) reflect a well-disciplined Christian discipleship. Indulging parents, dominated by the chase after power, prestige, success, and wealth, cannot effectively plead with their spoiled children to practice sexual self-restraint and expect to be taken seriously or even to be vaguely understood.

(2) Parents and parental models must do more communicating with their blossoming teenagers. Beyond the biological facts, we can teach them a rich, responsible approach to love, sex, and marriage. We can provide guidelines for our children's dating life. We can put emphasis on friendship dating. Many people, whether sixteen or twenty-six, would simply enjoy some companionship, without romantic intention, and they should feel comfortable about so doing. The test of a male's manhood is not his ability to kiss on the first date or undress a girl on the third, but his power to personally befriend her. A very warm, gentle friendship marked by feelings of closeness can give tremendous fulfillment and may very well constitute the basis for a lifelong friendship or a more intimate relationship leading to marriage. Most of us need the companionship of the opposite sex, but not in a manner that pushes one to either "get serious" or to stop dating. The traditional dating system tends to offer one the choice between the terrors of loneliness and the trauma of premature romance. This system drives desperately lonely people into premature sexual intimacy.

(3) We must forcefully contend that the greatest passions and deepest longings of human hearts are appropriately expressed in the climate of a well-developed and enduring marital relationship. Most students, especially females, still consider casual sex incompatible with their quest for meaning and belonging. Yet, most students also argue that love justifies premarital sexual relations. We must know by now that few things are more dangerous than sexual relations in an undefined relationship informed by an ill-defined love. Emotional and bodily intimacy without the security of a commitment to faithfulness leaves love *unnecessarily vulnerable* to all manner of cruelty. "Love" relationships may cloak a self-seeking that only serves to bring pain and disillusionment. One male student explained himself this way:

> I am somewhat troubled because I am not really looking for a wife but sort of taking advantage of nice girls who assume I am. It is just too much for me to turn down the chance to go all the way. Soon I begin

to become afraid of being trapped and usually drop the girl, and try to do it in a way to ease the hurt for her.[17]

(4) We must judge all Christian behavior in terms of Christian freedom (Gal. 4:1-7; Gal. 5:1-6; Gal. 5:13-15; Col. 2:20-23). God's Spirit liberates Christians from tyrannical conformity to the idolatrous values and mindless behavior of this world (Rom. 12:2). Christians are liberated to grow up in the image of Christ (Eph. 4:15-16). Christians seek to be more than legally correct; we seek the way most expressive of God's love in us (I Cor. 8:7-13; 19:19-23). One learns the secrets of freedom only through spiritual self-discipline. The words "I buffet my body daily" constitute the cry of a free man in Christ (I Cor. 9:27). Because sexual relations are a fragile gift, easily wounded by sinful carelessness, sexual self-control must accompany sexual celebration. It is possible in the name of freedom to enslave oneself, to pass under the authority of inexpedient practices, and of one's own desires (I Cor. 6:12-13). Thus, we must describe this freedom to our children with a clarity and power that does justice to the many responsibilities and opportunities of Christian man-woman relationships.

Masturbation

Because 95 percent of us masturbate at one time or another and many of us feel guilty about masturbating we cannot ignore the subject. Masturbation may express the lust of one who fears a personal encounter. Masturbation fantasy may also reflect the sinful dynamics of hatred and violence. Yet, masturbation, certainly a poor substitute for intimate love-making, may very well serve as a harmless release at appropriate times in our lives. Masturbation may be a means of sexual release for the unmarried, helping to prevent fornication; it may also serve the marriage when travel, illness or temporary marital incompatibility might separate a couple. It should never serve as a permanent substitute for a loving sexual encounter.

The fantasies accompanying masturbation do need disciplined control or they may very well wander as vagrants in the street. Yet, fantasies need not be vagrants; they may very well serve as

---

[17]Vance Packard, *The Sexual Wilderness* (New York: David McKay Company, 1968), p. 184.

promises of a healthier future. Do not married couples often need to dream of more intimate love-making before their love life can actualize that meaning? If we possess the will to shape it, fantasy can be a profitable servant. It can become an invitation to growth and wholeness for the one dreaming of a future married life or for one already married. Masturbation must always serve our desire for wholeness.

Adultery and Divorce

> Infidelity is a very chancy and unreliable means to use in searching for one's identity, in exploring one's true emotions, in struggling not only to find out what one's deepest feelings and beliefs and responses may be, but also communicating them to someone else.[18]

Masters and Johnson's words only serve to corroborate the enduring wisdom of the Hebrew-Christian tradition. Yet today, among some Bible-believing Christians, adultery has become not only unfaithfulness, but also the only act which cannot be forgiven. Adultery needs to be demythologized so it is removed from the land of witches and voodoo. Does adultery constitute a scriptural reason for divorce when it has been confessed, repented of, and growth is evident? Do not some adulterous acts indicate momentary weakness while others indicate long-standing marital unfaithfulness? Biblically speaking, can we ever speak of an "innocent" party? Are we not bone of our bones and lovelessness of our lovelessness? How can the couple, after experiencing an adulterous wound, find their way forward (not backward) to mutual acceptance and intimacy? Is it not possible to forgive an unrepentant adulterer while living separate lives? Does not this forgiveness express Christ's love while recognizing that it takes two to reconcile (become one again)?

When adultery is confronted we must not only penitently confess our sins, we must also ask questions of our relationship. Masters and Johnson, acknowledging that the sample with whom they talked might not be representative, noted that of the "swinging" marriages, in only one marriage did the partners seem to "have a relationship in which each partner felt safe with the other."[19]

[18]Masters and Johnson, *Pleasure Bond*, p. 146.

[19]Ibid., p. 185.

Homosexuality

At the present time the following attitudes toward the homosexual are notably missing within the Christian community: any contact with and understanding of the homosexual by the church; any understanding of the trap into which a homosexually-inclined person feels himself thrown; any community of responsibility for dispensing grace. We do not allow the problem to take its place with other offenses on Paul's list. If we take Paul seriously (Rom. 1:24-26; I Cor. 6:9-11) it would appear that he does not single out homosexuals for condemnation, but rather that having branded all men as idolatrous, he has learned to celebrate the grace of God for all. But what about I Corinthians 6:9-11? What about the homosexuals who "will not inherit the kingdom of God?" Paul goes on (6:11) to say, "Such were some of you." The verb, second person plural imperfect, clearly suggests ongoing activity in the past. "But," says Paul, "you were washed, you were sanctified, you were justified in the name of the Lord Jesus Christ and in the Spirit of our God." The verbs here are all second person plural aorist, referring, presumably, to that moment in time when they were baptized.

Does Paul mean here that once they were baptized all the tendencies to immorality vanished? If so, it is at least fair to point out that Paul would then have had no occasion to write to the Corinthians. If instant perfection is demanded, the gospel ceases to be the good news that while one lives imperfectly, he is nevertheless loved, accepted, and in right relationship with God (Rom. 7:25-8:2). However, because idolatry, adultery, homosexuality and the like are inconsistent with the nature of the new life in Christ, we must gratefully commit ourselves to the joy of Christ's disciplined freedom (I Cor. 9:27).

If we are to minister effectively to the homosexual we must create a climate of acceptance in which a homosexual will risk disclosure of himself. We must carefully listen to those who think of themselves as homosexuals. Only about 4 percent of all Americans are exclusively homosexual. Some are bisexual, able to relate sexually to men or women. Some are willful (more sinners than sinned against) promiscuous idolators of sex; being morally repulsed by responsibilities of heterosexual relationships, they seek gratification from their own sex. Others are more sinned against than sinners. Environmental factors such as a brutal father, a domineering mother, seduction by an older male or female, or the emotional trauma of rejection by numerous heterosexual lovers may very well lead many people into a homosexual relationship. Some (more sinned against than sinners) are far more conditioned to an exclusively homosexual orientation than are others. Many of these people hate their own tendency to homosexuality.

The deadly cycle of sin, repressed guilt, shame and self-hatred ceases when a penitent sinner accepts the grace of God and becomes a part of a *community of acceptance*. One afflicted with a thoroughgoing homosexual conditioning must seek to sublimate his homosexuality in constructive service. All homosexuals must seek the power to change their sexual identity—"For with God all things are possible" (Luke 18:25-27). Acceptance of the situation, leading to open acknowledgment with fellow strugglers in a similar situation, when combined with commitment to help others and new experiences in heterosexual relating, constitutes a positive therapeutic experience. The reading of John Drakeford's *Forbidden Love*, a chronicle of the Christian therapy of a Christian homosexual, should move us to be and become known as a Christian community of responsible involvedness.

Summary

Living in the end time between the first and second advent of Jesus, Christians know that Christ Jesus, not lord eros, is reigning at the right hand of God. Thus, we are liberated to spiritually discern the gifts, the disciplines, the celebrations, and the commitments that make sexuality human. The church as the people of God must be and become known as a people who celebrate their sexuality and who bind the wounds of those spiritually wounded sexual creatures who come, crying out for wholeness. The Word of the Living God must be proclaimed to the total situation and not just to an isolated issue (e.g. premarital sex). To do otherwise means the pews in the churches will be increasingly filled with fragmented believers, people confessing Jesus as Lord while wandering without guidance in a wilderness of confusion, lust, and guilt.

PERRY C. COTHAM

8

Mass Media Ethics and Christian Values

If the amount of public comment about the mass media in American society is any index to their power, persuasiveness, and general significance, then the mass media are very powerful indeed. A check with any volume of *Reader's Guide* in the last ten or fifteen years will turn up listings of scores of articles by critics of all mass media: newspapers, magazines, film, broadcasting, advertising, and public relations. Watergate-related scandals evoked a reexamination of journalistic ethics. The 1977 trial of 15-year-old Ronald Zamora focused on whether television caused the accused to murder the elderly widow living next door; his defense attorney claimed the lad "was just acting out a television script."

The rash of assassination attempts, hijackings, kidnappings, and other terrorist acts has led many to wonder if the media are creating a "climate of violence" and encouraging criminal activity by glamorizing criminals. With the stimulus of the bicentennial, a number of "docu-dramas" began production (the most publicized and controversial being ABC's "Washington: Behind Closed Doors") and many wondered if such shows fused too much fiction and fact, thus opening the door to subtle bias.

Perhaps it is true that comment and criticism about the mass media, when considered as a *percentage* of the vast outpouring from these same media, is not excessive. But whatever else

Americans are concerned about, there can be no doubt about their concern about the functions, roles, and performance of mass communicators.

A force in our lives that has been so pervasive, intrusive, and persuasive must not be overlooked by Christians. And it has not. Mass media, and particularly the television industry, have been subjected to varied criticism from all points along the religious spectrum—from the Church of God, which asked 175,000 families in its constituency to rank the ten "most offensive" shows, to a national convention of the United Church of Christ which charged that "predominant concepts expounded by television are poles apart from the Christian understanding of the human potential and God's purposes." The sum of most enlightened criticism of the media is that the quest for power and profits dominates all media decision-making processes and that ethical considerations are secondary at best; specific criticism against the broadcast media contends that networks and stations often flaunt federal standards, ignore obligations to the public, and manipulate audiences for profit while public officials remain largely indifferent.

Our purpose here is to focus on ethical considerations related largely to the entertainment media, especially, though not exclusively, to television. We will not review the vast literature on the subject nor cite the myriad of statistics available from hundreds of studies, most of which were completed since the release of the controversial report of the President's Commission on Obscenity and Pornography. Our purpose is served by an evaluation of mass media in light of general biblical principles and Christian values. Hopefully, the Christian, with an ever-increasingly wide range of media offerings from which to choose, will equip himself to use his time wisely as a good steward of Jesus Christ. Again, not all Christian principles and values will be examined in this essay; for example, standards of fairness and integrity which must be upheld in evaluating journalistic ethics. Such issues relate to constitutional law and public policy considerations, but they are not the heart of our present concern.

Christian criticism of mass media must be judicious and balanced if it is to be effectively heeded by the industry and the general public. Too frequently, well-intentioned church spokesmen have leveled wild attacks on the media and the criticism was not taken seriously because of its lack of discrimination or qualification. Media owners and managers have been depicted as greedy manipulators leading the United States down the road of decay, degradation, and ultimate doom. One recently published critique of television by a Christian writer is entitled *Telegarbage*. Newsletters and newsmagazines devoted to the subject have included gross generalizations and inflammatory articles and cartoons. Too few critics stop to consider how the mass media reflect our own greed, selfishness, immorality, and weaknesses. We must recognize that the strengths and shortcomings of television, for example, emanate from the 200 million or so people, in all walks of life, who, every week, are its voluntary viewers. Ultimately, people get the kind of media offerings they deserve, or at least desire.

We gladly concede that the mass media offer us a widely varied fare of entertainment and information and that they serve a pluralistic society with its many tastes and values. They have dealt with human problems of all kinds and the important public and social issues of our time. Anyone who recalls seeing "King" (the biographical series on the life of the late Dr. Martin Luther King, Jr.), "Roots" (which may have done more to increase understanding of American race relations than any event since the civil rights activities of the 60s), "A Case of Rape," "Holocaust," "The Autobiography of Miss Jane Pitmann," "The Execution of Private Slovik," to name but a few, knows something of television's potential worthwhile entertainment. "Sesame Street" has established measurable gains in the cognitive skills of preschoolers. Programs like these come from creative artists who have something to say and are reaching viewers who respond in large numbers and often with deep personal involvement.

No matter what appears on the stage and movie or television screen, someone may be unhappy with it. What one Christian finds moving, absorbing, and perceptive, another may find repugnant. For example, reviews in religious publications of the George Burns role in the movie "Oh, God!" were not neutral; many critics found the movie to be a wholesome and refreshing depiction of deity, not unlike the intent of biblical parables, while others found the movie's entire concept based on blasphemy of the name and nature of God. Some insist that sexual aberrations, abnormalities, and dysfunctions do not constitute fit subject matter for humor while others argue that such light-hearted treatment lifts a taboo on discussing such issues and paves the way for more serious public discussion. We may appreciate the heightened moral sense concerning our mass media without necessarily concurring with all the criticism that religious spokesmen are offering.

Sex and Violence Revisited

The way a culture depicts sex and violence, notes George Gerbner, is symptomatic of its definition of humanity and is indicative of the structure of its power. The representation of sex and violence in our mass media is the cause of greatest criticism against mass media.

Thoughtful criticism of television programming centered first on violence. A number of scientific studies were begun in the late 60s, spawned both by a significant increase in the national homicide rate and the assassinations of the two Kennedys and Martin Luther King, Jr. Taken as a whole, the studies present a strong indictment against media violence; in other words, one cannot deny there is a link of some kind between media's depiction of violence and the amount of violently aggressive behavior in the nation.

Two qualifications are in order. First, in scientific research one must be reluctant to conclude that one phenomenon is the cause of something else. Even in a laboratory under controlled conditions, scientists will conclude cautiously that "the most plausible single factor in obtaining this result is . . ." And when working outside the laboratory with human subjects, the task of distinguishing cause and effect becomes even more cumbersome. Second, and related to the first qualification, psychologists contend that the seeds of violence lie less in mass media than in one's social environment and personal experience. Neglect during a child's earliest years and the absence of consistent parental care are significant factors in the development of the kind of emotional disturbance which is likely to lead to violent behavior. Less significant factors are brain damage, mental illness, or some other abnormality.

A summary of the research findings in clarifying the link between media violence and real-life violence produces three generalizations that Christians must consider seriously:

(1) Media violence subconsciously makes the viewer, especially the child, more aggressive and hostile. Depictions of violence, some psychologists contend, "arouse aggressive tendencies" which are "readily translated" into harsh, aggressive action. Movie or televised violence is essentially different from traditional presentations of violent themes in paintings or literary forms, the

latter requiring willful participation and some degree of action on the audience's part. Such traditional participation was active and voluntary, but screened violence needs only a passive viewer who submits to both visual and aural stimuli. To the marked degree that television viewing encourages passivity, it may well constitute a danger for those children whose characters are still in the process of formation. Viewers of all ages may eventually become desensitized to depictions of murder, rape, maimings, and other torturings and there can be no doubt that directors and producers are developing and using more explicit and vivid methods to shock audiences. "Television coarsens all the complexities of human relationships, brutalizes them, makes them insensitive," asserts screenwriter Paddy Chayefsky in a pointed criticism of television. "The point about violence is not so much that it breeds violence—though that is probably true—but that it totally desensitizes viciousness, brutality, murder, death so that we no longer actively feel the pains of the victim or suffer for the mourners or feel their grief. . . . We've lost our sense of shock, our sense of humanity."[1]

(2) Media violence provides behavioral models to follow. Popular literature on this subject is replete with examples of violent crimes that appeared to be carbon copies of previously broadcast dramatizations of violence; there is no valid reason to deny the causal link between the two phenomena. The style of operation, in contrast with the substance of what is done, may be the most harmful. Televised and filmed violence can powerfully teach, suggest, even legitimize, extreme antisocial behavior. One psychologist claims that seeing violence on television not only gives "unstable people the idea of doing the same, but also teaches them exactly how to go about it—it cuts out trial and error."[2] Journalists concur that expectation of publicity helps create terrorist acts.

(3) Media violence generally teaches that violence is acceptable behavior. The New Testament has much to say about how disciples should resolve conflict and establish proper interpersonal relations among themselves and toward nonbelievers. A resort to pointless violence, an easy solution to conflict for screenwriters who want a shortcut to pleasing audiences already conditioned to expect "action," is at odds with Christian doctrine and reprehensible to concerned Christians.

---

[1]*Time*, December 13, 1976, p. 79.

[2]*Time*, March 28, 1977, p. 57.

Increased public furor over violence on television led to the industry's adoption of the family hour with programming intended to be family-oriented. Though the family hour encountered both legal and practical problems, a recent trend has been to reduce television violence, but to increase the frequency and explicitness of sexual themes. By 1978, Christian criticism of television concentrated on the treatment of sex, especially in such shows as "Soap," "Three's Company," and certain made-for-television movies. The most widespread suspicion was that prime time's emerging blue hue was a carefully calculated replacement for the old blood-red one. Although most of the "vid-sex" remained verbal and insinuative rather than visual and explicit, virtually no sexual themes have been neglected. The visual and verbal explicitness increased as the late hour broadcasting approached.

Sex and aggression are elements of life and no thoughtful Christian would insist that media purporting to portray the human condition should draw a curtain over such integral parts of human existence. Aggression is a necessary human characteristic that leads men and women to all kinds of constructive and creative activities and accomplishments. The aggressive tendency is obvious even in children who, whether through toy guns, water pistols, or sticks, attempt to project themselves into the world, yearning for power and impact in their social environment. But aggression may also be transformed into destructive violence, a distortion of the humane use of innate aggression.

Because violence is such an integral part of the human experience, the media must deal with it. In fact, most people would be bored if all dramatized or literary violence were banned; this would mean losing much of the writings of Shakespeare, Sophocles, Dostoevsky, Tolstoy, Dickens, as well as the Old and New Testaments (not to mention traditional fairy tales which are full of dire events—bloodshed, death, cruel punishment, and heartless revenge). No one would argue that the works of these writers, staged or in print, are damaging to the psyche of children or adults. In fact, most children would be bored by Greek tragedies and Shakespearan plays. Unlike films such as *The Omen* or *The Gauntlet*, the violence in these works is reported but not always depicted; in Macbeth, a drama of dark bloody deeds, every one of the violent actions takes place off-stage; what we see and hear is the rise of evil passions in the souls of two people, and their different ways of deteriorating.

Violence is one of literature's most common and most enobling themes. Ideally, media depiction of violence will accomplish several purposes: elucidate its historical role in the shaping of crucial events in history, such as the crucifixion of Christ or the persecution of the Jews in Nazi Germany; aid audiences in understanding and sublimating destructive forces in themselves; examine dangerous passions and the human character in which they emerge; help viewers reflect on the consequences of violent aggressiveness in a meaningful and manageable context, and, in experiencing terrible events vicariously, keep them from acting on their own violent impulses.

Media portrayal of human sexuality may be subjected to the same canons of criticism. The sexual revolution of the past fifteen or twenty years has had a major impact on all the mass media; now every conceivable lifestyle and taste, both natural and perverse, is catered to by one medium or another. For those satiated with old-fashioned pornography, child pornography ("kiddie porn" as the press likes to call it) is pandered in adult book stores. Television, the massest of media, was not left unaffected. In its formative years, and in keeping with prevalent views about the privacy of sex and with at least the lip service paid to traditional sex morality, television was carefully circumspect. The seldom-shown bedroom scenes involved long pajamas and twin beds for husband and wife; sex was denied more than suggested and marital status was unequivocally clear. Marital status now is irrelevant in many movies and shows and, far from denying sexuality, Mary Hartman lies in bed with her husband discussing his impotence. The writers of shows like "Charlie's Angels" use any pretext for getting the buxom trio into suggestive clothing that best displays their titillating body movements. Wildly improbable events make such shows among the poorest written on television, but the robust ratings for risque programs indicate they are in tune with society's newly liberated tastes.

Despite all the furor over hard-core pornography and X-rated movies, the greatest challenge to Christian moral standards may well be the exploitation of the human body and the gratuitous, excessive, and perverted treatment of sexual themes in general television programming and in advertising. At issue is not any single offensive line or scene, or even a specific comedy or drama. The real concern is the cumulative impact of show after show, night after night, that leads viewers to dull their sensitivities and increase their tolerance of lower standards. From the viewpoint of responsible Christian parenting, the impact on children may not be much less than devastating. Many motion picture and television productions tend to glorify sexual activity without impressing on viewers (a majority of whom may be adolescents) the responsibilities that go along with it or the consequences of the abuse of human sexuality. Have not the mass media only aggravated the problem of nearly one million unwanted pregnancies a year among teenagers in the United States? Artistic realism is hardly a defense for exploitative sex in the media.

Here, however, is a parallel with depictions of violence. The great literature of the world does indeed treat sexual themes and male-female relationships. The Bible has much to say, both directly and implicitly, about both sex and violence. The subject is the human soul stretched between the passions of nature and its intuitions of goodness and righteousness, so that sex and violence are often incidental and derive their meaning from the struggles, strengths, and weaknesses of human character. Violence and eroticism in the Biblical narratives emerge from a larger context and are in balance with the natural events in the lives of individuals depicted; such behavior occurs within the ebb and flow of more complete and complex relationships between men and women. The media often strip this mantle of meaning and present sex and violence in moral nakedness, making an act of sex or an act of violence an absolute in and of itself.

Media World View and Christian Values

The survival of any society depends on its maintenance of commonality or, to borrow Hannah Arendt's phrase, *consensus universalis*—common language, traditions, values, interests, goals, and assumptions about human existence. A nation creates, sustains, and alters this commonality through its institutions, and primarily through mass media. The media constitute, excluding perhaps the home, the most effective and pervasive agents of *socialization*, that all-important process by which human beings learn the complex rituals and value systems of their own culture. The media generally, and television especially, have assumed the teaching of values, goals, and traditions which in the past was largely conducted through parents, churches, peer groups, formal education, and the rites of initiation.

Knowledge acquired from television and movies can be far more pervasive and influential than the traditional means of awareness. Such value education and awareness training come, not from news and public affairs programming, but with entertainment. Although designed neither to teach nor to provide information, movie and television entertainment teach a great deal indirectly and by example about attitudes, values, styles of behavior, and self-perception. Fiction impels the impressionable audience toward empathizing with protagonists and vicariously experiencing their sensations and feelings.

By both necessity and nature, the media select and distort from reality. Television has often been described as a window to the world. The phrase is aptly chosen, for by its nature a window allows the one inside to see only a small part of the outside world. Seldom is the glass perfectly clear; though transparent, it may be tinted in order to change the color of everything in the outside world. Or it may act as a filter—selecting, coloring, and blocking out certain images in the real world. In essence, the real world and the mythical world are two different worlds indeed.[3]

How are the mass media defining personhood? What do they teach about the meaning of life and human existence? What are the values, goals, and traditions they are asking us to hold dear? How is the media world different from the real world and how is it different from the world that God wants disciples to work toward creating? For the concerned disciple of Christ, these questions are crucially important in evaluating the entertainment media.

Consider a demographic profile of the entertainment media. For the average American, the television world becomes *his world* anywhere from three to seven hours a day, every day, throughout most of his life. Sex-role stereotypes are reinforced by television programs and commercials, according to one study; men outnumber women three to one and females are twice as likely to display incompetence. By and large, men are portrayed as dominant, authoritative, and the sole source of their family's economic support. Another study showed that young black viewers regard whites as more competent than blacks, and model their behavior accordingly.[4]

---

[3]Much of the analysis here was provoked by an excellent article by William F. Fore, assistant general secretary for communication at the National Council of Churches. See his "Mass Media's Mythic World," *Christian Century*, January 19, 1977, pp. 32-38.

[4]Studies reported in a cover story, "What TV Does to Kids," *Newsweek*, February 21, 1977, pp. 62-70.

Violence occurs in the mythical world of television mostly between strangers, whereas in the real world it occurs mostly between relatives and acquaintances. Heroes initiate violence as frequently as villains; witnesses usually remain passive; neither legal consequences nor suffering usually follow. Media violence is not caused so much by hate, rage, panic, or despair as much as from a businesslike pursuit of personal gain, power, or duty.

Television violence teaches that the risks of victimization are high and unequal. George Gerbner notes that on top of the heap are mature white males; on the bottom lie the bodies of children, the poor, the old, the nonwhite, and young or single women. Both children and adults who spend much of their lives absorbed in the "world" of television learn and accept some assumptions of that world and then project them onto social reality. For example, research has shown that heavy viewing of television cultivates an exaggerated sense of risk and danger in real life, especially among the elderly and weak.

Television has some interesting messages about business and career people. Half of all TV-land characters are married, Gerbner tells us, but among TV teachers, only 18 percent of the women and 20 percent of the men are married. Failure in life and love is a requisite for teaching success and women "find themselves, and a man" by *leaving* teaching. TV teachers' problems are solved by *leaving* their profession—not by building new facilities, renewed community support, raising tax revenue, and granting higher salaries. TV journalists are honest and courageous. TV scientists are deceitful, cruel, dangerous; their research leads to murder in at least half the situations.[5]

Most adults expect such discrepancies in the two worlds. To interest and sustain an audience, popular programming necessarily presents highly active characters involved in exciting, glamorous, action-filled situations and events. In the real world, most people have dull, unglamorous, less significant, repetitive jobs; consequently, the proportion of people in fictional populations employed as criminals, detectives, lawyers, journalists, espionage agents, scientists, corporation executives, doctors, and wandering adventurers is unrealistically high. Most people in the real world solve their personal problems in more lengthy, but undramatic,

<hr />

[5]Information taken from George Gerbner's address at International Communication Association, April 21, 1972, and cited by Fore, "Mass Media's Mythic World." For media demographics, especially as they relate to sex and violence, see Gerbner's "Scenario for Violence," *Human Behavior*, October, 1975.

even anticlimactic, ways. Media characters resolve problems by quick, decisive, highly visible actions, often involving some form of socially disapproved action.

At least three important principles of the Christian doctrine and lifestyle clash mightily with the values communicated by the mass media on behalf of the American culture:

(1) The entire thrust of biblical morality is based upon the premise that people are ends in themselves, not means to another's end. Consequently, the disciple of Christ is called, both by the explicit teaching and the Lord's example, to a life of compassion for the needs of his fellow men and women. The mass media have the potential for aiding concerned Christians in learning more about the people of the nation and the world and their needs. There can be no doubt that we know much more about what is going on in the world—its celebrations and its tragedies—than any generation in history. Wars and rumors of wars, earthquakes, floods, droughts, terrorism, famine, epidemics, and the like do not seem so far removed from us because of our access to the window on the world. We have seen traumatized victims of violence, starving children, human and material wreckage caused by accidents, and grief-stricken survivors of all kinds of tragedy. The daily newscast at times seems to be an unending litany of human misery. The real issue: Do more and more information and images lead to greater commonality and deeper compassion?

Obviously, pornographic depictions in the media deny the basic subjectivity of individuals, treat others (regrettably, sometimes children) as objects, and evaluate their worth not in terms of potential for bearing the image of God but in terms of their capacity to arouse lust, titillation or morbid interest. Much less obvious is the fact that the massive exposure given from the media to human misery can lead, not to a sensitized conscience and expanded sense of compassion, but to psychic numbness. When we are bombarded with the multivaried miseries of the real world, we may shut off the content of newscasts from our innermost selves, lest we become overwhelmed by our own sense of helplessness and the apparent absurdities of human existence. The easiest response is to fuse the tragedies of the real world with the tragic experiences of the mythical world of action-packed, fictionalized series and then to dismiss both from our consciences. After all, both types of tragedy are reported with the same poised, ritualized tone of voice and facial expression and each regularly interrupted by happy people urging us to buy happy products for happy problems. The church ever has the task of personalizing human tragedy and calling disciples to intimate involvement in the plight of fellow-sufferers, however difficult and hopeless our efforts may seem.

(2) A fundamental teaching of the New Testament is that the child of God is called to a lifestyle of humble service to others. God's criterion for true greatness is the extent to which his creatures follow the example of Jesus in the path of committed servanthood. After the mother of James and John appealed to Jesus to grant her sons prominent positions in the kingdom, Jesus admonished his apostles, "Among you, whoever wants to be great must be your servant, and whoever wants to be first must be the willing slave of all—like the Son of Man; he did not come to be served, but to serve, and to give his life as a ransom for many" (Matt. 20:26-28). In this lifestyle of humble service, the Bible calls us to righteousness and social justice (Amos 5:23-24), kindness and humility (Mic. 6:6), and the correction of oppression (Isa. 1:17).

These values are seldom reinforced by the mass media for, as William Fore points out, power heads the list of values that the media communicates on behalf of our culture—power over others, power over nature. The trappings of power are made attractive; thus the lust for power is legitimized and its exercise is intriguing. Little wonder there is such fascination with media coverage of both actual and fictionalized treatments of American political life.

(3) Inherent within every human is a desire for happiness. Jesus often addressed himself to that desire and spoke of a blessedness and serenity that is not rooted in man's good health, wealth, or fortunate connections and outward circumstances. The blessedness of God is a gift to those who have espoused a new lifestyle in the kingdom and who seek it first (Matt. 6:33).

There can be no doubt that the central message of the Scriptures and the central lesson taught by most mass media productions are in diametric opposition. The Bible teaches that happiness comes to the one who seeks the kingdom of God; the media often tell us that the pursuit of happiness *is* the chief end of life. In his parables, Jesus taught about the futility of accumulating wealth while ignoring human need; the media reinforce the values of wealth and property. In one of Jesus' stories, the rich farmer planned to construct bigger farms but neglected to see that such accumulation did nothing to fill his impoverished soul. "Whoever cares for his own safety is lost; but if a man will let himself be lost for my sake and for the Gospel, that man is safe. What does a man gain by winning the whole world at the cost of his true self? What can he give to buy that self back?" (Mark 8:35-36).

The Bible teaches that pleasure was made for man, not man for pleasure (cf. Mark 2:27). The media bombard us with both explicitly and subtly persuasive messages that say the philosophy of the playboy is essentially valid, that there is joy in instant and unchecked sexual gratification and only despair and frustration in restraint and discipline. The varied and complex components that enter into human sexuality are reduced to "sex appeal"; and sex appeal is largely a matter of purchasing the right toothpaste, mouthwash, deodorant, and grooming products.

In contrast to the media values of immediate gratification, creature comforts, and narcissism, is Jesus' assertion that the one who wants to be his disciple must forget self, use material goods in the service of the needy, take up the cross, and follow his way (Matt. 16:24). To those who would exploit the earth and its animal and material resources to maintain a lavish lifestyle, the psalmist reminds us that "the earth is the Lord's and all that is in it, the world and those who dwell therein" (Ps. 24:1). In media dramatizations, the anxiety suffered by the man of the world about the meaning and purpose of human existence and about death is assuaged by making the right moves to step up into the envied position, inviting the right company to the dinner party, serving the proper mixed drinks and/or taking the appropriate drug, legal or otherwise. In real life, such solutions offer only a temporary relief. The Word of God calls us to examine our priorities and life direction, to repent and be born again, thus inaugurating a new life in the kingdom.

Mass Media and Family Life

In light of this basic conflict between media values and biblical values, perhaps the most important decision that Christians will make relates to the place media entertainment, and particularly television, will play in family life. Only the most radically detached and noninvolved in contemporary culture would attempt to extricate themselves from all media messages and influence. Some families have opted for removing the television set from their homes. However, most people are reluctant to relinquish all television entertainment; this was demonstrated recently by a Detroit newspaper offer which had few takers willing to be paid to give up television viewing for one month. And, even if adults were willing to submit to such regimen, such a ban merely cuts off their children from their peers and brands them as eccentrics. For children, a total ban would be ineffective, for they would be exposed to viewing at a friend's house, at school, or elsewhere. The more sensible solution is to avoid the excesses and be selective. One should read reviews, look for the excellent movies and programs that are available, encourage family members to watch them, and then watch them together. Through the ratings system the general public can control the content of programming. Meanwhile, control of the channel selection switch, and at times the on-off switch, lies with parents. It is obvious that no parents are totally powerless to control media input into their homes.

Nevertheless, there is a concern which should extend beyond the question of program selection: What is the Christian concept of leisure? And what changes are needed in leisure habits? Such questions are usually overlooked by critics of the media. Taking a cue from Luke's account of Jesus' maturation (Luke 2:52), the Christian is concerned about the development of the whole person. Life's fulfillment is not totally identified with work, and leisure time should contribute as vitally toward developing and sustaining the whole person as time spent in toil or rest. For in leisure one can explore the meaning of life, seek fulfillment of the human spirit, and search for truth. Recreation should involve restoration—the resting and recharging of tired muscles, frayed nerves, and overworked brain cells. Never before have Americans had as much time to spend in leisure as they now have.

Despite the wide variety of ways to spend leisure time and the availability of all kinds of sporting and recreational equipment with space and facilities for their use, not to mention the many expanded opportunities for continuing education, there are indications that some Americans have not developed an ethic for free time. Rather than the United States becoming one great "playpen," the greater danger, warns noted psychiatrist William Glasser, is that we may develop into a "don't care" civilization, because so much of our pleasure-seeking is the passive intake from television, drugs, and alcohol.[6] There is little or no social en-

---

[6]See special interview with Dr. Glasser in *U.S. News and World Report*, May 23, 1977, pp. 74-76.

richment and social pleasure from watching television; viewing can be done in the presence of others, but just about as much strength and growth can be realized when viewing is done in the presence of a pet or statue. Often, in fact, the pointless violence or exploitation of sex is not the worst aspect of some regular programming. The trite, bland, hackneyed—though morally innocuous—television productions can addict some, just as drugs can addict others.

A number of doctors and psychiatrists are concluding that excessive television viewing is an addiction which constitutes a growing threat to a child's mental and emotional health. Television does keep the child's mind occupied and stimulated, but in a passive way, acting on his mind much like a cast would act on his leg. Excessive viewing habits begin in many homes when the television is deployed as an electronic babysitter. Overuse of television interferes with the brain's capacity to handle simple problems of everyday living; it may also cripple the child's creativity, self-sufficiency, curiosity, and discovery of himself and others. Children still model most of their behavior after their parents' example, so Christian parenting means first and foremost that mother and father must be prepared to set the right example. The secret of a fulfilling leisure life is getting personally and actively involved in the kind of recreation that frees the mind and lifts the human spirit.

Conclusion

Three general ideas may be expressed in concluding this discussion of mass media and Christian ethics:

First, the solution to any given problem in the mass media is not to be realized in tighter governmental reins. Granted that much industry self-regulation is self-serving and inadequate, the dangers posed by censorship are greater than the evils which censorship is intended to eliminate. When most citizens speak of greater governmental strictures, they generally have in mind stopping the hard-core pornographer who panders to and profits from human frailties. By our analysis, however, the perpetration and inculcation of worldly values and philosophies through respectable channels of communication poses a far greater challenge to Christian ethics than does hard-core pornography. There are some areas in the "personal-morality-among-adults" business in which government does not belong. Government ought not to intrude on the right of adults to see or read whatever

they choose, provided that performance or publication does not
include the commission of, or incitement to, a crime. A balance of
rights is possible here, protecting those who do not wish to be
confronted by certain media content while defending the rights of
those who do.[7]

Instead of getting involved in the politics of the media, activists
should attack the problem at its economic roots. Action instituted
against sponsors of programs containing excessive violence have
met modest success. The National Citizens Committee for Broadcasting (NCCB) has ranked shows according to the amount of violence depicted, and the sponsors of the more violent programs
have been cited. Perhaps the most publicized victory, one which
did not involve violence at all, was won by Bob Jones III, who
waged a campaign against General Motors' sponsorship of "Jesus
of Nazareth," Zeffirelli's biblical epic on NBC. In proposing the
boycott, Jones declared: "Those who love and know the Lord
Jesus Christ, God incarnate, will, I am sure, make their protest
known both verbally and by spending automobile dollars elsewhere." General Motors withdrew at a cost of three million
dollars. It may be hoped that subsequent attacks by evangelicals
on the economic sponsoring of objectionable programming may
be aimed at productions more objectionable than Zeffirelli's.

Second, it should be obvious that media education involves
more than looking at movie ratings and other media reviews. The
line of analysis pursued here means that perhaps our first and
most difficult task as disciples of Christ is to spend a great deal of
time analyzing how the mass media are attempting to influence us
and to help others understand it also. Surely this is part of what
Jesus meant by stating his disciples must be in the world but not
of it. In recent years the religious media business has been boom-
ing, especially among evangelicals. But there is much that the
"secular" press, movies, magazines, journals, novels, and
programming have to offer Christians as they seek to understand
the social environment in which they are summoned to live.

---

[7]There is much literature on this subject. For a brief treatment, I recommend
Charles Rembar, noted attorney who won landmark literary censorship decisions,
"Obscenity—Forget It," *Atlantic Monthly*, (May 1977): 37-41. Rembar argues that a
citizen who has something he wishes to communicate may not be silenced completely, and may even be obscene about it if he likes, but the flow of his expression
can be channeled without infringing on First Amendment rights. Restraints may
be employed for the protection of children and the right of unwilling or captive
audiences not to have to confront what is offensive to them.

Media education would aid each religious group, each social class, and each subcultural group in discovering what the media say about them and how they define their problems and potentials. For example, evangelicals and parachurch movements and organizations have attracted a great deal of media attention, and it would be folly to impair our effectiveness by ignoring our media image and neglecting to listen to potentially constructive criticism.

Finally, the church should examine critically its own use of mass media. William Fore is on target when he criticizes those religious productions that "ape the images of secular media— images of prestige and power, of sex, escape and nostalgia, with all the trappings that reinforce the myths of secular society—and then somehow hope to turn the whole thing into a religious statement about the God who requires only justice, humility, and love."[8] In these years of religious renaissance we should beware of the obvious merging of pop religion and Madison Avenue technology where each borrows the language and images of the other.[9] One method moves toward sacrilege while the other moves toward desacralization; sensitive Christians condone neither trend. Church leaders should place themselves under special obligation to review for integrity purportedly religious productions, such as Hal Lindsey's film *The Late Great Planet Earth*, and those that allegedly deal with religious themes, such as *The Exorcist* or *The Omen*.

The varied mass media systems in this nation reflect all the diversity of our complex, pluralistic, and free society. The vast collective power of all the media can be harnessed for good or exploited for evil ends. Reform in our social institutions is not possible apart from changing and activating enough concerned individuals. Given the immeasurable impact of mass media in the lives of all of us, few tasks are more important for the church involved in the renewal of minds and the transforming of contemporary culture than that of shaping a theological critique of mass communications. The standards of judgment and criticism that evolve may be put to good use.

---

[8]Fore, "Mass Media's Mythic World," p. 37.

[9]D. G. Kehl offers illustrations of both points in his article, "Have You Committed Verbicide Today?" *Christianity Today*, January 27, 1978, pp. 18-21.

DAVID O. MOBERG

9

Ethical Dimensions
of Aging

Facts About Older Americans

There is no one age at which all persons give evidence of "being elderly." Aging is a process that begins at the moment of conception and continues until death. It has become customary, however, to deal with relevant information and data using age 65 as a statistical dividing point. This is largely a result of the Social Security Act of 1935, which established the sixty-fifth birthday as the age of eligibility for retirement benefits. That, in turn, has influenced the retirement practices and institutional arrangements in a wide variety of other American agencies. Thus an arbitrary dividing point has become a significant boundary between social groups for many practical purposes.

It should be recognized that there is great variability within the older population. There are differences from one nation to another; the "problem of aging" is characteristic of highly industrialized and urbanized societies more than of those which are relatively rural or preliterate. There are important variations between the respective regions, states, and communities within a large nation like America as well as among the various occupational categories, neighborhoods, families, denominations, church congregations, and ethnic groups. In spite of these limitations, the general statistical data which apply to the nation as a whole do suggest areas within which there are problems for individuals. Every social problem which has an impact upon masses of people also impacts upon the lives of individual persons, much as those persons vary.

In 1975 one in every ten persons (10.5 percent) in the U.S. was age 65 or over, and the proportion is expected to reach about twelve percent by the year 2000. The total number of such persons was equivalent to the total population of the twenty smallest states plus the District of Columbia in 1975. The number has increased from 3,080,000 in 1900 to 22,400,000 in 1975, and it is expected to reach 30,600,000 by 2000. During the twentieth century the proportion of the population age 65 and over will almost triple (from 4.1 percent in 1900 to 11.7 percent in 2000). If birth rates remain relatively low, the figure may be slightly higher; if birth rates rise, the figure will be somewhat lower at the end of the century.[1]

There are great variations from one state to another, however. The highest proportion in 1975 was found in Florida, with 16.1 percent of its population aged 65 and over, and the lowest was Alaska with only 2.6 percent. High proportions of aging people were found also in Arkansas, Iowa, Kansas, Missouri, Nebraska, Oklahoma, Rhode Island, and South Dakota, all of which had over twelve per cent of their population in that age category. In many villages in those states, one-fourth or more of the total population consists of "older Americans" or "senior citizens" past age 65.

Life expectancy in 1900 averaged about 47 years, but a child born in 1974 could expect to live to the age of 72. Women live longer on the average than men; a much larger proportion of them survive to the later years. Of all those who reach age 65, men can expect to live thirteen years more, but women eighteen years more. Over four-fifths (81 percent) of the females born in 1974 can expect to reach the age of 65 if there is no change in age-specific death rates, but only two-thirds (67 percent) of the male babies can expect to survive to that age.

As a result of that fact plus the tendency of men both to marry women younger than themselves and to become remarried upon widowhood, over half of all women aged 65 and over (52.5 per-

---

[1]National Clearing House on Aging, "Facts About Old Americans, 1976," Administration on Aging, U. S. Dept. of Health, Education and Welfare (DHEW Publication N. OHD 77-20006, 1976). Unless otherwise indicated, all statistics in the chapter are from this source, which summarizes data from various census studies and other government reports.

cent) but only one–seventh of all men (13.6 percent) were widowed as of 1975.

The increase in life expectancy has come in part from medical advances against the diseases and infirmities associated with old age. The development of new medications to control problems of the heart and circulatory system, improved detection and treatment of cancer, the invention of pacemakers to control the heartbeat, and the use of antibiotics and other drugs to control pneumonia, influenza, tuberculosis, and other infections have contributed to rising longevity. The greatest contribution of all, however, has come from medical attention during the early years of the life span. A much larger proportion of children and youth is surviving into adulthood than at the beginning of this century.

As other causes of death have diminished in relative statistical significance, those from heart disease have risen. It caused almost half (45 percent) of all the deaths of older persons in 1975, and cancer followed with seventeen percent. Two fifths (39 percent) of all older persons in 1974 were severely limited in activity due to chronic health conditions. A 1971 survey indicated that nine-tenths (92 percent) wore eyeglasses or contact lenses, and in 1972 almost one-fifth had some interference with their mobility due to chronic conditions (5 percent were homebound, 7 percent needed a mechanical aid to get around, and 6 percent had some trouble maneuvering alone).

Older people are more likely to be hospitalized than those under age 65. They then are likely to remain longer in the hospital, and they are more likely to have more than one hospitalization during the year. They also receive more physician visits than younger adults, and with each annual increase in age, they are somewhat more likely to die within the coming year. About three times as much is spent per person for the health care of the older population ($1,218 in 1974) as for younger adults. Almost one-third (30 percent) of the national costs for personal health care in 1974 was spent for older persons, with government programs like Medicare and Medicaid accounting for three-fifths of their health expenditures, compared to three-tenths for adults under age 65.

The death rate for persons past age 65 in 1974 was 70 per 1000 men and 48 per 1000 women. This combined rate of 56.8 per 1000 compares to four per thousand for people under the age of 65. Death is increasingly concentrated among older Americans.

The physical needs of the older population are paralleled by special material needs. Central to this is the level of income. Almost one in every six persons aged 65 and over in 1974 (15.7 percent) lived below the poverty level. When one considers that this was defined as an annual income of only $2,357 for a female and $2,387 for a male over age 65 (or $2,948 for a two-person family with a female head and $2,985 for a two-person family with a male head), it is obvious that this is a very conservative figure for the financial needs of the elderly. Half (51.2 percent) of all un-related persons aged 65 and over (individuals living alone) had incomes under $3,000, and over two-fifths (43.4 percent) of all couples with a husband aged 65 or over had incomes of less than $6,000 in 1974.[2] Although income decreases, the costs for food, shelter, clothing, taxes, transportation, and many other needs continue at a relatively high level during the later years, and those for medical care markedly increase.

The above financial statistics indicate that a very large proportion of older Americans live either below or only slightly above the poverty level. Inflation adds to their burden; those who are relying upon fixed incomes from pensions and investments have an increasingly difficult time coping with the rising cost of living. These financial needs spill over into problems with housing, transportation, dietary habits, recreation, social life, and even church participation.[3]

In the realm of social relationships, the majority of older people in 1975 (83 percent of men and 59 percent of women) lived in family settings, either with a spouse or other relatives, but over one-third (17 percent of men and 41 percent of women) lived alone or with nonrelatives. Only about five percent lived in institutions of all kinds. Four-fifths of the older men (79 percent) were married. Even among the married, the erroneous myth that it is abnormal or sinful to continue having active sexual relationships has caused considerable mental and psychological agony for large numbers of people. (Many married people continue to have active sexual lives well into their eighties and nineties.)

Other social interaction often suffers because of reduced income, transportation costs, physical limitations on mobility, membership dues which they feel they cannot afford, and other complications. During the later period of life in which there

---

[2]Consumer Income, "Characteristics of the Population Below the Poverty Level: 1974, *Current Population Reports*, series P-60, no. 102, January 1976.

[3]See Robert M. Gray and David O. Moberg, *The Church and the Older Person*, rev. ed., (Grand Rapids: Eerdmans, 1977), chap. 2.

usually is increased need for social relationships and more time is available for them, economic and physical complications frequently intrude to reduce those relationships.

The most serious among the social and psychological complications related to aging, however, pertain to attitudes and practices that are strongly entrenched in American society. Social scientists increasingly recognize that *ageism*, the discrimination against people merely because they have passed a certain chronological age, is as serious a social problem as racism and sexism.[4] Evident in compulsory retirement rules which give no allowance for differences in individual levels of capability at a fixed chronological age, it also is found in numerous social agencies and institutions which push the elderly aside. Our youth-oriented society does not respect the wisdom and knowledge of the elderly, thinking them instead to be relics from an outmoded past. While Americans show a nostalgic respect for antiques and other old things, they tend to push old people aside. Behind this phenomenon frequently is the psychological problem of *gerontophobia*, the tendency to unconsciously and irrationally fear one's own aging and hence to shun any reminder of it, including associations with aging people.[5] This unconscious attitude of gerontophobia may lie behind the practices of discrimination called ageism in much the same manner as attitudes of racial and sexual prejudice lend support to practices of discrimination.

The social and psychological problems of aging people are compounded by their losses through bereavement. Usually one spouse in a marriage dies before the other, and old friends pass one by one from this life to eternity. Those persons who have not cultivated a life-long practice of making new friends are gradually stripped of meaningful social relationships. In addition, complications often arise in family life as well-meaning adult children attempt to step in and manage the affairs of their parents, often against the parents' will.

All of these problem areas interact with each other, and all of them relate, at least indirectly, to spiritual needs. People desire and tend to develop a philosophy of life; their own formulation of

---

[4]Erdman B. Palmore and Kenneth Manton, "Ageism Compared to Racism and Sexism," *Journal of Gerontology* 28 (July 1973): 363-69.

[5]Joseph H. Bunzel, "Gerontophobia Pervades U. S. Life," *Geriatrics* 27 (March 1972): 41, 45, 49.

it may or may not satisfy them during the declining years and in their confrontation with impending death. During the 1970s increasing attention has been given to the human need for spiritual well-being by behavioral scientists and religious leaders. It was the focus of attention of one of the major sections of the 1971 White House Conference on Aging,[6] as well as of the National Intra-Decade Conference on Spiritual Well-Being of the Elderly sponsored by the National Interfaith Coalition on Aging in April, 1977. It is the focus of attention of a growing amount of social science research,[7] as reflected in sessions at the 1977 annual meeting of the Association for the Sociology of Religion and the Ninth World Congress on Sociology in 1978.

Older Americans face considerable ambiguity in our society.[8] There is no acceptable role widely developed in our society for retired persons, so people cannot be effectively prepared (socialized) for it. Rather, they must accept a devalued status in which the functions of restitution and social control are minimal and society gives no hope for their future.[9] The problem is compounded by the fact that even workers in their forties and fifties are labeled "older workers," experience age discrimination, and, if they become unemployed, often find it very difficult to re-enter the labor force because of age discrimination. Only about one-fifth of older men and one-twelfth of older women are in the labor force, and a large proportion of those men who do work are in low-paying agricultural jobs. This represents a significant shift since 1900, when two of every three older men were in the nation's labor force. The physical problems characteristic of many older people during their declining years (especially the "old old" aged 75 and over, in contrast to the "young old") are described vividly in Ecclesiastes 12:1-8. This passage stresses that people should remember their Creator in the days of their youth "before the evil days come, and the years draw nigh, when you will say,

---

[6]David O. Moberg, *Spiritual Well-Being: Background and Issues* (Washington, D.C.: White House Conference on Aging, 1971).

[7]David O. Moberg and Patricia M. Brusek, "Spiritual Well-Being: A Neglected Subject in Quality of Life Research," in *Social Indicators Research* 5 (July 1978): 303-23.

[8]Kurt W. Back, "The Ambiguity of Retirement," in *Behavior and Adaptation in Later Life*, ed. Ewald W. Busse and Eric Pfeiffer (Boston: Little, Brown and Co., 1969), pp. 93-114.

[9]Irving Rosow, *Socialization to Old Age* (Berkeley: University of California Press, 1974).

'I have no pleasure in them' " (v. 1). Those who commit their lives to him in their youth remember him all the rest of their days as well and benefit greatly from doing so.

Biblical Values and Aging

All of the ethical principles in Scripture which indicate what love in action means for our relationships with fellow human beings apply to our relationships with the aging. These are developed in other chapters of this book, so I will not attempt to discuss them systematically. Rather, I shall call attention to but a few principles which explicitly include reference to aging and the elderly.

Confronted with this subject, many Christians will immediately recall the commandment, "Honor your father and your mother, that your days may be long in the land which the Lord your God gives you" (Exod. 20:12). This idea is elaborated repeatedly in the Scriptures (Deut. 5:16; Matt. 15:3-9; Mark 7:9-13; Eph. 6:1-3). Proverbs 20:20, Colossians 3:20, and other passages more indirectly allude to it.

Significant questions can be raised concerning the relevance and meaning of that commandment for our day. Since husbands and wives also were commanded to depart from their parents and establish their own households (Gen. 2:24; Matt. 19:5; Mark 10:7), does it apply only to the period during which they are members of their family of procreation? At least in regard to material needs, this evidently is not the case, for the apostle Paul admonished the young minister Timothy that Christians who do not provide for their relatives, and especially their own family, have disowned the faith and are worse than unbelievers (I Tim. 5:8). Precisely how to fulfill such responsibility may vary with the individual persons involved. In many cases it may be more effective to implement that responsibility through collective action than as an individual all alone.

Leviticus 19:32 commands the Israelites to "rise up before the hoary head and honor the face of an old man." This respect is closely related to, if not also an aspect of, fearing God. In our society today, in which so much disrespect is demonstrated toward older people, we are tempted to think that that commandment was completely followed among the ancient Hebrews. In fact, however, the pleas in Psalm 71, allegedly the prayer of an old man, suggest that many elderly people were despised, rejected, and cast off when they lost their physical abilities and economic power. The psalmist pleaded to God that He would not do the same when his strength was spent but instead would revive him again, increase his honor, and put to shame those who brought disgrace and harm upon him. God is presented as the deliverer from social rejection, economic problems, physical decline, and psychological burdens.

The righteous, however, who are planted in the house of the Lord, still bring forth fruit in old age (Ps. 92:12-15) and are satisfied with good as long as they live, so they experience continual renewal (Ps. 103:5; see Prov. 16:31). This suggests that what social scientists call "activity theory" is more appropriate than "disengagement theory" as a basis for action in programs related to the aging.[10] Older people can continue to be fruitful if they are helped to recognize and accept significant responsibilities.[11] Even on the death bed, the Christian can engage in intercessory prayer for others; therefore among most people, fruitful activity can continue to the very end of this life. There is no need to disengage completely from other people and from usefulness in the world, even though circumstances may compel the tapering off of physically active forms of social participation.

Respecting the elderly is reflected in the instructions given to Timothy by the apostle Paul. Paul said that an older man should not be rebuked, but rather should be exhorted as a father. Older women should be treated like mothers. Widows who are "real widows," apparently those truly dependent and without any assets to meet their needs, should be sustained and helped by the church, but those who have relatives to support them should relieve the church of that burden (I Tim. 5:1-16).

A kind of reciprocity is built into many of the ethical teachings of the Bible. Both the "Golden Rule" to do to other people what you would have them do to you (Matt. 7:12) and Christ's summary of the ethical teachings in the Ten Commandments, that all are summarized in the one command to love one's neighbor as one loves oneself (Matt. 22:39-40), include this reciprocity. The teaching that every Christian is a part of the body of Christ, with all of the various members dependent upon all the others (Rom.

---

[10]Robert C. Atchley, *The Social Forces in Later Life*, rev. ed., (Belmont, CA: Wadsworth, 1977). This is one of the best textbooks in social gerontology, the study of the social and behavioral aspects of aging.

[11]Gray and Moberg, *The Church and the Older Person*, chap. 9.

12:3-8; I Cor. 12:1-31) conveys a similar norm of reciprocity; by doing good to others, including the elderly, we are helping to establish relationships, programs of activity and service, and examples which will presumably contribute to our own explicit benefit at some future date. But if there is injustice in this life, God is the ultimate judge; he will reward those who, with no thought of reward, provide food, drink, clothes, health services, and prison visits to Christ's brethren who need them (Matt. 25:31-46).

Since Jesus taught that it is more blessed to give than to receive (Acts 20:35), we ought to provide all of the aging who retain even a modicum of physical, mental, or spiritual energy with the opportunity to serve the needs of others. If, on the contrary, we merely serve them, we may be depriving them of the opportunity also to give. We must work with, as well as for, the aging, letting them serve us and others even as we serve them.

General biblical principles which apply to our ministries with and for the aging are numerous. For example, it is easy for us to become hypocritically oriented toward others, seeing their flaws while examining only our own virtues (Matt. 7:1-5). Cooperation with others is a better stance, for no single group can meet all of the material and social services needed by the aging (or any other group) in contemporary society. We must recognize our own flaws as well as our great ideals.

When we provide services to meet the needs of the aging and other groups, we soon discover that the problems of individuals reflect basic structural needs in the entire social system. These include such issues as unjust retirement policies, defects of pension systems, flaws in the Social Security program, the high costs of medical care, consumer exploitation, and the discrimination associated with ageism which grows out of gerontophobia. This means that to be "Good Samaritans" in the world today, we need to give attention to these collective needs while also dealing with the problems of individuals.

Another principle embedded in Scripture is that institutions are primarily instrumental. They are established to serve human beings; human beings do not exist to serve them. This means that even churches must remain tools of service. If they become institutions to which service should be given, goal displacement has occurred, and they need reform.

In a similar manner, the value of possessions is always far less than the value that is placed on human rights. Whenever there is an apparent clash between property rights and human rights, the latter must prevail. (This is not a secular humanist doctrine, nor one of Marxist socialism; see Luke 12:13-34 and related Bible passages.) Although all people are created in the image of God, each is unique. It is unjust to react to people as stereotypes, which imply that all members of a category have the same explicit needs and those needs may be fulfilled in the same ways. For example, far too often we respond to the aged as if they are *old*, instead of remembering that they are *people* who happen to be elderly, each of whom is a unique, distinct person. Indeed, the differences among the elderly are far greater than those which are apparent at earlier stages of the life cycle. To respect this uniqueness by treating each as a distinctive individual is one form of showing honor both to them and to their Creator.

At the core of all of the problems and experiences of the aging are spiritual needs. Solutions to many problems can be found in the context of a community of faith; so can comfort, hope, and the assurance that justice eventually will be done by the Judge of all the earth. Comfort in time of sorrow, joy in the face of despair, spiritual fulfillment in days of deprivation, acceptance by God when rejected by human beings, and assurance of the eternal love of Jesus Christ are spiritual assets which help to provide meaning for life and a context of assurance and hope when earthly burdens are heavy upon one. Spiritual insights and dedication are primary prerequisites of progress toward the solution of problems by the individual elderly person, as well as of others in society.

Applications of Christian Ethics

In order to be doers of God's Word, we must not only learn biblical principles, but we must apply them diligently in our daily conduct as individuals and as members of the body politic. The precise applications must always be related to the specific persons involved, the community context, the roles and relationships of sponsoring churches and other organizations, and similar practical considerations. Hence it is impossible to lay down a blueprint which specifies precisely what should be done in every instance for every person in every place. Nevertheless, there are some general principles about important areas of applied Christian social ethics to which attention should be given on the individual, congregational, regional, denominational, state, national, or even international levels.

The recommendations given here are not intended to be an exhaustive list; they are only suggestive of the wide range of possibilities which can enhance life for the elderly and others in contemporary society. We shall examine the same areas as were mentioned earlier in this chapter in our discussion of special needs of the aging, specifically, physical needs, material needs, socio-psychological needs, and spiritual needs.

Physical Needs

Continuing investigation and development of research findings which may contribute to alleviation of the health problems of the elderly certainly are desirable. Through them additional medical and technological advances ought to facilitate improved health for older people.

Meanwhile, those persons whose physical condition introduces limitations of mobility or strength need various kinds of services. Transportation for medical care, shopping, and church attendance, assistance with household work, and other supportive services ought to be available in order to facilitate independence of action as long in life as possible.

Gaps in current facilities in typical communities today force many people to remain in nursing and convalescent homes when such intensive and expensive services are not fully needed. Additional intermediate and minimal care residences can serve as halfway houses between nursing homes and private residences in the community. To some extent this need can be met by day-care centers for the elderly at which adults who go to work daily can leave the elderly person who is in need of care and pick him up again at the end of the day. Services ideally should also be provided so that people who have dependent elderly persons in their homes can take an occasional vacation, by letting the elderly persons move in for residential care during the departure of the adults who normally care for them.

Many older persons no longer can afford the relatively expensive maintenance needed to retain their own homes, or they may find that the work is too heavy for them. It is not uncommon for a single person, usually a widow, to reside alone in a six-room or eight-room house. Independent living can be extended many more years if two or more such persons join in a cooperative residential arrangement by which they live on a congregate basis like a family, each member having his or her own bedroom while sharing meals, household duties, taxes, and other responsibilities and costs. Unfortunately, many cities make such cooperative arrangements illegal by ordinances which prohibit unrelated people from living together except in licensed rooming houses or boarding facilities. Helping people who wish to cooperate with each other in such communities requires political involvement to have those ordinances changed.

Demonstration projects can be sponsored to show how older people can successfully overcome their problems by helping each other. These projects can be very effective in spreading the vision of possibilities among older adults who have the mistaken impression that there are only three options ahead of them when they slow down because of physical limitations—a retirement home, nursing home, or living with children or other relatives. Fearing all three of these, many older people cling much too long to their own individual residences, and their inability to do necessary maintenance work causes premature deterioration of their properties and unnecessary worry about their own future.

Helping older adults to discover other alternatives can be a distinct service facilitating their independence. It can help to prevent the forceful action against their personal dignity and autonomy that all too often is taken when some physical, mental, or economic emergency strikes.

Material Needs

The need for a variety of housing arrangements to fit the individual physical and mental conditions of older adults has already been mentioned. Many church groups sponsor retirement homes. Unfortunately, the majority of these are for people of middle and upper incomes, not for the large numbers which live below or near the poverty level. Whether it is wise for church groups to use their limited assets to satisfy such needs is something for each of them to decide. Many government-financed housing projects require trustworthy sponsoring agents, without which low-income housing may be unavailable within a community. Therefore, cooperative ventures by church groups of one or several denominations may be an appropriate step in the direction of meeting such needs.

By receiving various kinds of services, many older people would be able to remain in their own homes. There are high rates of unemployment among young people in most communities.

Church youth groups can be of service to God and their neighbors through giving their time at low rates of pay or even on a completely voluntary basis to care for household needs of the older people. In this way, it may be possible to deal with some aspects of the youth unemployment problem and at the same time enable many older people to remain in their own homes for months or years beyond the time when they otherwise would be forced to move.

Work exchanges among retired people also can be a very helpful means of getting services for which they are unable to pay at standard rates. Many retired persons have the ability to do household repairs, cleaning, clothes washing and maintenance, landscaping, tree-trimming, sewing, and such skills which other retired people need. By using simple bookkeeping devices to keep records of the hours contributed to and the hours received from the skills bank, many older people can receive services which otherwise would be financially and physically beyond their reach. Some might even build up credit that could be applied years in the future during their own declining years. All would be helped in the process by the fact that they were a part of a community, and as they contributed, they would find that even the act of giving constitutes an act of receiving.

In some communities protective services are greatly needed. If there is fraud against the purchasers of services, swindling of people who are easily confused, and failure of businesses and service agencies to stand behind their work, it may be necessary for people to work together to bring about desirable changes in the institutions, laws, and operating procedures of the community. Where crime rates are high, citizen cooperation with the police can be a major force to detect and report crimes and even to provide clues to the capture of offenders.

Special issues of justice are involved in the problems associated with the limited incomes of the majority of elderly people. Many of them have put money into pension funds for most of their working lives, but have discovered that those funds were not vested in them personally. As a result, when they lost employment before retirement, all of their savings in the pension fund were lost. Other older people have been penalized by rules and regulations that forced them to retire long before it was physically or mentally necessary. Nearly all elderly people have found that the money they saved when working is now worth far less in buying power, in spite of its increase through dividends and interest, than it was at the time it was put aside for their retirement years. All of these necessitate basic structural changes in the economic institutions and practices of the larger society. The inflation problem is worldwide and cannot be resolved by any one nation alone. The very best socioeconomic research and political leadership, sustained by Christian social ethics, is required in order to reverse the trends which are so inimical to the well-being of people.

An example of constructive correction of abuse of the elderly by structural injustices is a change in the rules and regulations of the Social Security Administration. Until January 1, 1979, a widow aged 60 or above who remarried found that her Social Security benefits were cut in half. As a result, many elderly people entered into illicit living-together arrangements in order not to lose a significant portion of their combined incomes. The 1977 amendments to the Social Security Act corrected this unfortunate flaw, so it will no longer discourage marriage.

Socio-psychological Needs

Many older people's need to love other people is less-than-satisfied because of the circumstances they experience and suffer. Some older people can be helped considerably when they are given the vision that they still can be of help to others. The Foster Grandparents program has helped many older people overcome problems of loneliness while also providing loving care for institutionalized children. When the picture of total human needs in a community is clear, other arrangements through which especially the "young old" can help also may become evident. Those who accept such opportunities unintentionally fulfill some of their own needs as well.

Counseling services to help people cope with their psychological problems, anxieties, fears, and concerns about the future, as well as deal with legal and financial complications, can be incorporated into cooperative community service centers for older adults. The congregate meal facilities provided in many churches, community centers, and schools with the help of federal funds do much more than merely meet dietary needs. They bring people together in social relationships through which they informally help each other to fill social and psychological needs which all human beings have.

People who themselves have experienced the guilt, grief, and burdens of bereavement are often the most capable of helping others who experience them (II Cor. 1:4). In many communities and church congregations widowed persons services assist men and women when they are bereaved of a spouse. The needs are often much greater after the funeral than before. Compassionate Christian love involves acts of kindness even more than words of sympathy.

Lifelong learning centers, of which the Shepherd's Center in Kansas City and the La Farge Institute of Life Long Learning in Milwaukee are outstanding examples, can deal with many practical needs of older people. They can also be an outlet for the interest many older adults have in enriching their lives through arts and crafts, liberal arts learning, increased knowledge of the sciences, and other educational ventures. Church-related or community senior centers can satisfy many recognized and latent needs as well; McClellan's description of the frontier for ministry which they provide can be of significant help in developing such programs.[12]

One of the greatest needs of all in regard to the psychological and social problems of the aging is internalized in the American population in general—the need to gain a clearer and more correct understanding of the characteristics, problems, potentialities, and privileges of aging in contemporary society. Gerontophobia must be overcome, and the erroneous attitudes and behavior associated with ageism must be eradicated from children, youth, young adults, and the middle aged, as well as from the mentalities and actions of the elderly themselves. All too often, older people are self-fulfilling prophecies of what they were taught to anticipate and expect in the later years. Stereotyped images of the aged become flesh in derogatory self-images. We all must learn to respect the elderly rather than to denigrate them.

Spiritual Needs

The primary focus of the church and its subgroups ought to be the spiritual needs of people. Whatever else it does, that is an area the church cannot afford to overlook, for no other agency in

---

[12]Robert W. McClellan, *Claiming a Frontier: Ministry and Older People* (Los Angeles: Andrus Gerontology Center, University of Southern California, 1977).

society has spiritual needs as its primary focus of attention. If churches fail in this, society will fail.

All of the conventional activities of worship, fellowship, Christian education, social service which ministers to the needs of others, and evangelistic outreach can contribute to that goal. At the same time, however, unless explicit attention is given to the special problems associated with aging, the church is not likely to meet the full gamut of human spiritual need. While it is true that the elderly can participate in groups designed to meet the needs of all adults, they have special limitations and interests which usually are not recognized. Obviously, since most of them no longer have any children at home, their needs as parents are greatly different from the needs of parents of preschool or even high school children. The relationships between husband and wife also are considerably different after retirement from those of younger adults who are employed on a full-time or more than full-time schedule. The death of friends and relatives occurs at a faster rate during the later years, and there is sharper awareness of the fact that one will soon face death oneself. The construction of one's own life story through reminiscing also puts a somewhat different slant upon the needs and requirements of older people from those of young and middle-aged adults.

For these and many other reasons, no church has an adequate program for its aging members unless it includes one or more group activities oriented explicitly toward their particular needs. In addition, unless it also gives them opportunities to serve others, it is cheating them out of many spiritual, social, and psychological blessings.

Conclusion

As Herrman has indicated, "Old age provides a perspective on life which is invaluable to the church fellowship. . . . Old age is a sobering stock-taking, a reappraisal of the meaningful in life, a reassertion of spiritual as opposed to material values."[13]

Living as we do in a society that is materialistic and secular in its orientation, Christian social ethics must focus most of all upon the spiritual dimensions of human need. Since people are holistic beings, however, spiritual needs cannot be severed from material,

---

[13]Robert L. Herrman, "Old Age," in *Baker's Dictionary of Christian Ethics*, ed. Carl F. H. Henry (Grand Rapids: Baker, 1973), pp. 468-69.

physical, and socio-psychological needs. All of these areas interact, and all of them affect and are affected by the ways in which spiritual needs are or are not satisfied. This means, among other things, that cooperation in the designing, administration, and interpretation of social and behavioral science research projects is one of the applied aspects of Christian social ethics. The findings of scientific research can be of significant service in promoting the well-being of the aging.

Basic to the problems of older people in modern society are the acts of discrimination, *ageism*, and the underlying attitudes of prejudice, *gerontophobia*. To a considerable extent these can be interpreted as violations of biblical principles, and hence of Christian social ethics. Christians above all others should take the lead to change the situation to one of *gerontophilia*—love for older people—and to demonstrate that love through national and state policies, as well as through the actions of individuals, church organizations, and other groups.

W. STANLEY MOONEYHAM

10

Christian Ethics in a Hungry World

What would it take to make your life complete?
A new home? A better job? More money?

Those would be typical answers in an affluent society. But suppose you lived in a village in the West African country of Upper Volta? Saidou Sawadogo is not your typical eight-to-five, forty-hour-week laborer. He is a farmer who lives in the village of Kaya. His nation is among the poorest in the world and Saidou is among the poorest of Upper Volta's generally impoverished population.

Saidou tries to provide for his family as best he can, but that is difficult in this largely desert nation where the gross national product averages out to about $90 a year per family. In America, by comparison, a family's average share in the gross national product is about $24,000.

Saidou is not a greedy man. His modest answer to that question was simply put: "If I can grow enough vegetables to feed my family the year round, then my life will be complete."

Mr. Sawadogo, his six million countrymen, and at least one-fourth of the earth's people are struggling to survive amid poverty, ignorance, disease, and injustice. Sawadogo cannot spell it out in those terms. All he knows is that circumstances always seem to conspire to keep him and his family hungry.

Hunger

Hunger is not an intimate word to most of us. If we ever think about it at all, the thought is usually brought on by a mild discomfort, quickly relieved by a visit to the refrigerator or a quick trip to one of the fast food outlets nearby. To most of the world's people, however, hunger is a gnawing feeling in the stomach that forms the context for all of life.

Hunger drains the body, dulls the mind, and crushes the spirit. It narrows the parameters of life to one unencumbered thought—survival.

Hunger is one of the great facts of life—and death—in our world. What is tragic is that so few of us who are well-fed are even aware of it.

Hunger is not a "thing." It is a symptom of many diseases, a result of many causes. Hunger is a sign of the lack of buying power; in other words, poverty. It is an indicator of unemployment or underemployment, of inefficient farming methods and lack of fertilizers, of insufficient water and unpredictable weather. Hunger is also the result of governmental policies that do not encourage food production, international trade that discriminates against developing nations, and attitudes of unconcern by those who have wealth and power.

Hunger is also nothing new to mankind. Perhaps that fact makes us insensitive. But an inescapable question for a follower of Jesus Christ is this: "Must it always be so?"

References to food abound in both history and the Scriptures. The Bible speaks of food for eating, food as a symbol, and food as a blessing and a celebration. There are also many descriptions of how the lack of food—even famine—has affected God's people through the centuries. It was famine that drove Abraham to Egypt (Gen. 12). Joseph's wisdom in food conservation prevented disastrous starvation in pharaoh's kingdom (Gen. 37—47). Famine in Samaria gave Elijah an opportunity to demonstrate God's power (I Kings 17—18).

In the New Testament, Luke speaks of the great famine during the reign of Claudius (Acts 11) and of how this became an opportunity for the Christians at Antioch to send relief to the believers in Judea. Famine is one of the four horses of the apocalypse, according to Revelation 6.

A list compiled in 1878 showed 350 famines known to that time, the earliest being in Rome in 436 B.C.[1] Famines, often

[1]Cornelius Walford's 1878 chronology, cited in Paul R. Erlich and Anne H. Er-

with drought and disease, have brought death from North China to Ireland—and these are only the disastrous shortages of which we have records.

Russia, 1600: 500,000 died of famine and plague.

India, 1769-70: Three million are thought to have died in this first extensive famine recorded in India.

Ireland, 1845-47: The "potato famine" caused over one million deaths.

Central India, 1876-78: Five and a half million died.

North China, 1876-79: Ten to thirteen million died.

If this seems like ancient history, Lester Brown, director of the Worldwatch Institute, estimates that starvation was responsible for more than 700,000 deaths in Bangladesh between 1971 and 1975, and that nearly one million persons died in India in 1972 when monsoon rains, and therefore crops, failed.[2] The Sahel drought and famine in West Africa made headlines from 1972 to 1974. An estimated five to ten million people were seriously short of food and as many as 200,000 died.

Despite greater attention to food production and the establishment of an international "early warning" system for agriculture, famine on a large scale is likely to occur again. Director of the United Nations Food and Agriculture Organization (FAO), Edouard Saouma, believes that greater efforts are needed to prevent or at least minimize the famines that may come: "Not only are individual countries and regions as subject as ever to devastation from natural calamities, droughts, plant diseases and so forth, but each cyclical food crisis tends to be worse than its predecessors. . . ."[3]

Famine is the dramatic and extreme form of hunger. The undramatic but even more pernicious expression is malnourishment.

Malnutrition

Chronic, widespread malnutrition is a greater concern right now than is famine for most developing nations. Estimates of the

lich, *Population, Resources and Environment* (San Francisco: Freeman, 1970), p. 14.

[2]Lester Brown, *Worldwatch Institute Report*, October 1976, reported in *Facts on File*, 1976, p. 863.

[3]Quoted in *The New York Times*, January 2, 1977.

number of malnourished people in the world range from 460 million to well over one billion. Whatever the number, hundreds of millions of people are not getting enough of the right kinds of food to lead active, healthy lives.

The human body needs about 2,400 calories each day to maintain good health, although this total can go up or down depending on such things as individual size and energy exerted. With as few as 1,500 calories the body is in trouble, and if it receives less than 1,200 calories for a prolonged period, the body will deteriorate and starve.

The average intake of calories in the United States is 3,300 per day—far in excess of daily needs. The average in India is about 2,000, although in some places in the country and during certain seasons, the intake may be less than 800 calories a day for one or two months. That is barely staying alive.

Ethiopians, Indonesians, Vietnamese, and Filipinos also show similarly low levels of caloric intake. But remember that these are averages; millions of people are below the average.

But caloric intake is not all there is to adequate nutrition. The key element in health- and body-building is protein. Dr. Georg Borgstrom, professor of nutrition at Michigan State University, believes that "the prime global deficiency is that of protein. . . . Indeed, 10 to 15 percent of the world is short of calories, or 'undernourished.' But vastly more people—perhaps 1.5 billion—suffer from the calamity of inadequate nutrients, or 'malnutrition.' A shortage of protein is the number one problem everywhere in the hungry world."[4]

What does this mean in human terms? I talked to Gokal Walji Christie, a laborer who lives in Singhali village in Gujarat state, India. Gokal does his best to feed a family of six. In normal times they have two meals a day. If drought comes—as it did when I was there—they are thankful to eat once a day.

On the day I was there they had started the morning with a cup of tea, no milk or sugar. In the evening they would have a small millet cake with tea and, perhaps, a raw onion or other vegetable. This was their one "meal." Some of Gokal's fellow Indians might vary the diet slightly with boiled rice or a soup called *dahl*, made from peas, beans, or lentils. Another common dish is *chapatties*, made from whole wheat flour and water. A little fish or some fruit are luxuries.

---

[4]Georg Borgstrom, "The Dual Challenge of Health and Hunger—A Global Crisis," *Population Reference Bureau Selection* 31 (January 1970).

For people like Gokal, malnutrition is a constant companion, and it is the children who suffer most. In the villages and on city streets you can see tiny bodies with sunken cheeks and loose skin wrinkled over bony limbs. They move listlessly, almost too tired to respond. Ironically, one form of malnutrition—kwashior-kor—causes the body to swell because the tissues are filled with fluid. This fills out the face and bloats the stomach, deceptively look-ing as if one had enjoyed too many good meals.

The list of diseases that result from malnutrition is not pleasant reading—blindness, beriberi, scurvy, rickets. And malnutrition in expectant mothers affects the unborn children. After birth, more often than not the infant continues to be undernourished, resulting in stunted growth and the possibility of irreversible mental retardation.

I remember the pert, smiling face of little six-year-old Marli as she scampered around the playground of the Methodist school and nutrition center in Rio de Janeiro. She looked normal in every way. But she couldn't learn. Her teachers had finally discovered that Marli, one of eleven children from the slums of Rio, was un-able to learn because, as an infant, her malnourished body could not produce a healthy brain. Marli would never achieve her God-given potential, and the awful finality is that nothing can be done about it now.

I have heard the same diagnosis repeated around the world. Millions of children have suffered irreversible brain damage because of chronic protein deficiency. They are condemned forever to the cruel twilight world of mental cripples.

Poverty

One cannot talk about hunger without mentioning poverty, for the two conditions are bound together. The poor are hungry. The hungry are poor. Someone has said: "Hunger and poverty are two sides of a coin that buys nothing but misery."

For most of the world's hungry people, there really is no standard of living—only a "standard of survival." These are people who are so poor that they cannot buy food regularly and who are so malnourished they have barely enough energy to work, and so are caught in an impossible cycle of hopelessness.

In the affluent nations, we refer to "poor" or "underdeveloped" countries. But the language of international politics is not as straightforward. "Developing" is a less offensive term and in more common usage. In the international alphabet, these are the LDCs, or less-developed countries. The hunger problem has become so acute, however, that "developing" or LDC was not an adequate descriptor for those nations in desperate need of assistance. The United Nations, therefore, designated MSAs, or "most seriously affected" nations, as those countries most hurt by the shortages of food, fuel, and foreign exchange. More recently, MSAs have given way to FPCs, "food priority countries," those most in need of food assistance and trade on easy credit terms.

Whatever the designation—LDC, MSA, or FPC—the meaning is hunger, poverty, and misery. These nations are what has been termed the "Fourth World," defined by British economist Barbara Ward as "the one that is about to fall off the edge of the global economy." The forty-three nations designated as FPCs contain 1.25 billion people, or almost 32 percent of the world's population. And those one billion-plus human beings are trying to exist on an average of 27 cents a day.

"Total poverty" is the only term that can adequately describe the condition of masses of people in the Fourth World.

Compare that 27 cents a day with the poverty level for a family of four in the United States, which is now over $5,800, or about $1,400 per person per year. That poverty income level is fourteen times greater than India's official poverty line of about $96 per year per person. How much food a person eats depends not only upon how much food is grown but also on how much money that person has. No one who has money goes hungry, anywhere in the world.

An article in the *National Observer* described the crowded, filthy slums of Calcutta where more than two hundred thousand Indians sleep and live on the streets. In this same issue of the newspaper were classified advertisements that read: "Guide to Fine Real Estate Around the World is yours . . . a 288-page book of fabulous homes, glamourous villas, chateaux steeped in history, ranches with huge acreage, islands floating in emerald seas, contemporary ski lodges for the sports minded . . ."; "Castle in the Sky. Completely furnished, two-story luxury home overlooking lake (has piano, stereo and freezer)." For that latter piece of property, the owner felt he should set a minimum bid. How much? A modest $70,000.

How far from the world of fine villas is the world of Calcutta's slums. But perhaps no more distant than is your world and mine from that of our one billion hungry cousins in places like Niger, Haiti, and Bangladesh.

Rich vs. Poor

It is hard for us in the developed nations to see how we appear to the less developed countries. Our surroundings affect the way we look at the world. Most of us are well fed, educated, and employed. Our nations are not obviously overcrowded, our population growth rates are low, and our food production is at least adequate. How can we empathize with the hungry of our world?

Charles Mount, Jr. comments: "We may know intellectually that world hunger could mushroom rather than disappear, that population growth could do us in, and that something must be done. Yet we may also avoid getting agitated about these twin terrors . . . because hunger and crowded conditions have not been part of our experience."[5]

Mahub ul Haq, a senior economic advisor at the World Bank, in his book *The Poverty Curtain*, tells of some of the differences in the way rich and poor nations look at the world. The rich are concerned with the quality of life; the poor are concerned with life itself. The rich have become vocal in their demands for conservation of nonrenewable resources. The poor nations argue for a fair distribution of those resources. The rich are suffering from industrial pollution due to excessive development. The poor are suffering a "pollution of poverty" due to inadequate development.

On a major issue such as population growth, the developed and developing nations may both understand the problem, but they see it in different perspectives. Although the current annual population increase in developed nations is less than one percent, that growth, says Haq, "places eight times as much pressure on the world's natural resources as the 2.3 percent annual population increase of the Third World. This is simply because each new member of a rich nation enjoys about twenty times the income of an individual in poor nations. It costs our planet about thirty times more to feed a North American than an Indian or Pakistani."[6] Where, then, is the *real* population burden?

---

[5]Charles Mount, Jr., "The Squint," in Estelle Rountree and Hugh Halverstadt, *Sometimes They Cry* (NY: Friendship Press, 1970), p. 92.

[6]Frank Meissner, *Review of The Poverty Curtain by Mahbub ul Haq* (1976), *International Development Review* 1977.

If you say that we in the developed world "earned" our affluence because we worked for it, let me suggest that we did not do it alone. There is some validity to the claim that our affluence was built upon the resources and efforts of the less developed nations. Considering food items alone, rich nations import more food *from* poorer nations than we export *to* them. United Nations figures from 1955 to 1973 show that developed nations imported almost twice as many dollars' worth of food from developing nations as they exported to them. Although the United States is one of the few nations that regularly exports more food than it imports, U.S. food imports from *developing* nations have consistently exceeded our exports to those nations. In 1972, these developing nations sent us $1.4 billion worth of food *more* than we sent them.[7] Who, we are forced to ask, is helping whom?

I have referred to the Third World nations as "less" developed. This suggests the more affluent nations are "more" developed. From the Third World viewpoint, our condition might be better described as *over*developed.

The average American consumes well over 3,000 calories of food energy per day, while most people in the Third World receive an average of less than 2,300 calories per day. While lack of food is the worry of millions in the Third World, too much food is the concern in affluent nations. According to the American Medical Association, 40 percent of the U.S. population is overweight. There is even a dog food on the market for our overweight pets.

And this overconsumption goes beyond food. The typical Indian uses about one-twenty-fifth as much energy and scarce materials as does the typical North American. Even the poorest American will consume more than most of the people in the poorer nations. Harold Shane of Indiana University has said: "Even now the purchasing power of Americans at the U. S. *poverty* level is above the consumption level of the top 25 percent of whole populations in the so-called undeveloped countries."[8]

Do you wonder at the Third World demands for restoring some balance? Or that those demands have a sharp tone?

Julius Nyerere, president of Tanzania, who is trying to make

---

[7]Ronald J. Sider, *Rich Christians in an Age of Hunger: A Biblical Study* (Downers Grove, IL: InterVarsity Press, 1977) pp. 156-58.

[8]Harold Shane, "Education for Tomorrow's World," *The Futurist* (June 1973), p. 104.

his nation more self-sufficient, has said, "I believe that the poor nations have the right to demand assistance from the rich nations as a matter of justice, and in compensation for continuing exploitation."[9]

Mubashir Hasan, Pakistan's former minister of finance, planning, and development, made the same point to the United Nations:

> The antagonism between the rich and poor is natural. You have to be poor to realize it. The poor are increasingly beginning to believe that the rich have not become rich by divine desire but by expropriating the fruits of their labor; that some nations are affluent and others are impoverished as a result of the cumulative effect of the years of imperialism, colonialism, and neo-colonialism, and not because of any inherent defect in themselves.[10]

And Indira Gandhi, while still prime minister of India, said to a 1974 conference on international law: "Is it not a new form of arrogance for affluent nations to regard the poorer nations as an improvident species whose numbers are a threat to their own standard of living?"

Third World leaders object, quite rightly, to the unthinking assumptions and arguments made by many in the developed nations. A dialogue between rich nations and poor nations might look like this:

Rich: Why should we care about you? We have our own problems.

Poor: All the things you want for your country and your families, we would like to have, too. Are you the only ones that have a right to them? We have contributed to your development; don't you think it's time you contributed to ours?

Rich: But why don't you work harder? If you worked as hard as we have done, you'd get ahead.

Poor: You may have pulled yourselves up by your bootstraps but we don't have any straps, much less boots. We do work hard; often harder than you do. But many of us are hungry, malnourished and sick. We aren't able to work as we would like. Then too, a lot of us can't find work. Our economies are struggling. Unemployment is high. Sometimes that unemployment is the result of trade policies of you

---

[9]Julius Nyerere, "Aid and Development from a Recipient's Point of View," quoted in *Africa* (May 1974): 66.

[10]*Los Angeles Times*, May 5, 1974.

rich nations that prevent us from competing in the international markets. We often don't have your tools or knowledge, and when you offer them to us, they may be too expensive or inappropriate for our conditions. Help us find new ways which are less complex and less expensive.

Rich: Why don't you do something to control your growing populations? If we are going to help you, we want to be sure we're not just helping produce excess numbers of children.

Poor: How would you feel if we were to demand that you affluent nations stop having children because each child in a rich nation puts a much greater demand on the world's scarce resources than the average child in a developing nation? Some poor countries are overcrowded, but some are not. There is room to grow if we can get help to develop the land. You rich nations have educated people, reasonably decent living conditions and good health care. You know how to limit your families and you have a good hope that your few children will live to become adults. Many parents in poorer nations would like to limit the size of their families but they are ignorant of family planning. Then, too, for many parents large numbers of children are their security in old age. We don't have Blue Cross, pension plans, or social security programs. Our security comes from our children. Don't forget that so many children die before the age of five that a family must have eight or ten children to insure that three of four will live. Remember that we love children just as much as parents in rich nations. We want to enjoy their warmth and smiles. Will you deny us that privilege?

The divisions and misunderstandings between rich and poor nations have grown over the decades and will not be settled in a short time. There is also much anger and hostility and shouting when people do not wish to listen. Yet, if each side can really hear what the other is saying, there is hope for the future.

Faced with the dismal reality of world hunger, the vast disparity between rich and poor nations, and the injustices of international economics, how are Christians to respond? Where do followers of Jesus fit into this world of overwhelming need?

The Right to Food

Hunger is unquestionably a moral and ethical issue as well as an economic and political one. Dr. Norman Borlaug, former director of the International Maize and Wheat Improvement Center in Mexico, and one of the creators of the "Green Revolution," has said, "It is my belief that food is the moral right of all who are born into this world. . . . Without food, all other components of social justice are meaningless."[11]

The concept of a "right to food" has been emphasized by Bread for the World, a Christian citizens' lobby for political action on food policy. It has published a statement which says, "As Christians we affirm the right to food: the right of every man, woman and child on earth to a nutritionally adequate diet. This right is grounded in the value God places on human life and in the belief that 'the earth is the Lord's and the fullness thereof.' "[12]

Is there a right to food? Not everyone agrees.

Before we look at biblical ethics, let me deal with two other viewpoints on world hunger that have been widely publicized but which, in my opinion, are amoral at best and certainly not Christian. One of these is known as the "lifeboat ethic"; the other is the concept of "triage."

The lifeboat ethic is propounded most forcefully by Dr. Garrett Hardin, a biologist at the University of California at Santa Barbara. Dr. Hardin says that rich nations have no obligation to provide food or aid to poor countries. He uses the metaphor of a lifeboat. Each rich nation is like a lifeboat full of comparatively rich people and their resources. In the ocean surrounding each lifeboat swim the poor of the world, who would like to get in to one of the boats. When a boat is full and its resources are limited, the ones on board are faced with the unhappy—but understandably necessary—task of pushing away the others who are thereby doomed to drown. Since many poor countries are permitting unrestrained population growth, says Hardin, giving them aid only delays inevitable starvation. Giving aid also robs the rich (and presumably provident) nations of their limited resources.

In other words, each nation must do what it can to care for itself and leave others to make their way as best they can.

Sink or swim.

The metaphor has a fatal flaw. It is this: No country is a "lifeboat." All nations are part of a single world; no one can be completely independent of the others. In the United States, we would quickly find ourselves in difficulty if we tried to do without copper from Chile, lumber from Indonesia, rubber from Malaysia,

---

[11]Commencement address, New Mexico State University, May 12, 1973, quoted in *Vital Speeches* 7-1:556.

[12]"The Right to Food," A Statement of Policy by Bread for the World, March 1975, reprinted in Arthur Simon, *Bread for the World* (NY: Paulist Press, 1975), p. 165.

and coffee from Brazil and Costa Rica. And we cannot ignore our growing dependence on oil from the Arab nations.

Dr. Hardin also ignores data which show that many developing nations can and have cut population growth significantly. Nations such as China, Barbados, Sri Lanka, Taiwan, Cuba, and South Korea, among others, have all been able to reduce the rate of growth of their populations, even in the face of generally low income levels.

Dr. Hardin does not seem to recognize that the affluent nations have had a part in bringing on the desperate conditions found in many developing nations. I have already described the demand of developed nations for resources, including food, and how this demand has worked against the needs of the poorer nations. Professor Ronald Sider, in his book *Rich Christians in an Age of Hunger*, says, "In a world where the rich minority feed more grain to their livestock than all the people in India and China eat, it is absurd and immoral to talk of the necessity of letting selected hungry nations starve. The boat in which the rich sail is not an austerely equipped lifeboat. It is a lavishly stocked luxury liner."[13]

The other viewpoint, "triage," is taken from the concept of military medicine, where the wounded on a battlefield are sorted out to determine who shall be cared for first. There are three categories: Those who will recover with minimal aid; those who can be saved if given immediate attention, and those who are so badly hurt that recovery is unlikely. For those in the last category, the policy is to make them comfortable, give them something to ease their pain, and move on to care for those who may recover. Sounds callous, perhaps, but such are the necessities of battle.

Applied to global economics, triage becomes a moral nightmare. Triage advocates contend that the developed nations should give aid and assistance only to those nations that are willing to take positive steps in such matters as population control and agricultural reforms. Those countries unwilling to discipline themselves in the "approved" manner would be left to go their own way. Millions might starve, revolutions might follow, and human life might degenerate to animal level, but those conditions would not be our concern.

There is an incredible presumption that developed nations, especially the United States, can and should "play God" with other

---

[13]Sider, *Rich Christians*, p. 55.

countries. We would decide which nations would survive and which would die. Some nations would be helped while others would be consigned to oblivion.

Again, there is a fatal flaw in this viewpoint. Nations are not soldiers on a battlefield. Individual citizens may die but nations struggle on. Bangladesh or Mali or Angola will not disappear from the earth simply because we decide to ignore them.

Economist Barbara Ward writes that triage is "so shot through with half-truths as to be almost a lie, and so irrelevant to real world issues as to be not much more than an aberration. . . ."[14]

Biblical Ethics

Lifeboat and triage may be ethical views but they are not the ethics of biblical Christianity. The history of Israel, the words of the Bible, and the record of the New Testament church are filled with exhortations, commands, and examples of the importance of feeding the hungry, caring for the impoverished, and showing justice to the poor and the powerless.

Ancient Israel had a strong tradition of concern for the under-privileged and the needy. In fact, so much was the practice of charity considered a duty that one of Job's friends suggested that Job's sufferings were due to his failure in that area: "You must have refused water to the thirsty, and bread to the starving." (Job 22:7, LB).

Jews were exhorted not to live in any city which had no alms box, for almsgiving was of paramount importance—so much so, that "righteousness" and "almsgiving" came to be interchangeable terms. Blessedness meant sharing actively in the misfortunes of others.

During the wilderness experience, God himself was the provider of food, and the Israelites were told to depend exclusively upon him. Elisha fed a hundred men with seemingly little to offer them, yet he had some food left over, a foreshadowing of Jesus' feeding of the thousands. God is described as the one who brings justice and who feeds the hungry (Deut. 10:16-19; Ps. 146:5-9).

We are objects of God's mercy and grace. But his blessings also bring responsibility. He expects us to show the compassion of

---

[14]"Not Triage, but Investment in People, Food and Water," *The New York Times*, Nov. 15, 1976.

Christ to others. The Bible makes very clear that we cannot claim to be faithful followers of Jesus if we fail to actively care for others: "But if any one has the world's goods and sees his brother in need, yet closes his heart against him, how does God's love abide in him?" (I John 3:17).

When we see photographs of hungry people or hear of their plight, can we recognize this terrible truth? In a very real way, it is Jesus Christ who is starving. It is Jesus who has tattered robes. It is Jesus who is cold. You cannot avoid that conclusion when you hear him say, "I was hungry and you gave me food. . . . As you did it to one of the least of these, my brethren, you did it to *me*" (Matt. 25:35, 40). To feed the hungry is to render a personal service to Christ himself. To fail to do so is to neglect and reject Christ.

That may be hard to accept, but if we who claim Christ as Lord say that we have faith in him and love him, our love and faith must be expressed in deeds. James points to those who are poor and hungry and says, "If a brother or sister is ill-clad and in lack of daily food, and one of you says to them, 'Go in peace, be warmed and filled,' without giving them the things needed for the body, what does it profit? So faith by itself, if it has no works, is dead" (James 2:15-17). Love only talked about is easily turned aside, but love demonstrated in action is irresistible.

Former Prime Minister Nehru of India once said, "It is really folly to talk of culture or even of God when human beings starve and die." In the face of world hunger and poverty, words—even religious words—are empty. Action is called for.

Another Indian leader, Mahatma Gandhi, spoke directly to Christians: "In my judgment the Christian faith does not lend itself to much preaching or talking. It is best propagated by living it and applying it. . . . When will you Christians really crown [Jesus Christ] as the Prince of Peace and proclaim him through your deeds as the champion of the poor and the oppressed?"

Practical caring is not something added onto spiritual concerns; caring is at the heart of spirituality. The Russian theologian, Nicholas Berdyaev, said, "Care for the life of another, even material, bodily care, is spiritual in essence. Bread for myself is a material question: bread for my neighbour is a spiritual question."[15]

---

[15]Nicholas Berdyaev, cited in Victor Gollancz, *Man and God* (Boston: Houghton Mifflin, 1951) pp. 211-12.

Some of the Bible's strongest condemnations are for those people who neglect and oppress the poor. The Law, the Prophets and our Lord himself are stern in declaring that God destroys and brings low the rich and powerful when they fail to help the poor. Scripture seems to assert that God often casts down the wealthy, because they became wealthy *at the expense of* the poor and because they failed to share with the needy.

James warns those who have gotten rich unjustly: "Your gold and silver have rusted, and their rust will be evidence against you and will eat your flesh like fire. . . . You have lived on the earth in luxury and in pleasure . . . you have condemned, you have killed the righteous man; he does not resist you" (James 5:1-6).

In Luke's account of the rich man and Lazarus (Luke 16), it does not say that the rich man exploited Lazarus, just that he showed no concern for the beggar at his gate.

Sodom was destroyed not only for its immorality but for its failure to aid the poor and the needy (Ezek. 16:49-50).

In Matthew's description of the judgment of the nations (Matt. 25), failure to feed the hungry and care for the needy results in God's disowning. Those who neglect the poor and oppressed are not really God's people. And if we, as comparatively affluent Christians, fail to respond to the cries from those in need around the world, how can we say that we have God's love in us? The twin sins are injustice and neglect. Is it a coincidence that these two sins are the ones the less developed nations most often charge against the rich nations?

The Lord God is a God of forgiveness. But there comes a point, emphasizes Dr. Ronald Sider, "when neglect of the poor is no longer forgiven. It is punished. Eternally. Is it not possible—indeed very probable—that a vast majority of Western 'Christians' have reached that point? North Americans earn fourteen times as much as the people in India, but we give a very small amount to the church. Most churches spend much of that pitiful pittance on themselves. Can we claim that we are obeying the biblical command to have a special concern for the poor?"[16]

Dr. Lewis Smedes points out that there are three moral concepts that bear directly on the issue of the Christian response to hunger: justice, responsibility, and stewardship.

Justice

Smedes says that we should think of our duty in responding to

---

[16]Sider, *Rich Christians*, p. 83.

world hunger as a matter of meeting the claims of justice rather than as matters of charity and mercy. Justice has a stronger and broader claim on our response, it demands a longer commitment, and it requires that we think beyond private charity to matters of public policy.

If we, as Christians, believe that there is a oneness to mankind, we must see that starving people are not merely citizens of some other nation but that they are members of *our* family, part of *us*. In Smedes' words, "This being true, they have a just claim on the resources we glibly call ours, resources that God put on the earth to be shared equitably by all his earth-bound family. And we are obligated to share these resources."

At a minimum, justice appears to require that every person have enough food to provide energy for a productive life, and the opportunity to produce food or to have enough money to buy needed food. Justice also means that those of us with more than the minimum must seek a fair distribution of the earth's food supply and help with the development of the poorer nations.

Responsibility

Responsibility, the second concept, requires Christians to seek appropriate and useful responses to the challenge of world hunger. There are many things we might do, individually and corporately. We need to understand the alternatives and choose those that we believe we should undertake.

At the same time we must recognize that our personal responsibility is a limited one. We cannot increase the acreage of food-producing land, or provide political expertise to leaders of developing nations, or decide how land reforms should be instituted. As Smedes says, "God does not ask us to bear responsibilities beyond our limits. This does not negate the claims of the poor. . . . It does say that our accountability is limited by our power to grant their claims. Responsibility has limits, but it compels us to respond personally *within* our limits; it urges me to respond even when I sense that there is not much I can do effectively."

Stewardship

Finally, the concept of stewardship helps us to relate our manner of living to the needs of others. We too often forget that we are stewards, not owners, of God's property. We have no absolute claim to whatever wealth we may possess; God, as the owner, places limits on its acquiring and use. The basic constraint is that use of wealth must be subordinated to caring for people.

Says Smedes, "Being stewards means that we find the most responsible way of taking care of God's goods in our place and time. What we are called to do is cope with a problem we cannot solve. And coping as God's stewards means finding the right thing to do with what we have, at least to keep things from getting worse and maybe making them a little better for others."[17]

Not only are we to use our wealth to care for others, but we are warned that the very pursuit of wealth can lead to the sin of covetousness and then to the neglect of the poor. Paul writes that "those who desire to be rich fall into temptation . . . that plunge men into ruin and destruction" (I Tim. 6:9). Abundance of possessions can even lead to forgetting that God is the source of all wealth and good. "Take heed," warns the writer of Deuteronomy, "lest, when you have eaten and are full, and have built goodly houses and live in them . . . and your silver and gold is multiplied, and all that you have is multiplied, then your heart be lifted up, and you forget the Lord your God. . . . You shall remember the Lord your God, for it is he who gives you power to get wealth . . ." (Deut. 8:11-18).

We need to see that our style of life, as individuals and as nations, stands under God's judgment. "Are we not guilty of covetousness," asks Ronald Sider, "when we demand an ever higher standard of living while a billion hungry neighbors starve?"[18] Possessions and wealth are not inherently evil; God does permit us to have things which will enrich our lives and allow us to help others. But we surely are urged to use diligence and care to see that we do not desire and consume to excess, nor to waste that which could help others.

William Law, in his classic, *A Serious Call to a Devout and Holy Life*, makes the point that one of the reasons for special care in the use of our wealth is that it is capable of being used for so much good.

If we waste it, we do not waste a trifle . . . but we waste that which

[17]Lewis Smedes, "Hunger and Christian Duty," (unpublished paper presented to Fuller Theological Seminary, 1975).

[18]Sider, *Rich Christians*, p. 124.

might be made as eyes to the blind, as a husband to the widow, as a father to the orphan. We waste that which not only enables us to minister worldly comforts to those that are in distress, but that which might purchase for ourselves everlasting treasures in heaven. So that if we part with our money in foolish ways, we part with a great power of comforting our fellow-creatures, and of making ourselves for ever blessed.[19]

Dietrich Bonhoeffer put it this way:

To allow the hungry man to remain hungry would be blasphemy against God and one's neighbour, for what is nearest to God is precisely the need of one's neighbour. It is for the love of Christ, which belongs as much to the hungry man as to myself, that I share my bread with him and that I share my dwelling with the homeless. If the hungry man does not attain to faith, then the fault falls on those who refused him bread. To provide the hungry man with bread is to prepare the way for the coming of grace.[20]

Some Christians may say, "We don't neglect the poor. We believe in good stewardship. We just want to be sure that our aid will be used wisely, not wasted through corruption or inefficiency." That is a valid concern, but let us be careful that we do not apply a standard more strict than the one God uses.

An old Hasidic story tells of a rabbi who was rebuked by his students for giving his last coin to a beggar. He replied: "Shall I be more particular than God who gave the coin to me?"

William Law describes Miranda, the epitome of Christian virtue, and her attitude toward the poor:

It may be, says Miranda, that I may often give to those that do not deserve it, or that will make an ill use of my alms. But what then? Is not this the very method of divine goodness? Does not God make his sun to rise on the evil, and on the good? Is not this the very goodness that is recommended to us in Scripture, that by imitating of it, we may be children of our Father which is in heaven . . .? And shall I withhold a little money or food from my fellow-creature, for fear he should not be good enough to receive it of me? . . . Shall I use a measure towards him, which I pray God never to use towards me?

Besides, where has the Scripture made merit the rule or measure of charity? On the contrary, the Scripture saith if thy enemy hunger, feed him, if he thirst, give him drink.[21]

---

[19]William Law, *A Serious Call to a Devout and Holy Life* (London: Ogles, Duncan & Cochran, 1816) p. 81.

[20]Dietrich Bonhoeffer, *Ethics* (NY: Macmillan, 1955), p. 137.

[21]Law, *A Serious Call*, p. 113.

Miranda relates her charity directly to the matter of salvation:

> As far as I can, I give to all, because I pray to God to forgive all; and I cannot refuse an alms to those whom I pray God to bless, whom I wish to be partakers of eternal glory. . . .[22]

The danger is not that salvation of souls will become second priority, but that we will feel that the salvation of souls is alone sufficient, and neglect the very real need for the "salvation" of bodies.

Christ never conditions his love. Jesus does not tell us, "When the government of Ethiopia gets rid of its corrupt bureaucracy, then you can help the Ethiopian people." He does not say, "When the Africans, or the Indians, or the Brazilians get their populations under control, then give them aid." Love will not wait.

But how are we to think about helping others? In a world of scarcity, starvation, and poor distribution of resources, is there such a thing as a food ethic?

The Bible does not spell out a food ethic as such. There are, of course, the great themes of charity and mercy found throughout the Bible. In Old Testament Israel, Jews were forbidden to gather the leftovers of the harvest from the fields, for these were to be for "the stranger, for the fatherless, and for the widow" (Deut. 24:19, KJV).

There is plenty of comment on the use of abundance (the rich fool and his barns) and on self-indulgence (the rich man and Lazarus). There is much about sharing (the Good Samaritan and the teachings of the Epistles).

I believe there is a food ethic, but it is part of the comprehensiveness of the Christian life. It is included in mercy, in charity, in love, in compassion, in Christlikeness, and in respect for our Creator God. It is an inescapable part of being our brother's keeper.

The Good Samaritan

Jesus' account of the Good Samaritan has been so much used to illustrate Christian charity and compassion that the familiarity may cause us to miss its pointed teachings. Let me suggest three.

First, we must help those in need when they bring trouble on

---

[22]Ibid., p. 115.

themselves. The road from Jerusalem to Jericho was known to be infested with robbers, and those who did not take another route at least traveled in groups. The man Jesus described chose to go this dangerous way alone. So it could be claimed that he brought his trouble on himself.

There are those in the developed world who say that the less developed nations have only themselves to blame for their difficulties. They argue: "Their governments are corrupt. They don't control their populations. They could work harder."

The Bible makes clear that we are to help others, no matter what the source of their problems. We should not presume motivations. The unfortunate Jew may have had a legitimate reason for traveling the road alone. Perhaps there was some emergency and he was taking the shortest route, willing to risk the dangers. The Samaritan did not know his motivation—nor did he care. He simply helped.

Second, our help must be without regard to racial, religious, or other differences. The Samaritan could have rationalized not helping by saying that the Jews were hated enemies. But he did not make such an excuse.

There are those who say that "charity begins at home" and that we should care for our own poor first. These same people would probably also complain of the "lack of gratitude" by nations that have received our help in the past. The Bible makes no distinction. Any person of any nation who is in need is our neighbor.

Finally, our help must be practical. Feeling sorry is not enough; compassion must become reality. The Samaritan bound up the wounds of the hurt man, carried him to place of safety, and provided for his continued care. His practical help was not only immediate but it provided for the longer term.

Our practical help to poorer nations must also be appropriate. Sending tractors, which require fuel and maintenance, to poor farmers is not practical; helping them move from hand plowing to ox or buffalo power is practical. Instruction manuals are of no use unless the recipients have been taught to read. To be truly practical, our help must go beyond short-term needs to deal with underlying causes.

Involvement

But what can *you* do? The size of the task is immense. The issues are complex. You would have difficulty supporting a needy

family down the street, much less the millions of people who in-
habit the world of hunger. So let us start by realizing that there
are many things that you and I *cannot* do.

God has given you the ability to enjoy life; I doubt that he
wants you to replace that enjoyment with continual feelings of
guilt. Among those joys is food itself. Even while He was feeding
hungry people, Jesus did not refuse to attend an occasional ban-
quet or feast.

As an individual, you cannot change the complex and in-
tricately-constructed U. S. policies toward hungry nations. But
your voice added to thousands and millions of others can make
any congressman take notice. National leaders respond to the
voices—and letters—of a concerned and knowledgeable elec-
torate.

You cannot respond to the appeals of every charitable organization that asks you for a donation. You too have your emotional
and financial limits. Do not feel badly about saying no when you
can do no more.

Nor can you force your views upon others. You may become
aware and sensitive to the needs of the hungry but not everyone
has reached the same level. Avoid being argumentative and judg-
mental. Otherwise you may alienate more than convince.

There is one more thing you cannot do. After having come this
far in increasing your awareness of world hunger and poverty,
and as a Christian, you cannot remain uninvolved.

But let us look at some things that you *can* do.

Caring is the crux of the matter. Knowledge will not produce
change. It will not make any difference for you to know that ten
thousand people die every day from starvation and diseases
related to malnourishment unless you care—unless you care
enough to do something about it. Knowledge can motivate but
action grows out of caring.

How will you respond to the little girl from Brazil whose malnourished body may prevent her from ever reaching womanhood? What will you say to the father in India who seeks
desperately to feed his family but there is no rain and crops are
poor? Would you respond differently if that person lived next
door? Why should it make any real difference that he is half a
world away?

T. S. Eliot once said, "We know too much, and are convinced
of too little."

Might that be true of the problem of world hunger? We know

too much in one sense. We have been exposed to books, television programs, photographs, and thousands of words in print depicting the horrors of a starving world, yet despite this intense exposure the real meaning has not sunk in to our emotions and our souls.

Perhaps Eliot was right. Perhaps part of the reason for our indifference is that we are not really convinced that there is anything that we can do about hunger that would really make a difference. The problem seems so big, so complex.

We seem to have forgotten the power of one. Revolutions have toppled governments because one person had seen enough of injustice. The writings of individuals have changed the course of history. One man with a dream made the phrase "civil rights" a household word. And One Solitary Life became the pivot point around which human history revolves.

As an individual, you can be willing to expose yourself to the issues that make up the hunger problem. You can be willing to learn more and to sensitize yourself. You will need to make a conscious decision to do this, because it is so easy to turn away.

You can examine yourself and your family. Look at your style of life and consumption of resources and ask yourself, "Can I live more simply?" or "Is this purchase really necessary?" There may be several benefits from this self-examination. There is psychological value which comes from your conscious awareness of the needs of others. Making changes in how you consume or use can have important symbolic value as you take visible steps to put your beliefs into action. There is great spiritual value in seeking to follow the commands of Jesus in caring for others. Fasting will not put food on a table in India but fasting may give you a greater awareness of your own spiritual condition and of your dependence upon God for all that you have.

There is material value as well. As you seek to simplify your manner of life, you will probably find that you have more money to use for other purposes. That money becomes a form of power to influence and help those in need. You may contribute it to agencies which are doing what you believe should be done. You might use it to enable you personally to become directly involved in helping those in need.

I have already suggested that you believe in the power of one. Crucial to providing large-scale assistance to the less developed nations is the direction of U. S. policies. As one person you can write or telephone your elected representatives. You can also stimulate others to do so. Arthur Simon, executive director of Bread for the World, says that the urgent need is for Christians *as citizens* to contact decisionmakers. "Acts of charity are not enough. We will lose the battle on hunger if we do not change our public policies. Become a voice for the hungry to your member of Congress."[23]

Churches, civic groups, and other organized bodies can have greater awareness of hunger by making local communities alert to the needs of the hungry and by expressing the group's views to elected officials. Groups can also be effective in raising money for organizations involved in relief and development. For example, college and high school students have fasted for a designated number of hours, with pledges for each hour they participated. The money collected has gone to fight hunger.

U. S. Senator Mark Hatfield has outlined four suggestions for Christians who really want to respond to the needs of our hungry world:

> 1. Every congregation could establish a specific budget amount directed to meeting the needs of starving people in some particular point of the world.
> 2. Christians can be asked to give a specific tithe just for the purpose of relieving hunger; further, we should consider a graduated tithe, which increases its percentage according to the amount of one's income.
> 3. We should renew the Christian discipline of fasting as a means of teaching us how to identify with those who hunger, and to deepen our life of prayer for those who suffer.
> 4. We must all analyze, in prayer before God, our own habits of food consumption. Specifically, we can drastically alter our consumption of meat, and the money we save we can give to alleviate world hunger.[24]

But, you may ask, can these efforts really make any difference? How will they feed a hungry world?

Development

I believe the answer is in the process called "development." In the language of international politics and economics, develop-

---

[23]Arthur Simon, *Bread for the World*, p. 138.

[24]Quoted in W. S. Mooneyham, *What Do You Say to a Hungry World?* (Waco, TX: Word, 1975) pp. 246-47.

ment has several meanings but it is essentially a people-oriented effort to raise the quality of life of entire communities or nations. Edgar Stoesz, an experienced Mennonite development worker, describes development as "the process by which people are awakened to opportunities within their reach (conscientization). Development is people with an increasing control over their environment and destiny. Development is people with dignity and a sense of self-worth. Development is freedom and wholeness and justice. Development is quality of life. Development is people living in the full realization of their God-given potential."[25]

In other words, development is not one thing but a balanced combination of elements which must aim at meeting total human need—mentally, morally, economically, physically, and spiritually.

This concept of developing people instead of nations goes counter to much of the conventional wisdom of development which has tended rather to focus on factories, dams, and capital-investment projects. These projects have too often been alien; they have been imposed on communities from the top and from the outside, based on plans created thousands of miles from where they were to be put into practice.

Development, to be effective, must start where the people are. It must deal with their perceived needs and must use their level of technology. These same people must also be involved in the planning of projects that affect them. E. F. Schumacher says in his influential book, *Small Is Beautiful*, "Development does not start with goods; it starts with people and their education, organization, and discipline.[26] Development seeks qualitative changes; therefore, it takes time.

For organizations like World Vision International, development has been a necessary and logical step beyond relief. Emergencies will continue to happen and relief programs will always be needed. But development deals with underlying problems and seeks to make long-lasting improvements in the lives of people. If relief is handing out bread, development is building a bakery.

I have seen some beautiful examples of development that give me hope for our hungry world. In southwestern Niger, World Vision worked with an American philanthropic foundation and the government of Niger to bring the fertile Niger River flatlands un-

---

[25]Remarks to Mennonite Economic Development Association, 1974.

[26]E. F. Schumacher, *Small is Beautiful: Economics As If People Mattered* (NY: Harper & Row, 1973) p. 185.

der cultivation. At least two crops can be grown in this region each year, cultivated by farmers who would be given twelve-acre plots to work. Villages will have to be created to house enough people to till the land. Health clinics and safe water will be priorities, helping bring better health and improve living standards for thousands.

The potential is tremendous. If all the river lowlands within Niger were brought into production, it is estimated they would provide fifty percent of the grain requirements of the nation. And this can be done in a way that will not destroy local customs and traditions; there need be no Westernizing of the concept. It is a program that has potential for making lasting improvements in the lives of thousands of poor people.

In Nicaragua, following the disastrous earthquake of 1972, most of the Protestant churches in the country agreed to form a cooperative relief committee, known by its initials (from the Spanish) as CEPAD. CEPAD provided a channel for relief aid from churches in other countries and coordinated its distribution. As emergency conditions eased, the churches faced the question: "Should we stop our efforts?" They believed that practical Christian concern must be shown in more than immediate relief, so the churches decided to continue CEPAD as an agency for development assistance in Nicaragua. In providing this help aimed at long-lasting improvements, the churches are showing that Christian love does not stop with the "cup of cold water" in Jesus' name; it goes on to provide wells for safe water, earthquake-resistant housing, tools and equipment for farmers, and basic health care.

Development is clearly a complex process, something far beyond what one person might undertake. But individuals are involved. Jeanne and Denny Grindall, florists from Seattle, Washington, once visited Kenya in East Africa as tourists. But they saw some things that were not on the usual tourist itinerary, such as the poverty and desperate need of the Masai, the brown-skinned herders of the East African plains. They lived in huts made of sticks and cow dung. Sick children lived with filth and flies. Malnourished mothers were trying to nurse malnourished babies.

The Grindalls returned home but the need they saw would not let them rest. As a result, since 1969, Jeanne and Denny have been spending six months of each year working among the Masai. Denny has helped them build earth-filled dams, designed a simple and easy-to-clean house, introduced vegetables into the diet, and encouraged the Masai to have fewer but healthier cattle. Jeanne has taught the women to bake bread, to sew and to care for their children in more hygienic ways. Most important, Denny emphasizes strictly self-help work.

The Grindalls are also concerned for the spiritual welfare of the Masai—along with the community development projects, eight churches have been built and attendance is growing.

"We are just ordinary people," say Jeanne and Denny. "We knew it was almost time to think about what to do with our retirement years, and we just feel the Lord told us what we should be doing."

I think, too, of missionary Tom Crosier in the tiny African nation of The Gambia. As he began working there some years ago, he saw the serious malnutrition among the people and decided to do something about it. In late 1975, he began raising chickens at the town of Somita, about fifty miles from the capitol, Banjul. He offered twenty-five chicks to any farmer who would build a suitable chicken coop and have ready a supply of feed and grit. For a while, no one took him up on his offer. Finally, one farmer built a coop and received his chicks. "Then everyone all around was making chicken pens," Tom said.

Now, more than fifty Gambian farmers have been given a start in chicken raising. The eggs produced in the first two or three months of business are given in payment for the twenty-five chicks. Then these eggs are sold to buy locally-produced feed. After one year, the farmers return their hens to the Somita farm and receive new stock. Farmers are also encouraged to invest a part of their earnings in additional hens and buildings. The result is farmers who are becoming self-sufficient, and many Gambians are getting a better diet by eating much-needed eggs and poultry.

Yes, the world can be fed. More land can be put into cultivation. Existing lands can be cultivated more intensively. New equipment and high-yield seeds can be used in many places. This can and must be done in the very nations that are most in need. Lester Brown makes the point: "Over the long run, the key to coping with world food scarcity lies in the developing countries. It is here that the population pressures are most severe and furthest from solution; it is here also that the unused potential for expanding food production is the greatest."[27]

---

[27]*Washington Post*, July 15, 1973.

Development is the process. Political action is an essential ingredient. And vocal, determined concern by Christians is required.

Christian Response

Christians have been meeting the needs of the poor and hungry since the earliest days of the church. In Acts 11, we read that the prophet Agabus, moved by God's Spirit, predicted that a severe famine would come. It came about A.D. 44 and the Christians in Antioch decided that each would send as much as he could to help fellow believers in famine-struck Judea. They gathered their contribution and sent it to the church elders by Barnabas and Saul.

In the second century, the Athenian philosopher and Christian, Aristides, gave a defense of his faith to the emperor Hadrian. Here is how he described the way Christians of that day cared for those in need: "They love one another; the widow's needs are not ignored, and they rescue the orphan from the person who does him violence. He who has gives to him who has not, ungrudgingly and without boasting. . . . If they find poverty in their midst, and they do not have spare food, they fast two or three days in order that the needy might be supplied with the necessities."[28]

In our own day Christians by the thousands have been responding to world hunger in many different ways. A small Lutheran church in the northeast decided to borrow $100,000 against the church property for use in emergency aid. The Episcopal Diocese of Southern Ohio designated a minimum of $150,000 from its funds for world hunger.

A clergyman and his family in California regularly give two percent of their gross income—above their tithe to their church—to development projects. The Mennonite Central Committee has asked its supporting members to reduce their food consumption and expenditures by ten percent and contribute this remainder toward meeting the food needs of others.

Colleges and universities in all parts of the country have held seminars to raise awareness and events to raise funds for hunger.

People in all walks of life have shown that they care enough about the cries of the hungry to take even small steps toward

---

[28]Marcianus Aristides, in Helen H. Harris, *The Newly Recovered Apology of Aristides*, 1893, quoted in S. E. Wirt, *The Social Conscience of the Evangelical* (NY: Harper & Row, 1968) pp. 29-30.

helping. From World Vision's television specials on world hunger, we have been reminded over and over again of the generosity and caring that springs from compassion.

A woman confined to a wheelchair for thirty years pledged ten dollars a month for the rest of her life to help feed hungry people. A six-year-old girl shared fifty-nine cents from her piggy bank "to buy a glass of warm milk" for a hungry person.

A family of five was living on welfare. After watching the television special, they realized how fortunate they were. They all decided to go without one meal a week in order to give five dollars a month to help feed hungry people overseas. A ninety-year-old lady living on Social Security sent fifteen dollars to help hungry people in Bangladesh. She said, "I wish I could do more . . . when I read about all the suffering and starvation in other parts of the world, I feel rich."

Have you ever felt rich? No matter what your economic situation, I challenge you to think about the hundreds of millions of people who live in the "hungry world."

An IBM employee told me how he and his family had been affected by seeing the needs of the hungry. They watched the television program on hunger. Then they looked around at their style of living, their beautiful home and all the material blessings that they possessed. After much prayer they decided to sell their expensive home, move into an apartment, and give the equity in their home, amounting to $47,000, to help fight hunger. That is what I call compassion—and commitment.

But it is not how much you possess or give that makes the difference in God's sight. Jesus' account of the widow's mite makes that clear. One of the most moving responses to hunger that I have witnessed came from a third grade class in Shawnee, Oklahoma. The fifteen children in this class come from many ethnic backgrounds and from families that are certainly not affluent. The teacher, Rosemarie Haddock, was seeking for a way to turn the children outside of themselves to see the world around them and its needs. Rosemarie told them about some of the hungry people in the world and showed them a picture of a Vietnamese child whom she had been sponsoring through World Vision. The class talked about what they might do to help hungry children and they agreed on tasks and class behavior that would "earn" money. Later, the children decided they needed to do more. They organized a popcorn sale for their school mates. And the money came in.

Then came the big day when their goal was reached: One hundred dollars. What excitement! Said little Petir, "God wants us to care about each other because He created us and them, too. They're worth all the money in the world."

Kelly shook her blonde hair and said, "It isn't fair for them to be hungry when we have our tummies full of peanut butter and jelly."

Jann expressed his mixed feelings. "There's a happy part and a sad part. The happy part is selling popcorn and feeling good about helping starving children. The sad part is knowing about starving children and not being able to help them all. But I'm glad I know."

And now you also know.

I have described something of the numbing, sickening, crushing hunger and poverty that is the daily life of so many fellow human beings. I have pointed to some of the teachings of Scripture that urge and command us to respond. And I have shown you how a few people have made decisions to do what they can.

A decision to act. That is what we come down to. It is a matter of the will, not of resources or technology. Do we have the will to get involved?

Perhaps the real miracle of the feeding of the five thousand was not the fact that they were fed. The real message may be that the owner of the few fish and loaves was willing to share them.

We are certainly talking about more than five thousand people who are hungry, lonely, and afraid. They number in the many millions—people who are hungry for love, for a touch, for a meal. Together with others, you and I have the resources. Our world can be fed. The fragile miracle takes place when we will to do it.

The apostle Paul commands, warns, and promises: "Command those who are rich in this present world not to be arrogant nor to put their hope in wealth, which is so uncertain, but to put their hope in God, who richly provides us with everything for our enjoyment. Command them to do good, to be rich in good deeds, and to be generous and willing to share" (I Tim. 6:17, NIV).

ROBERT G. CULBERTSON

11

Perspectives on Punishment and Sentencing

Do you believe in capital punishment? Do you believe the criminal justice system in American society is a fair and just system and that the rich and poor are treated as equals? Do you believe that we need longer prison terms for most offenses? Do you believe that prisons rehabilitate offenders and return them to society as better persons capable of leading productive lives?

If your attitudes on these issues concur with a majority of your fellow citizens, you are a supporter of capital punishment and longer prison terms. However, as a member of that same majority, you also believe the criminal justice system is neither fair nor just, and that the powerful and affluent hold a favored status and can avoid prosecution when they violate the law. Furthermore, although you support longer prison terms, at the same time you are convinced that prisons do not rehabilitate offenders. In fact, if you have any knowledge regarding prisons, you are convinced that the probability of continued criminal behavior is increased by incarceration. Generally, public opinion surveys indicate that we want a greater intensity of the kinds of punishment mechanisms we have used in the past even though we readily acknowledge they have not worked.

The Purpose of Criminal Law

How do we account for the present state of affairs? Why does the criminal justice system, which has the responsibility of providing protection and maintaining order, have so few friends and so many enemies? The criminal justice system has failed in a number of areas. Continually rising crime rates seem to indicate that we have neither order nor protection. In our search for answers to these and other questions, we find that the criminal justice system is restrained by a number of factors.[1] The most serious restraint emerges from the array of conflicting attitudes in our society.

There is very little agreement regarding the purpose of the criminal law and even less agreement on the function of punishment. Herbert Packer contends that "the criminal law is caught between two fires."[2] On one hand, there are those who want retribution and hold, very simply, that when we are injured, we are right and proper in our desires to seek revenge. The Mosaic law is cited and recited *ad nauseum* to justify the contention that the wicked must suffer and the purpose of the criminal law is to make certain punishment is inflicted.[3] For this group, punishment of the moral derelict is its own justification and no further explanation is needed. On the other hand, there are those who hold the utilitarian position and contend that the purpose of criminal law and punishment is the prevention of antisocial behavior. Punishment, this argument continues, must be assessed with the goal of modifying the future behavior of the criminal.

This philosophical debate, which apparently will not be resolved in the near future, has contributed significantly to a criminal justice system with conflicting goals. On one hand, we contend that punishment must be utilitarian, and we develop institutional programming for inmates as a part of the utilitarian

---

[1]For a comprehensive discussion focusing on barriers to an effective criminal justice system, see my "Corrections: The State of the Art," *Journal of Criminal Justice*, vol. 5, no. 1 (1977): 39-46. The article, focusing on issues in the area of corrections, examines internal and external constraints which function to guarantee failure for rehabilitation programming.

[2]Herbert Packer, *The Limits of the Criminal Sanction* (Stanford, CA: Stanford University Press, 1968).

[3]Many Christians have a conception of justice based on the principle of *lex talionis*—an eye for an eye, tooth for tooth. . . ." Supporting citations include Deut. 19:21; Exod. 21:23-35, and Lev. 24:20. Often overlooked is the fact that Jesus quoted these principles only to repudiate them, as noted in Matt. 5:38-39. The evidence further indicates that even in the time of Jesus, rabbis were beginning to reinterpret the harsh commands. Eventually, many devout Jewish jurists took the lead in condemning retaliation as a principle of justice.

goal to modify their future behavior. On the other hand, because we have a commitment to the philosophy of retribution, we demand that programming function in environments that are extremely punitive and in contexts where attitudes are hostile toward the concept of rehabilitation. The present attacks on the concept of rehabilitation have merit; however, the critics ignore the fact that rehabilitation programming was doomed from the outset because of an overwhelming desire for retribution and revenge. It is the latter set of attitudes which pervade the criminal justice system in America and function to prevent successful efforts in the area of rehabilitation.

Another problem area for the criminal justice system is the probability that crime and the criminal are functional in our society. A number of sociologists, including Emile Durkheim and George Herbert Mead, have called our attention to the fact that crime helps maintain an essential factor in the social order, the collective conscience. The criminal, while stimulating negative attitudes in the community, also enhances the level of solidarity and at the same time provides a negative model. This somewhat complicated process is referred to as the "psychology of punitive justice." Mead notes that our revulsions against criminality reveal themselves in a sense of solidarity: "The attitude of hostility toward the law breaker has the unique advantage of uniting all members of the community in the emotional solidarity of aggression."[4] The object of our hate becomes a rallying point, and as we assimilate hostile attitudes toward persons who have committed crimes, the level of social solidarity increases. The Christian political rightist, whose political attitudes are somewhere between conservative and reactionary, is especially quick to note that this hatred has a biblical foundation. Richard Pierard has outlined the role of hate in some perspectives on Christianity in our society:

> The believer is repeatedly instructed to despise sin and evil. 'Hate evil and love good' (Amos 5:15). 'The Lord loves those who hate evil' (Psalm 97:10). 'The fear of the Lord is hatred of evil' (Proverbs 8:13). 'Thou hatest all evildoers. Thou destroyest those who speak lies' (Psalm 5:5-6).[5]

Although Pierard's remarks are not specifically addressed to the criminal justice system, his citations are frequently used by the

---

[4]George Herbert Mead, "The Psychology of Punitive Justice," *American Journal of Sociology* 23 (1918), 591.

[5]Richard Pierard, *The Unequal Yoke* (Philadelphia: Lippincott, 1970).

Christian political rightist in supporting the most despicable of all social institutions—the prison.[6]

When these attitudes of hatred find expression in sentencing policies, we find a society helpless in the grip of the hostile posture it has taken toward the criminal:

> Hostility (hatred) toward the lawbreaker inevitably brings with it the attitudes of retribution, repression and exclusion. These provide no principles for the eradication of crime, for returning the delinquent to normal social relations, nor for stating the transgressed rights and institutions in terms of their positive social function.[7]

In the long run, the hatred and hostility are self-defeating; the more stigma and deprivation experienced by the criminal, it seems, the greater the probability of continued criminal behavior—and the cycle continues. The consequence for persons incarcerated in our prisons is expressed in *An Eye For An Eye* by Griswold, Misenheimer, Powers, and Tromanhauser. While incarcerated they wrote:

> With the absolute certainty of offending many people, we have to say that the American people want, desire, lust for and need crime and criminality. They need, albeit on a subconscious level, an easily identifiable group whom they can look down upon, feel superior to, castigate, segregate and inflict emotional, psychological, and physical punishment upon. The public needs its criminally deviant individuals so that through an act of catharsis they can expunge their own guilt feelings, and every once in a while call up from the darker side of their souls all the repressed hate and fury that dwells within.[8]

Some may find this commentary shocking and perhaps frightening. However, certain segments of our society support the kinds of attitudes discussed by the inmates, and their writing is a reflection of their feelings of being victimized by those attitudes through the process of incarceration. Incarceration is, of course, a frequent outcome of the sentencing process. Unfortunately, discussions focusing on sentencing issues tend to be abstract and ignore the degradation that is a part of the process.

Inequities in the System

In addition to the philosophical debate regarding the function

---

[6]The Christian political rightist tends to ignore the commands to love our enemies as noted in Matt. 5:43-48. As a result, hostility develops unchecked. Some Christians tend to selectively study the Bible, singling out those citations which support their preconceived notions of the nature of punishment.

[7]Mead, "Punitive Justice," p. 591.

[8]Griswold, H. et al., *An Eye For An Eye* (New York: Holt, Rinehart and Winston, 1970), p. 24.

of the criminal law and the potentially positive functions of crime and the criminal, the criminal justice system must cope with the pervasive nature of crime in American society. John Alexander has noted that in our affluent society we define a criminal act as a crime only if one wears a mask and carries a gun. George Jackson served twelve years for stealing seventy dollars at gunpoint, while Edith Irving served one month for conspiring to defraud a publisher of $650,000. We all know about street crimes, the kinds of crime to which Alexander refers. However, we have little information about the extent of "respectable crime." This imbalance is a strong indication of the structural immorality in our society.

Edwin Schur has provided a detailed discussion on violations of antitrust laws, tax laws, and rules and regulations of regulatory agencies. It is Schur's position that crime is deeply rooted in our legal, political, social, economic, and military institutions—to the extent that we can define our society as a criminal society.[9] The scandals following the Watergate burglary and the Korean bribery incidents provide current evidence that Schur is accurate in his assessment.

In a journalistic effort, Donald Bacon has summarized what he describes as the new American way of life: "ripoffs."[10] Noting the extent of white collar crime and economic exploitation, Bacon cites a number of authorities and incidents to demonstrate the pervasive level of criminality in American society. The contagious nature of criminality is also indicated as increased levels of crime function to enhance the cynicism prevalent in our society. Cynicism in turn inhibits any kind of corrective action and, in fact, stimulates others to cut corners and commit crime. As more and more persons come to see some types of crime as "respectable," responsibility and accountability are effectively "neutralized" as the offender perceives, and correctly so, an extremely high tolerance level for certain kinds of criminal behavior. As the societal blur between right and wrong increases, the offender comes to define his/her illegal behavior as normal. This is especially the case for upper class persons who are well insulated from the criminal law and penal sanctions.

---

[9]Edwin Schur, *Our Criminal Society* (Englewood Cliffs, N.J.: Prentice-Hall, 1969).

[10]Donald C. Bacon, "Ripoffs, New American Way of Life," *U. S. News & World Report* 81 (1976): 29-32.

Tolerance for criminal behavior in the affluent classes creates serious inequities in the sentencing process. When affluent, powerful political figures receive relatively light sentences for serious crimes because of their political influence, we establish national models that prove crime indeed pays. When that behavior is emulated in the lower classes, however, the insulation from punishment is absent and incarceration is often the result.

These issues compound problems for the criminal justice system. When critics contend that the criminal justice system has failed or that it is not working, we should keep in mind that one of the reasons it is not working is because affluent, upper class members of our society do not want it to work when their behavior is defined as criminal. But we cannot have two systems of justice, one for the poor and one for the rich. Any injustice undermines the moral order, enhances cynicism and bitterness, and functions to destroy the stability of our society.

Before examining issues and problems in the sentencing process, it is important that we examine one of the outcomes of sentencing—incarceration. A number of the sentencing reform proposals call for increased use of incarceration as a punishment mechanism for those convicted of crime.

Incarceration

There are numerous biblical references to prisons. Christians, for the most part, seem to select those passages which support their preconceived notions about crime and tend to ignore responsibilities mandated in the Scriptures.

The New Testament clearly indicates that visitation of the prisoner is a Christian virtue. Instructions to visit those in prison are outlined in Matthew 25:36-39, Hebrews 13:3 and in II Timothy 1:16. In spite of these teachings, many of us have not seen a prison, and most of us have not witnessed the dehumanization and degradation thousands of men and women suffer on a daily basis. The number of persons incarcerated in prisons will likely exceed 300,000 by the time this book is published.

Many Christians are naive about the conditions in prisons and the kinds of behavior that occurs behind the walls of concrete and steel. This lack of understanding is personified in comments by Judge Randall Hekman writing for *The Banner*, the official publication of the Christian Reformed Church. Judge Hekman notes that "physical conditions in most prisons are probably better than ever before. Mentally, emotionally, and spiritually, however, conditions are at an all-time low. The rehabilitation 'reform' movement has caused the problems."[11] There is no evidence to support Judge Hekman's commentary regarding physical conditions in prisons or his contention that the "reform" movement is the cause of other problems he lists. The fact is that conditions in prisons today are probably at their very worst.

Because of these dehumanizing conditions in many prisons, prisoners are turning to the federal courts for relief by alleging cruel and unusual punishment, a violation of the Eighth Amendment of the Constitution of the United States. The Christian political rightist has, for the most part, been critical of the federal courts and especially of decisions which have established civil rights for those accused and convicted of crimes. However, evidence revealed in testimony in court proceedings on prison conditions justifies a firm, positive response from the judicial system. A number of court decisions can be cited; such litigation has occured in nearly every state.

In the case of James v. Wallace, a Federal District Court in Alabama found the following conditions:

> In general Alabama's penal institutions are filthy. There was repeated testimony at trial that they are overrun with roaches, flies, mosquitoes, and other vermin. A public health expert testified that he found roaches in all stages of development—a certain indication of filthy conditions. Plumbing facilities are in an exceptional state of disrepair. In one area at Draper [prison], housing well over 200 men, there is one functioning toilet.

> Food service conditions are equally unsanitary. Food is improperly stored in dirty storage units, and is often infested with insects. Inmates drink from used tin cans, and have to wash and save their own utensils from meal to meal.[12]

A United States public health officer toured the facilities and testified that he found them wholly unfit for human habitation according to virtually every criterion used for evaluation by public health inspectors. Efforts in the area of inmate classification and rehabilitation programming had failed because of the intense overcrowding and lack of staff. As a result, inmates were housed in massive cell blocks without regard to offense pattern or personality. As in many other state prisons, homosexuality and homosexual assault had become a way of life. In the Alabama

---

[11]Randall Hekman, "Is Punishment a Crime?" *The Banner* 109 (1974): 14.

[12]406 Fed. Supp. 318, 1976.

case one inmate testified he was raped by a group of inmates on the first night, and on the second night he was almost strangled by two others. After the second assault, he agreed to become the property of the inmates who had assaulted him. They sold his body for profit.

Some might contend that conditions in Alabama's prisons are unique. But a review of correctional case law indicates that Alabama is not unique; many state prisons have equally serious problems in the area of living conditions, inmate programming, and sexual assault. The recently publicized gang rape of a pacifist held in a Washington D.C. lockup personifies both the tolerance for this kind of assault and an inability to control prison violence. A study done in Philadelphia found that rape occurred even in vans moving inmates to and from institutions.

An inmate who lives in these conditions and circumstances stands no chance of leaving the prison with a more positive attitude than the one he or she brought in. In fact, inmates often leave prisons extremely bitter and angry. Predictably, they seek out innocent victims who become scapegoats for their anger. That is one reason American prisons annually release thousands of persons who are more violent than they were before they were incarcerated. In the end, we become potential victims because of our gross neglect.

Turning for a moment to jails, we find similar problems. For example, Richard Velde, former administrator for the Law Enforcement Assistance Administration, has stated:

> Jails are festering sores in the criminal justice system. There are no model jails anywhere; we know, we tried to find them. Almost nowhere are there rehabilitative programs operated in conjunction with jails. It's hard to say, but the truth is that jail personnel are the most uneducated, untrained, and poorly paid of all personnel in the criminal justice system.

> The result is what you would expect, only worse. Jails are without question brutal, filthy cesspools of crime—institutions which serve to brutalize and embitter men to prevent them from returning to a useful role in society.[13]

It is important to note that nearly every county in the United States has a county jail, and many cities have lockups where persons are held for brief periods of time. Organized religious institutions, for the most part, have not considered the county jail

---

[13]Richard Velde, *The Correctional Trainer* (Fall 1970): 109.

as a part of their mission field. There are noted exceptions to this general neglect, but in those instances it is common to find workers with minimal resources and little support from the larger religious community. The county jail is often the first contact accused persons have with the criminal justice system. It is at this point where intervention is needed to limit the potential for further criminal behavior. However, because we tolerate miserable conditions in many of our jails, jails have come to be referred to as pipelines to prisons.

Why do these conditions exist in America's prisons and jails? First, men and women incarcerated in our penal institutions are devalued people. Society considers them to be failures and has labeled them accordingly. Seldom does one have contact with a white collar offender in a county jail or a state prison, for as noted earlier, the criminal justice system is discriminatory. Individuals sentenced to these institutions almost universally come from lower income and "non-income" groups. Alcohol and drug consumption is pervasive in these groups and is symptomatic of the complex problems of the individual inmate. Through society's devaluation processes, these people have been judged worthless and are treated as such.

Second, by selectively incarcerating the poor, we can ignore the vast amount of discrimination against groups in the lower income strata. In some instances, we punish people because they are poor. Examples of this can be found in the bail system, a system which frees people who have money and results in incarceration for those who cannot "make bail." In this discriminatory punishment process, we legitimize an economic value system and lessen our responsibility to restructure a society which places a heavy emphasis on exploitation. Again, we note the emphasis on retribution which justifies the perspective on punishment stated earlier, that the punishment of the moral derelict is its own justification.

However, if one takes the opposite perspective, the utilitarian perspective, punishment must have as one of its goals the modification of future behavior. To accomplish this, we must look beyond the individual and examine the society from which he or she comes. The retribution position allows us to avoid these complex implications and to continue to focus our hostility on the lawbreaker.

Third, conditions in prisons and jails reflect the history of these institutions. Robert Caldwell has noted that many prisons are antiquated; almost half of the state prisons now in use were constructed over eighty-five years ago. A large number of these institutions have been in operation for over one hundred years. Many of them are overpopulated; prison cells built for one person are used to house two, three, and sometimes four inmates. At the time these institutions were constructed, the correctional goal was simple—punishment through retribution.

An inmate in one of our large penal institutions, reflecting on the incarceration process, recently commented to me, "You cannot treat me like a person part of the time and like an animal most of the time and expect me to be a person all the time." Treatment of persons incarcerated is exemplified in the monotonous and oppressive institutional routines described by Caldwell, all of which result in degradation, dehumanization and eventually "devalued" persons.[14]

Returning to the original question, "Why has the criminal justice system failed?", we see an answer that is now more obvious. The criminal justice system is committed to the retributive (revenge) ideal rather than to the utilitarian ideal, and the consequences are with us: massive punishment mechanisms which enhance dehumanization, degradation, hatred, and the potential for further violent behavior.

Sentencing Reform

Criminal justice is an area in which we seem to have a surplus of "experts." As a result we have what appears to be an unlimited number of reform proposals. Every area of the criminal justice system has been subjected to scrutiny. However, the area of sentencing is the major focal point for a number of critics, and the recent fascination with this area is understandable. First, as indicated earlier, many believe that persons convicted of crimes should spend more time in prison. This can only be accomplished through modification of the sentencing structure. Second, if we are also committed to the concept of retribution (revenge), it is the sentencing system which allows us to increase the level of retribution. Third, changing the sentencing system does not result in restructuring any of the large criminal justice bureaucracies, so change can be accomplished more rapidly. Fourth, and most important, a large segment of society, including both conservatives

---

[14] Robert Caldwell, *Criminology* (New York: Ronald Press, 1965).

and liberals, are extremely dissatisfied with the present sentencing systems.

Much of the criticism has as its target the indeterminate sentence. Indeterminate sentencing is closely linked to the concept of rehabilitation. The goal of the traditional rehabilitation model, utilizing the indeterminate sentence, is to provide an individualized response to criminal behavior. It was the contention of a number of professional groups in the 1950s that it was more important to respond to the needs of the criminal than to simply react to the crime. This required a vast amount of flexibility in the sentencing process. Theoretically, a person sentenced under an indeterminate sentence could be incarcerated from zero days to life, regardless of the offense. The goal was to provide individualized rehabilitation programming to meet the individual needs of the offender.

Most states did not adopt the theoretical model of zero to life, but a number of states did adopt partially indeterminate sentencing statutes, that is, depending on the offense, an individual convicted of a crime would be sentenced to a minimum and maximum number of years. Under the partially indeterminate sentence, persons are sentenced to institutions for one to ten years, five to ten years, and so forth. Under this sentencing policy the decision of when the individual is to be released is left to a parole board. The parole board determines when the individual is "ready" for release to the community and bases its decision on the individual's response to rehabilitative programming while incarcerated.

The attack against the indeterminate and the partially indeterminate sentencing models has been justified in part because of the failure of rehabilitation programs. But while many of the criticisms of the present sentencing system are well documented, it must be noted that most of the reasons rehabilitation programming has failed have little relationship to the sentencing model. Indeed, rehabilitation programming was introduced into hostile environments and was often doomed from the outset. In the following section, we will examine three determinate or "flat-time" sentencing models.

Determinate Sentencing Proposals

There is a substantial collection of literature suggesting sentencing reforms. While the proposals vary in style, precision, and

vocabulary, they generally agree that most of the powers currently delegated to judges and parole authorities should be
reallocated to the legislature through the establishment of
determinate sentences, which carry a fixed number of years for
each offense. Some writers refer to this as "flat-time" sentencing.
Another proposal is conceptually close to determinate sentencing
but referred to as "presumptive" sentencing. Andrew von Hirsch,
for example, suggests that each crime category be assigned a
presumptive sentence based on the seriousness of the crime, with
a specific number of years assigned to each category where incarceration would be in order. Judges would be able to depart
from the presumptive sentences in cases where there were aggravating or mitigating circumstances. In addition, prescribed increases in prison time could be made for offenders with prior
records.

The result is a two-dimensional penalty scale indicated in the
following diagram provided by von Hirsch:

The penalty scale would look something like this—with the P's
representing the presumptive sentences.

HYPOTHETICAL PENALTY SCALE

Seriousness level of most recent offense				
5	$P_{5,1}$	$P_{5,2}$	$P_{5,3}$	$P_{5,4}$ (most severe)
4	$P_{4,1}$	$P_{4,2}$	$P_{4,3}$	$P_{4,4}$
3	$P_{3,1}$	$P_{3,2}$	$P_{3,3}$	$P_{3,4}$
2	$P_{2,1}$	$P_{2,2}$	$P_{2,3}$	$P_{2,4}$
1	$P_{1,1}$ (least severe)	$P_{1,2}$	$P_{1,3}$	$P_{1,4}$
	1	2	3	4

Rating for seriousness of prior record
(based on number and seriousness of prior offenses)

The penalty in the lower left-hand corner ($P_{1,1}$) is that prescribed for
someone convicted of a minor offense who had no prior record. It
would be the least severe penalty on the scale. That in the lower

right-hand corner ($P_{1,4}$) is for the person whose current offense is minor but who had a record of serious prior offenses. (This penalty would be somewhat severer, but not very much so, since the offense of which the defendant now stands convicted is still a minor one.) The penalty in the upper right-hand corner ($P_{5,4}$) is that prescribed for someone convicted of a very serious offense who already had a record of major crimes. It would be the severest on the scale. That in the upper left ($P_{5,1}$) would be for someone convicted of a serious crime who had no prior record. Thus the penalties would increase in severity as one goes from left to right and from bottom to top.[15]

The four-by-five matrix provides twenty different penalty levels or sentences. In theory, the matrix has some appeal. However, when von Hirsch moves to the area of application, he encounters problems which he does not handle well. In attempting to develop precise punishments, von Hirsch turns to the principle of "just deserts." After noting that there is an absence of data to determine how much punishment should be prescribed for each offense, he concludes that the scale of punishments should be based "on a best guess of what its deterrent effect is likely to be."[16] Changes in the scale of punishments could be made from time to time and would be linked to crime rates. The problems encountered with this linkage are too complex to be discussed here; however, the overwhelming evidence is that von Hirsch has attached to his punishment scheme the worst data base in the area of federal statistics.

A second model, somewhat more specific than that proposed by von Hirsch, is the "justice model" proposed by David Fogel. Fogel's model is a departure from the "just deserts" theme, for imprisonment would not be utilized unless there was a finding of such "clear and present danger" that the offender would have to be incarcerated. "Imprisonment should be the court's last available sanction following an affirmative action by authorities seeking other alternatives."[17] The justice model includes a "good-time" provision that would reduce the inmate's sentence one day for every day of good behavior while incarcerated.

Fogel's flat-time proposal broadens the flexibility available to the trial court and sets standards for lessening and increasing sen-

---

[15] Andrew von Hirsch, *Doing Justice: The Choice of Punishments* (New York: Hill and Wang, 1976), p. 134.

[16] Ibid.

[17] David Fogel, *We Are the Living Proof* (Cincinnati: W. H. Anderson, 1975), p. 247.

tences. A pre-sentence investigation would be mandatory and a prison term could be imposed only in cases where there was "an affirmative showing by the state that the felon could not be safely supervised in a non-incarcerative program before permitting the imposition of a prison term."[18]

Fogel has established three types of sentences. Type A sentences include (both alone and in combination) probation, restitution, periodic imprisonment (work-release), and fines as sentencing alternatives.

Fogel's flat-time sentencing scheme turns out to be more bark than bite when one examines the mitigating factors which are to be considered in withholding a sentence of imprisonment and imposing Type A sentences:

Factors in Mitigation

The following grounds shall be accorded weight in favor of withholding a sentence of imprisonment:

(1) the defendant's criminal conduct neither caused nor threatened serious harm;

(2) the defendant did not contemplate that his criminal conduct would cause or threaten serious harm;

(3) the defendant acted under a strong provocation;

(4) there were substantial grounds tending to excuse or justify the defendant's criminal conduct, though failing to establish a defense;

(5) the victim of the defendant's criminal conduct induced or facilitated its commission;

(6) the defendant has compensated or will compensate the victim of his criminal conduct for the damage or injury that he sustained;

(7) the defendant has no history of prior delinquency or criminal activity or has led a law-abiding life for a substantial period of time before the commission of the present crime;

(8) the defendant's criminal conduct was the result of circumstances unlikely to recur;

(9) the character and attitudes of the defendant indicate that he is unlikely to commit another crime;

---

[18]Ibid., p. 250.

(10) the defendant is particularly likely to comply with the terms of a period of mandatory supervision;

(11) the imprisonment of the defendant would entail excessive hardship to him or his dependents.[19]

At the same time, Fogel proposes that sentences could be increased. Type B and Type C sentences are distinguished by length and by the standard required for increasing the length of the prison term. Type B is the ordinary term; Type C is the enhanced (increased) term. The following "Factors in Aggravation" are to be considered in imposing a Type C sentence:

Factors in Aggravation

The following factors shall be accorded weight in favor of imposing a term of imprisonment, and in the instances specified shall mandate a term of imprisonment.

(1) that in the commission of a felony offense, or in flight therefrom, the defendant inflicted or attempted to inflict serious bodily injury to another. Serious bodily injury as used in this Section means bodily injury which creates a substantial risk of death, or which causes death or serious disfigurement, serious impairment of health, or serious loss or impairment of the function of any bodily organ.

(2) that the defendant presents a continuing risk of physical harm to the public.
    If the court so finds and in addition finds the factors specified in subsection (1) of this Section, and that an additional period of confinement is required for the protection of the public, the defendant may be sentenced as provided (see below for sentencing schedule) in this Code whether or not the defendant has a prior felony conviction. However, a sentence under this Section shall not be imposed unless the defendant was at least 17 years of age at the time he committed the offense for which sentence is to be imposed.

(3) that the defendant is a repeat offender whose commitment for an extended term is necessary for the protection of the public. A defendant of this type shall have sentence imposed pursuant to (the sentencing schedule of) this Code. Provided, however, a sentence shall not be imposed pursuant to the Section unless:
    (a) the defendant was at least 17 years of age at the time he committed the offense for which sentence is to be imposed;
    (b) the defendant has been convicted of at least one other Class I or Class 2 felony or two or more lesser felony offenses within the 5 years

---

[19]Ibid., p. 251.

immediately preceding commission of the instant offense, excluding
time spent in custody for violation of the laws of any state or of the
United States.

(4) that the defendant committed a felony offense that occurred under
one or more of the following circumstances:
    (a) the defendant, by the duties of his office or by his position, was
obliged to prevent the particular offense committed or to bring the offenders committing it to justice;
    (b) the defendant held public office at the time of the offense, and
the offense related to the conduct of that office;
    (c) the defendant utilized his professional reputation or position in
the community to commit the offense, or to afford him an easier
means of committing it, in circumstances where his example probably
would influence the conduct of others;
    (d) if the court, having due regard for the character of the offender,
the nature and circumstances of the offense, and the public interest
finds that a sentence of imprisonment is not the most appropriate disposition under this Code, the grounds listed in paragraphs (1) and (4)
above shall be considered as factors in aggravation of the sentence imposed (non-imprisonment).[20]

Under Fogel's justice model, the power of the courts would be
increased immensely at the cost of parole agencies, since parole
would be abolished. This proposed transfer of power from the executive branch of government to the judicial branch poses some
serious problems. First, the issues of sentencing disparity are not
resolved; in fact, disparities would probably be increased under
the justice model. Second, increased flexibility for the courts is increased discretion, regardless of what it may be called. There
appears to be an implicit assumption that discretion, when
delegated to parole authorities, is bad policy. At the same time it
is assumed that increased discretion delegated to judges is good
policy.

The proposed shift in discretionary power to the judiciary
reflects Fogel's negativism toward the correctional process, and especially parole, as well as his undue optimism toward the judiciary. However, though the parole process has received just
criticism, the judiciary component of the criminal justice system is
plagued with problems which exceed those in the area of parole.
Shifting discretion is not the answer. A restructuring of the parole
process is a better resolution.

A third effort in the area of sentencing reform is provided by
the Twentieth Century Fund's Task Force on Criminal Sentencing. The task force, noting the many evils of the indeterminate

---

[20]Ibid., pp. 252-54.

sentence and the rehabilitation–therapy model of incarceration, proposes a list of presumptive sentences. The proposal is more specific than others previously discussed, and the proposed sample penal code deserves special consideration. The following presumptive sentences are established for homicide:

(1) The premeditated, deliberate killing of another: 10 years. (Though this may seem an extremely low sentence, even when the possible 50 percent increase for aggravating factors is considered, it is congruent with the average term of imprisonment actually served by persons currently convicted of murder in the first degree.)

(2) The intentional killing of another under circumstances in which the defendant was not initially the physical aggressor or subject to serious provocation: 6 years.

(3) The intentional killing of another during the course of a felony by any of the participants in the felony who did not actually commit the murder: the sum of the presumptive sentence for the felony plus the presumptive sentence for either (a) manslaughter or (b) second-degree homicide, whichever is the proper measure of the defendant's culpability in the particular felony-murder. (In essence, this provision recommends the abolition of the felony-murder rule; it advocates, instead, that such offenders receive consecutive sentences for the constituent parts of the crime.)

(4) An unintentional killing of another resulting from reckless conduct under circumstances in which the risk of death was extremely high and that risk was known to the defendant: 4 years.

(5) An unintentional killing of another resulting from gross negligence that the defendant did not contemplate as posing a risk of harm to another: probation for 1 year.[21]

It should be noted that the task force proposal also includes aggravating and mitigating factors, and a sentence hearing would be required to establish those factors. It would appear that deterrence is not a major goal of the presumptive sentences proposed in this model, for the penalty for premeditated murder is the same as the average term presently served by those convicted of murder in the first degree.

While one might concur with the aims and priorities of the task force as well as the proposals presented by Fogel and von Hirsch, there are a host of problems which have been ignored by these

---

[21]Twentieth Century Fund, *Fair and Certain Punishment* (New York: McGraw-Hill, 1976), pp. 57-58.

authors. Franklin Zimring has identified several. First, the inco-
herent nature of the criminal law has been ignored. For example,
in Illinois, burglary is defined in such a manner that an armed
burglar who breaks into an occupied dwelling is guilty of the
same offense as an eighteen-year-old who enters an unlocked
automobile and opens the glove compartment. The efforts of
Fogel, von Hirsch, and the task force are academically
stimulating; however, each has ignored the hard fact that "we
lack the capacity to define into formal law the nuances of situation, intent, and social harm that condition the seriousness of
particular criminal acts."[22]

The task force's handling of rape, for example, is certain to
raise the ire of feminists, although it demonstrates the complexity
of the problem when an effort is made to set a determinate sentence for a specific criminal act. According to the task force, rape
should have three punishments:

(1) Any person who commits a rape and also assaults the victim and
causes bodily injury: 6 years.

(2) Any person who commits a rape but causes the victim no additional serious bodily harm: 3 years.

(3) Any person who commits an unaggravated rape upon another
who has previously been a sex partner: 6 months.

Aggravating factors that, if found by the sentencing court, may increase the sentence shall include: (1) the fact that the victim was under
15 or over 70 years of age and (2) the fact that the victim was held captive by the offender for a substantial period of time (over two
hours).[23]

But what is bodily harm? Is it painfully twisted but undamaged
arms, or broken arms and a fractured jaw? Was the insertion
made with grace or violence? Was the victim intoxicated or otherwise handicapped, making assault unnecessary but in no way
diminishing the vileness of the act? Zimring does not attack the
efforts reflected in the determinate sentencing proposal; rather, his
concern is that "we may simply lack the ability to compre-
hensively define in advance those elements of an offense that
should be considered in fixing a sentence."[24]

---

[22]Franklin Zimring, "A Consumer's Guide to Sentencing Reform: Making the
Punishment Fit the Crime," *Hasting Center Report* (December 1976): 13-17.

[23]*Fair and Certain Punishment*, pp. 58-59.

[24]Zimring, "A Consumer's Guide," p. 16.

A second problem area ignored by Fogel, von Hirsch, and the task force is the "paradox of prosecutorial power." Practically speaking, it is the prosecutor who determines the sentence for any offense, because it is he who determines the charge. And prosecutors will continue to plea-bargain under any proposal. For example, under the criminal code proposed by the task force, the prosecutor could file a charge of "premeditated" killing and reduce the charge to "intentional" killing in exchange for a plea of guilty. The former results in a sentence of ten years; the latter, five years.

Zimring's position is that there is no assurance that sentencing disparity will be decreased under flat-time sentencing proposals. The level of discretion in the system is not diminished; it is simply reallocated. The consequences of shifting more power to the prosecutor has serious implications which have not been carefully examined.

Third, legislatures do not have a meritorious record in developing criminal codes. Shifting power to the legislature may only compound problems. Simply stated, "the penalty provisions in most of our criminal codes are symbolic denunciations of particular behavior patterns, rather than decisions about just sentences."[25] Legislators enjoy "barking" very loud; they are not affected by the consequences of their decisions to the extent that the judiciary and corrections systems are affected when it is necessary to "bite," that is, to incarcerate those guilty of crimes. Our overpopulated prisons reflect an absence of planning in the legislature.

Fourth, consensus on appropriate penal sanctions may be exaggerated. Research conclusions cited by von Hirsch and others which note a strong consensus are questionable. The climate in which a respondent completes a questionnaire indicating appropriate sentences for particular offenses is quite unlike the climate in which the legislature functions. On occasion, overwhelmed with their own rhetoric, legislators have been known to be less than rational in adopting criminal sanctions. Previous comments on symbolic denunciations are applicable here as well.

Fifth, each of the aforementioned proposals for flat-time sentencing has mitigating or enhancement clauses which provide for aggravating or lessening the sentence. As noted by Joseph Goldstein[26] these clauses are thinly-conceived thowbacks to individu-

---

[25]Ibid.
[26]von Hirsch, *Doing Justice*, p. 172.

alization, concern for the offender's failure to learn from prior offenses and their punishment. Applications of these clauses could well function to enhance sentencing disparities. Recent examination of the plea-bargaining process clearly indicates that a wide range of factors is included in the bargaining process, especially the offender's social status. Under the proposed sentencing plans, the prosecutor accrues even more power, for we note that previous bargains become a determining factor in the immediate sentence. Consequently, the proposals tend to move full circle and return to an abuse-prone discretionary sentencing system not unlike the present system which each of the proposals thoroughly discredit.

Sixth, by advocating determinate sentences, the proposals ignore the conditions of incarceration discussed earlier. Sentencing of the Watergate defendants reminds us that the disparities in sentencing time are paralleled with disparities in the effects of incarceration on the offender. Five years in a hundred-year-old state prison is in no way comparable to five years in a minimum security federal prison in California. Parole, which would be eliminated under the justice model, has a number of functions in addition to those outlined in traditional discussion on rehabilitation. A number of parole experts, while hesitant in their criticism, concede that the parole process is necessitated by the conditions of incarceration. In other words, the effects of incarceration in some prisons are so overwhelmingly negative that parole becomes a necessary and essential mechanism in reintegrating the prisoner into a normal living situation.

Seventh, the proposals have grossly oversimplified the problem of crime and effective social control. Flat-time sentencing, if intended to establish a uniform standard of justice, ignores totally the complex issues raised by relative deprivation. Examination of the proposals clearly indicates that we will continue to incarcerate the same racial, ethnic, and income groups presently incarcerated. Consideration has not been given to the probability that incarceration for the unemployed, black ghetto resident has considerably different psychic implications than incarceration for the middle-class, affluent white collar suburb resident. The mitigating clauses in the flat-time proposals relate to the latter category, while the aggravating clauses are likely to relate to the former category. The proposals ignore the fact that while the criminal justice system has developed a number of innovative diversion-type programs for low-risk offenders, little other than traditional incarceration has been done to examine alternatives for high-risk offenders.

In addition to ignoring the possibility that the deterrent effect of any punishment is relative, the proposals also ignore the potential implications of the mitigation schemes. As indicated, those schemes could function to insulate white-collar offenders from incarceration. When a sentencing scheme sorts out one group for incarceration and at the same time provides insulation mechanisms for a second group, the latter group functions as a model that crime pays with minimum personal risk. The proposed clauses for mitigation and aggravation function to further legitimize societal power dimensions and consequent discriminatory sentencing practices which are already institutionalized.

In the following paragraphs, an effort has been made to develop a reintegration model. The discussion is by no means exhaustive, but rather reflects an effort to move beyond offenders and sentences and overcome the temptation to provide simplistic solutions for complex problems.

The Reintegration Model

Before examining the potentials of a comprehensive reintegration model, further attention should be given to one of the factors which contributed to the failure of the treatment model. John Conrad has appropriately noted that "we should never have promised a hospital."[27] Conrad's critique of the medical model in corrections exemplified the complexity of the problem. Concepts and definitions which emerged from the medical model sold to us by psychiatrists, social workers, and their entourages, resulted in criminality being defined as a "disease" to be cured by the same group imposing the definition. Similarities between the treatment model for corrections and the medical model for hospitals is obvious as indicated in the following comparison:

Medical model: $P + HTP = S/F$
Treatment model: $O + OTP = S/F$

In the medical model we note, very simply, a patient (P) plus a hospital treatment program (HTP) results in success—good health

---

[27] John Conrad, "We Should Have Never Promised a Hospital," *Federal Probation* 39 (1975): 3-8.

(S) or failure—death (F). Likewise, correctional treatment programs under the direction of psychiatrists and social workers assumed that an offender (O) plus an offender treatment program (OTP) would result in success—law-abiding behavior (S) or failure—recidivism (F). The simplistic nature of the medical model made it attractive to corrections officials, and the reassurances provided by the treatment professional reinforced the basic notion that criminal behavior could be treated by focusing the therapeutic effort on the inmate. The treatment model espoused by psychiatrists and social workers was a failure at the outset because it was based on the erroneous assumption that the criminal was "sick."

> The general model for classification (and treatment) is a variation on the caseworker plan, adopted from the social work profession, which assumes that the offender is 'sick' and therefore, requires 'help' from the treatment team whether he wants it or not.[28]

Having grossly oversimplified the problem of criminal behavior, the treatment model ignored a number of complex variables such as community reaction, peer contacts, the economy, and the family.

Because inmates constitute a relatively powerless client system, the social work profession was able to impose the treatment model on the corrections process. In doing so, social workers ignored two basic tenets of their profession. First, the individual must perceive that he has a problem and be motivated to seek help. Second, goals in the casework process must be established by the client. The issues, respectively, are voluntarism and self-determination. The imposition of the assumption that all offenders are sick created a "Catch-22" situation:

> That is, we know you're sick. If you deny that you're sick, you're really sick. But if you acknowledge that you're sick, then you really must be sick or you wouldn't admit it.[29]

Corrections, pervaded by groupthink, has refused to face the enormous and growing body of literature which indicates the ineffectiveness of the medical model. Instead, social workers in

---

[28] Harry E. Allen and Clifford E. Simonsen, *Corrections in America: An Introduction* (Beverly Hills, CA: Glencoe Press, 1975), p. 145.

[29] National Advisory Commission on Criminal Justice Standards and Goals, *Corrections* (Washington, D.C.: U. S. Government Printing Office, 1975), pp. 197-99.

corrections complain about inadequate budgets, an intolerant society, and an ungrateful and recalcitrant client system. Erroneous assumptions, faulty diagnoses, and ignorance of the complex variables cited above have resulted in useless treatment programs. That the programs have lasted so long reflects far more the economics of the need for jobs for the treatment agents than the success of their efforts.

The reformers, those who advocate determinate sentencing, have much in common with the present failure group of treatment agents in that their proposals have also grossly oversimplified the problem. Determinate sentencing is simply a different inmate "treatment program," based, of course, on a set of assumptions different from the traditional treatment model advocated by social workers. The outcome is much the same, for complex variables ignored by the treatment model are ignored in the determinate sentencing proposals.

Turning to our comprehensive reintegration model, we should note that the model is based on the assumption that the criminal's behavior is a result of interaction with several systems and thereby includes a number of variables ignored by the traditional treatment model and the determinate sentencing proposals. The reintegration model is reflected in the following formula:

$$O + OTP + F + E + PC + CR = S/F$$

Both the traditional treatment model and the determinate sentencing proposals ignore the complex issues in the area of family (F), economic situation for the inmate (E), peer contacts or differential association (PC), and community reaction to the inmate (CR). The reintegration model starts with a set of assumptions about the criminal that differs from those advocated by the traditional treatment model. While some criminals may engage in criminal behavior as a result of some type of emotional problem, the basic assumption is that most criminals have normal psychic structures and that their involvement in criminal behavior is situational or value-oriented. Criminal behavior which is situational is personified in Donald R. Cressey's work in the area of embezzlement. Cressey found embezzlement to be the result of a unique non-sharable problem for a person who was generally conformist. Value-oriented criminal behavior, on the other hand, is systemic criminal behavior supported by commitment to criminal value structures. In the first case, the probability of recidivism is minimal; in the second case, the probability of recidivism is great.

In either case, punishment is considered an appropriate treatment program (OTP).

These assumptions about the criminal and criminal behavior call for new kinds of assessment techniques which reflect the complexities of the interaction process experienced by the criminal; that is, the assessment procedures must go beyond the traditional battery of psychological tests sometimes administered by reception and diagnostic centers. The assessment techniques must provide data on several dimensions of each of the variables cited in our reintegration formula. Each individual, after conviction of a crime, would have an extensive pre-sentence investigation which would focus on the above variables.

Discretionary Power

In applying the appropriate offender treatment program (OTP), and assuming for a moment that the decision will be to incarcerate, consideration must be given to an appropriate sentence. The complex issues in sentencing have been discussed earlier and with the exception of the work by Zimring, the proposals have not asked the right questions. As a result, the recommendations add chaos to the problem. The following issues must be resolved:

(1) Should there be provision for discretion in the sentencing process?

(2) If so, where should the discretionary power be placed?

(3) How much discretionary power should be granted?

(4) What kinds of guidelines should be established to regulate the discretionary power?

The sentencing process should provide for discretion, not because one approves of the concept of discretionary judgments in the sentencing process, but rather because a system without discretion is impossible. As noted by Zimring and others, it is impossible for a legislature to construct a penal code which will cover all the nuances of each crime which can occur in a variety of social contexts.

The second issue is, where should discretionary power be placed? Discretionary power should be given to a parole authority, autonomous and independent from the corrections bureaucracy. Although I am aware of the weaknesses in the present process, I nevertheless reject the notion that determinate sentencing returns power to the legislature. Determinate sentencing reallocates the discretionary power to the prosecutor and not to the legislature as proponents contend. Contrary to contentions made in several proposals, it is not the judge who determines the sentence. The sentence, as noted earlier, is determined when the prosecutor determines the official charge. And determinate sentencing increases the prosecutor's power considerably.

Analysis of the plea-bargaining process, sanctioned by the criminal justice system, indicates that socio-economic factors play a greater role at this point in sentencing than at any other time in the criminal justice process. Bargained justice is bought justice with the best bargains going to the highest bidders. It is the prosecutor who determines the price to be exacted and the resultant bargain. Fogel and others have noted that when the corrections process internalizes injustice, the entire criminal justice system loses credibility in the offender's eyes. While I concur with Fogel's position that too much discretion in the sentencing process has aggravated the problem, Fogel's solution is short-sighted. Simply stated, Fogel's model does not appreciate the politics of prosecution and the role the prosecutor plays in the local political context. It is in this context, behind closed doors, out of public view, and beyond due process that a community's power dimensions, prejudices, and politics interact. Allocations of power to the prosecutor should be reduced, not increased.

The third issue is, how much discretionary power should be granted? The amount of discretionary power should be extremely limited. The problems addressed by Cesare Beccaria in his 1764 treatise, *An Essay on Crimes and Punishments*, were not unique to the politics of that day. Discretionary power, regardless of the rationale, is often a euphemism for tyranny. Whether it be the tyranny of the king or the tyranny of the psychologist, the outcome is the same—loss of liberty. For this reason, each criminal sanction should carry a maximum, and in no case should the minimum be more than two-thirds of the maximum. We should realize that the major function to be served by punishment is retribution, and efforts should be made to minimize its effect on persons incarcerated. To contend that punishment has more important functions is to ignore the realities of the sentencing process.

The fourth issue is, what kinds of guidelines should be established to regulate discretionary power? Guidelines should be stringent, and the paroling authority should be obligated to follow the guidelines with appropriate accountability mechanisms established; that is, when parole is denied, the inmate should have the right to appellate review. Accountability for the parole process is long overdue. Sentencing time is a major component of the offender treatment program (OTP) and it is extremely important that it be equitable. The parole system, often pervaded by politics, is a serious barrier to reintegrating the offender into the community. The issue of incarceration is complex, and every effort should be made to develop programming which minimizes incarceration and maximizes reintegration into community life. This is not to say that incarceration should not be used. Obviously there are a number of individuals who cannot be adequately supervised in community-based correctional systems, and protection of society must be the primary goal of the process. At the same time, the irrational incarceration of thousands of convicted criminals, without differentiation between those who are a threat to society and those who are not, is a waste of resources. Furthermore, there is considerable evidence that through the incarceration process offenders often become increasingly sophisticated in their criminal behavior patterns. There is also evidence that some offenders become more violent. The criminal justice system has a number of criminogenic characteristics; characteristics of the system which enhance the potential for further criminal behavior. Unfortunately, because we have ignored these issues, problems have been compounded.

The Need for Reform

Beyond the issues of sentencing, delivery systems for programming must be totally restructured. The present delivery system is based on another erroneous assumption: that the interests of the warden and of the inmate are the same. If you were in prison, would you hire the warden's lawyer as your attorney? Can the clinical worker who delivers the "treatment" be an employee of the prison warden and at the same time function as an advocate for the inmate? The answers are obvious. Consideration should be given to a voucher system whereby inmates contract for the clinical services they believe they need. Obviously, if the inmate does not perceive a need for clinical services, none would be purchased. Parole would not be linked to the inmate's participation in programming per se, but rather to self-improvement strategies the inmate develops.

Industries in prisons, better known as "slave shops," should be contracted out to the business community. In this way, industries could be developed which would respond to market conditions for both products and employment. Wage levels should reflect realistic job market conditions with inmates reimbursing the state for maintenance costs incurred as a result of their incarceration. Restitution programs should be established for victims as well as support programs for the offender's family. In these efforts, programming should be developed which focuses on two important sub-systems in which the offender must be prepared to interact: the economy (E) and the family (F).

Finally, the collateral consequences of conviction must be eliminated wherever possible. The successful reintegration of the offender, is, to a large extent, determined by the nature of the community reaction (CR) and avoidance of participation in criminal subcultures with continual interaction with former peers (PC). It is a grim fact that punishment does not end when an inmate is released from one of our prisons. A study completed by the American Bar Association found 1,948 different state statutory provisions that prohibit the licensing of ex-offenders and thereby limit career development in a number of fields.

> The public is not generally aware of the fact that at the very time when it is approving efforts to develop job skills and employment for offenders and ex-offenders there exists a major body of legal barriers to meaningful and gainful employment of persons released from correctional systems. . . .
>
> We are thus involved in a system which defeats itself, in a system where through the work ethic and the values of our society, we applaud hard work and productive activity, while at the same time denying exactly that opportunity to do hard work and productive activity to persons we expect, in fact demand, to act responsibly. We try to rehabilitate, and then we place barriers to rehabilitation and in fact initiate an active impetus back to a life of crime.[30]

The resultant loss of self-esteem enhances considerably the potential for recidivism. If we do not radically alter the legal barriers which now function to severely limit the reintegration process, the vicious cycle of incarceration-release-incarceration will continue regardless of the sentencing model used. The

---

[30]American Bar Association, *Law, Licenses and the Offender's Right to Work* (Washington, D.C.: National Clearinghouse on Offender Employment Restrictions, 1973). p. 2.

present community reaction (CR) to the ex-offender is often one of negativism and continued stigma. We should not be surprised that ex-offenders often return to previous lifestyles, maintain commitments to old values, and become recidivists. The problem was identified by Frank Tannenbaum in 1938:

> The process of making the criminal, therefore, is a process of tagging, defining, identifying, segregating, describing, emphasizing, making conscious, and self-conscious; it becomes a way of stimulating, suggesting, emphasizing, and evoking the very traits that are complained of. . . . The person becomes the very thing he is described as being. Nor does it seem to matter whether the evaluation is made by those who would reform. . . . The harder they work to reform the evil, the greater the evil grows under their hands. The persistent suggestion, with whatever good intentions, works mischief, because it leads to bringing out the bad behavior that it would suppress. The way out is through a refusal to dramatize the evil.[31]

The advice given by Tannenbaum in 1938 has seldom been followed. The way out is to reject the retribution philosophy as it has been practiced and turn instead to the philosophies of reintegration, restitution, and reconciliation. We can no longer focus our efforts on the individual offender by blaming the offender when our efforts fail. The philosophy of reintegration requires that we examine the structure of our communities in addition to dealing with the offender. Crime occurs in a social context, the community. Some may seek change based on the flaming demands of Amos; others may rely on the sober words of Micah. Regardless of one's perspective, all Christians are under God's command to pursue justice in their communities.

If we can limit retribution and the brutal forms of punishment which have followed this concept, we can enhance restitution. In our somewhat barbaric system of justice we have ignored the victim. Rather than forcing an offender to "pay for his crime" by suffering, we must emphasize payment to the victim in the form of restitution. Because of our commitment to retribution, the criminal justice system has been unimaginative in developing mechanisms to compensate victims. Even as victim compensation programs are developed, we find very few involving the offender. The payment of cash to victims from a tax-supported fund is not restitution. Offenders must be given the opportunity to make restitution.

---

[31]Frank Tannenbaum, *Crime and the Community* (New York: Columbia University Press, 1938), pp. 19-20.

Restitution is important in reconciliation. To reconcile is to bring the offender back into the community. Our refusal to provide offenders reconciliation is unbiblical and un-Christian. Completion of a five-year prison term does not mean that one has paid for his/her crime in our society. We have a label for persons having served time: "ex-con." We use that label to deny persons jobs, training, and the opportunity to earn a decent living and to support themselves and their families. By our refusal to reconcile we stimulate the crime-incarceration-crime cycle. We literally guarantee failure to thousands of persons each year as they leave our prisons and enter the society that is terribly concerned with retribution and unconcerned with reconciliation.

Change will not come easily; it seldom does. At the same time the guiding principles are clear. Ignoring these issues today will result in judgment tomorrow—not only for criminals but for ourselves as well.

HAROLD O. J. BROWN

12

Biomedical Ethics

Ethics and the Technological Society

The 1978 announcement of the birth of a "test-tube baby" in England brought to the fore the complex ethical problems in our rapidly changing world. As Jacques Ellul repeatedly warned in *The Technological Society*, ethics cannot control technology.[1] Whatever can be done will be done. In World War II, the repeated use of the atomic bomb against a virtually prostrate Japan—after surrender offers had been made—demonstrates the force of Ellul's argument.

Before the fact, many religious ethicists found the idea of the test-tube baby (*in vitro* fertilization of the ovum of a married woman by her husband's sperm) objectionable. Paul Ramsey of Princeton University, the outstanding Protestant voice on medical and biological ethics, had already flatly stated in a 1972 article that such a procedure, as yet untried, constitutes "unethical medical experimentation on human beings and therefore is subject to absolute moral prohibition."[2] After the fact, however, most writers were willing to live with it—particularly as it was used to provide a direct biological offspring to a married couple.

---

[1] *The Technological Society* (New York: Knopf, 1961).

[2] Paul Ramsey, "Shall We 'Reproduce'? (I) The Medical Ethics of in Vitro Fertilization," in *JAMA* 220 (June 5, 1972): 1346-50.

However, similar technology could be used to provide a couple with non-homologous offspring (the ovum of another woman, or the sperm of a man other than the husband, used to produce the embryo then implanted in the womb of the mother-to-be). It could also be used—as a group of lesbian women demanded—to provide babies for lesbian mothers.[3] Such women, in Paul's words, "change the natural use into that which is against nature" (Rom. 1:26). The comment of Dominican friar and bishop Thomas C. Kelly, general secretary of the United States Catholic Conference, may serve both as a resumé of what has happened and an ominous prediction of the future.

> This episode points to a readiness to implement new technology *before its moral implications have been thoroughly considered* [fulfilling Ellul's prediction]. The consequences of this mentality—from the atomic bomb to uncontrolled use of carcinogenic pesticides—have become clear in recent years. We should proceed cautiously when the same mentality manifests itself in regard to so sensitive and sacred a matter as the transmission of human life.[4]

With the long-expected, yet astonishing announcement of the birth of a test-tube baby, the proposals concerning cloning,[5] and childbearing by the artificial insemination of homosexual women, a new light is cast on Ellul's prophecy and Kelly's warning. But we must recognize that the discipline of ethics lacks the power to impose its convictions on society in general and cannot prevent or punish violations of "absolute moral prohibitions." Indeed, in many cases ethicists, biblical Christians as well as others, have not even begun to grapple seriously with the emerging problems, not to speak of having established well-founded principles for resolving them.

The Background of Biomedical Ethics

The new field of biomedical ethics has its roots in medical ethics, a part of medicine that goes back at least to Hippocrates, the "father of medicine" (circa 460-360 B.C.) Practitioners of the

---

[3] Report in *Denver Rocky Mountain News*, August 5, 1978.

[4] Cited by Darrell Turner, *Religious News* (N. Y.) *Service*, July 26, 1978, my italics.

[5] Cloning is a procedure resulting in the asexual reproduction of an offspring that is the genetic copy of one parent, not two. It has been accomplished in some lower animals, but seems still distant in mammals.

art—and more recently, science—of medicine have long been feared as well as admired. Into their hands we entrust the most precious and irreplacable of our possessions, our own lives and those of our loved ones. For this reason the practice of medicine has been highly rewarded. It has been entrusted, at least ideally, only to those who have demonstrated their aptitude by completing a long course of study and who have indicated personal commitment to a noble standard of professional ethics—long summarized in the ancient Hippocratic Oath.

From the days of "the father of medicine" to the early years of our own century medicine was, in the words of Dr. Jean Bernard, "inexpensive and relatively ineffectual." Today, within the professional lifetime of still-practicing senior physicians, it has become much more effective—and frighteningly expensive. And thus are combined within one discipline three factors which invariably bring great ethical and moral pressure: power, vital interests (health, children, life itself), and the potential for wealth (of the physician) or financial ruin (of the patient and his family).

Hippocrates warned against burdening one's patients with apprehension about the cost of treatment, urging free assistance to those in financial straits.[6] This fear affects those even in wealthy America, so that many people dread the cost of illness more than illness itself and sometimes more than death. Even the progressive assumption by the state of medical care costs has not relieved these fears. Indeed, it is possible that by multiplying the cost of medical and hospital services, even while assuming much of the financial responsibility, government financing in America has increased the burden on the patient. In the United States today, Medicare, Medicaid, and other programs guarantee payment on behalf of the old and poor—yet paradoxically increase the burden on others. Physicians seldom and hospitals virtually never heed Hippocrates' mandate, "Consider carefully your patient's wealth or poverty. . . . Sometimes give your services for nothing." As a result, even a relatively mild illness may be a financial disaster for a patient.

The combination of vast power to heal and to transform lives with enormous financial consequences for patient, physician, and society as a whole is one of the most troublesome issues in medical ethics. If a modern society were to provide each of its

---

[6]Hippocrates *Precepts* 6. Cited in Stanley Joel Reiser, Arthur J. Dyck, and William J. Curran, eds., *Ethics in Medicine* (Cambridge: MIT Press, 1977), p. 5.

citizens with all the medical attention that might be helpful to him, the cost could exceed that society's gross national product.[7] How is society to decide which of many potentially helpful procedures shall be employed on a particular patient? Who decides which patients shall receive heroic, formidably expensive measures—such as the use of dialysis ("kidney machine")—when sufficient equipment is not available for all sufferers? But it is obvious that no amount of government financing can solve a problem whose magnitude exceeds a nation's gross productivity.

Related to these issues are the problems connected with three areas in which medical science has developed possibilities that were only dreams half a century ago—the "issues of life": birth, chronic and deadly illness, and death.

The Ability to Prolong Life

After the immediate goal of relieving suffering, the next natural goal for the phsyician is to prolong life. Nevertheless, as more and more individuals push toward and even surpass the biblical "threescore years and ten," the prolongation to fourscore—and more—often becomes "labor and sorrow" (Ps. 90:10). When the body's vital functions—heartbeat, respiration, digestion, elimination—fail or are blocked, medical science can sustain or supplant them, sometimes almost indefinitely. Occasionally such aid helps an otherwise doomed patient to survive a crisis and restores him to full or partial health. But often it merely prolongs his dying—incidentally making it terribly expensive to his survivors.

How is one to distinguish between the patient who will (or at least may) recover and the one whose final agony will merely be lengthened? Making this distinction is often beyond the ability of relatives and friends, and even of the best physicians. In critical cases, the exercise of such judgment on a physician's part is difficult, especially in the United States, where the physician may be afraid to trust his own judgment. He knows that if the patient or his survivors disagree with his choice of treatment, and if a jury of non-physicians can be persuaded likewise, he will be punished for his judgment with an immense malpractice penalty.

"Miracle Cures"

As a result of modern medical progress, illnesses that once

---

[7]Jean Bernard, *Grandeur et tentacions de la médicine* (Paris: Buche Chastel, 1973).

were irremediable or fatal have become merely chronic—but they require costly treatment to maintain or prolong life. Cancers of various kinds, kidney failure, and many other degenerative diseases can be arrested or retarded. Here the ethical problem is somewhat different from the case of the dying patient. Today, certain possible treatments may be withheld from a dying patient because they would not benefit him, but seldom because they would cost too much. In the case of a long-drawn-out, chronic condition, help for which is possible but very expensive, the question someday may no longer be one of therapeutic effectiveness but of expense. (Can the patient, or his family, or society, afford this help?)

At the present time, most of those with chronic illnesses in America *somehow* receive the treatment their physicians think best, regardless of cost. Unfortunately, as new treatments become more readily available—and certain types of chronic illness, including various cancers, become more frequent—the cost factor may eventually come to be of inescapable consequence. A limit will be reached and potentially helpful treatment will be withheld. But who will continue to receive it? Will it be the wealthy, the famous, the politically powerful? Or will the receivers be chosen by a governmental commission according to certain bureaucratic guidelines?

The prospect of future developments in this area is troubling. While we may hope for dramatic breakthroughs that will reduce the incidence of disease and the cost of treatment, we cannot confidently predict them. And, unless not one but many such breakthroughs take place, the cost of medicine will inevitably exceed even the wealthiest society's ability to pay.

Accelerated Death

Medicine has developed remarkable means to prolong life even *in extremis*; now physicians must question the extent to which they are ethically *obliged* to do so. At the other end of the human life cycle, however, it is not an increasing perfection of technology but a dramatic transformation of moral sense that has created a new ethical dilemma. The possibility of abortion has been known since antiquity. It has also been widely condemned—as in the Hippocratic Oath, the touchstone of medical ethics for twenty centuries.

Until the late nineteenth century, when antiseptic techniques and anaesthesia became common, abortion, although possible, was extremely risky for the woman. From mid-century onward the advanced scientific nations began to enact stringent anti-abortion laws, not to protect the health of women, but because an increasing understanding of fetal development made it clear to physicians that each embryo, from conception, is an individual human being.[8]

In the second half of the twentieth century, many of the same advanced countries, faced with a rise in unwanted pregnancies, liberalized restrictions on abortion. No new medical knowledge permits late twentieth-century man to define the fetus as anything other than an individual human life. In most countries, no effort was made to do so. It was simply argued that the social cost of unwanted babies was too great to permit the state to attempt to protect them from "termination" before birth. In the United States, the Supreme Court affected to disregard the question of when human life begins, but then made its decision as though life definitely did not begin until live birth, a supposition that is medically and biologically absurd. *Roe* v. *Wade* (January 22, 1973) *in effect* permits abortion on demand at any time up to live birth.

The wave of "elective" abortions released by *Roe* v. *Wade* and by earlier legislative action in a few states has now reached a rate of perhaps 1,300,000 legal abortions per year in the United States and is continuing to rise. The annual figure as recently as 1969 was only 20,000 (all claimed to be for therapeutic reasons, because of serious threats to the pregnant woman's life or health). But now abortion causes more deaths annually in America than any disease.

The first "biomedical" problems we considered were caused by advancing technology as yet unmatched by clear ethical principles—test-tube babies, extreme measures to prolong life, the possibility of securing remission or cure of otherwise fatal diseases. Science, so to speak, has outrun ethics. The abortion wave, however, confronts us with an ethical issue of a different nature. It is not caused by the failure of ethics to keep pace with science. The ethical principles were laid down before Christ by Hippocrates, well in advance of abortion technology. They have been affirmed and reaffirmed countless times since then—until the twentieth century.[9]

---

[8]Cf. John T. Noona, Jr., "Dispelling Two Legends," in *Human Life Review*, vol. 4, no. 3 (Summer 1978): 111-12.

[9]See my discussion, "What the Court Didn't Know," in *Human Life Review*, vol. 1, no. 2 (Spring 1975).

The most striking feature of *Roe* v. *Wade* is that it does not acknowledge that the developing human child has any human rights: it has only such rights as the state is willing to grant. Human life is considered worthy of protection only if "compelling state interest" is guaranteed by what the Supreme Court calls "capability of meaningful life." The fact that an unwanted child might force on its mother, in Justice Douglas' words, "a distressful life and future" is sufficient reason for terminating its prenatal development. Little effort was made, compared to the German Federal Constitutional Court decision of 1975, to examine the nature of the developing child or to weigh his rights—totally extinguished in abortion—against the various rights to privacy, an untroubled future, and so forth, which the woman must relinquish to some extent as a result of pregnancy.

When criteria such as "state interest," "meaningfulness," and "distressful future" take precedence over the fundamental principle of the sanctity of innocent human life, then it is pointless to speak of medical decisions as subject to ethical principles. In the climate in which abortion on demand—in the words of dissenting Justice White, "for any reason or no reason"—has become the law of the land, it is easy to predict that traditional ethical values will break down.

The abortion question has been termed by Malcolm Muggeridge a "life and death question" for Western civilization. In most Western countries (exceptions: West Germany, Switzerland), it is being resolved in the direction of death. Again we must note that what has happened to transform legal, popular, and sometimes even religious attitudes on abortion is *not* a scientific breakthrough, but an ethical breakdown that reduces the absolute value of human life to a relative good that may readily be forfeited in the quest for "privacy," "self-expression," or various other personal goals.

Implications of the Abortion Issue

Muggeridge and others recognize just how crucial is the abortion issue for the following reasons, among others: (1) Underlying the new abortion dilemma, as we have said, is not a scientific advance but a transformation of moral values. The danger is the relativizing of the value of human life to the extent of justifying its destruction on a cost-effectiveness basis. (2) The goals that abortion seeks to achieve could be obtained, in a great number of cases, without destroying developing life, simply by providing better facilities to assist the pregnant woman to bear and support her child, or to give him up for adoption. The fact is that these alternatives are not given serious public policy support—the courts having decided, in some cases, that the state not only may not *prohibit* abortion, it may not even seek to *discourage* it.[10]

It is possible to imagine a sane society that places a higher value on the developed life and the set of human responsibilities of an expectant woman than on the as yet undeveloped potential of the child in her womb. But it is difficult to comprehend a society that places *no* value on developing life. Clearly this is the dangerous trend of public policy in the United States.

One of the factors leading to the readiness of a segment of society to attribute zero value to developing human lives is the Malthusian dread of the "population explosion." The danger of a disastrous population increase has been greatly exaggerated, for most industrialized nations are confronting not an explosion but stagnation or decline. For our purposes it is sufficient to note that a widespread fear of such a population explosion exists—whether or not the threat is real. It ought to be evident that if the discretionary killing of developing babies is accepted *because* it helps achieve the priority goal of population control, then we have a situation in which the end—population reduction—justifies means that would otherwise be rejected—for example, killing.[11]

Our society prefers relatively cheap and quick abortions to the moderate social cost of state-assisted childbirth with the possibility of further state aid to a dependent child, even though the child may be expected someday to be a socially valuable, tax-paying citizen. In the same light, will society expend great and ever-increasing sums for the care and maintenance of the chronically ill, severely handicapped, and very aged who in all probability will never again be of service or value to the state? The *New Statesman* predicted some years ago that the (British) abortion wave of the sixties would become the euthanasia wave of the eighties. The logic is inescapable. If society cannot shoulder the moderate burden of pregnancy care and child assistance—despite the prospect of an active citizen who may someday benefit the

---

[10]Extreme decisions of this tenor have recently been somewhat moderated, as in *Poelker* v. *Roe* (1977). Government is given a modest scope to encourage childbearing in preference to "termination of pregnancy" by abortion.

[11]Those who wonder whether abortion should be classed as killing should read the pro-abortion editorial in the *New Republic*, July 2, 1977, in which abortion is admitted to be scarcely distinguishable from infanticide, yet deemed socially necessary.

state, how can it be expected to assume much greater burdens for the old and helpless who have no real expectation of ever being productive again?

Technology, Money, Morals

The early development of medical ethics was motivated by two chief factors: (1) the power of a physician more easily to do harm than good; (2) the therapeutic and social necessity of trust between physicians and their patients: unless they trust their doctor, many patients just will not improve. The rapid rise of biomedical ethics began as a consequence of a technology whose potential to change and accomplish pushed us into areas where we had not yet clearly decided what should be changed and what new possibilities ought to be accomplished or avoided. But whatever hopes ethicists may have of holding back dramatic developments until sound principles can be laid down must fade in the light of the abortion situation, where we have seen even well-established ethical norms repudiated or ignored because of a new quest for convenience.

Consequently, all of us who are concerned with the ethical and moral foundations of society have to look on present developments with great concern. This is particularly important for biblical Christians who believe that we have an obligation, on hearing a word from the Lord, to warn the general public accordingly (Ezek. 3:17). The quandary of biomedical ethics exists at every level—individual, familial, social, and governmental. It also has a past, present, and future dimension. The past has already accustomed if not committed us to some very ominous reversals of traditional Christian and Hippocratic values. In the present we are continuing to build patterns of conduct that relativize absolutes and make them readily vulnerable to sacrifice for the sake of economy, convenience, and other transitory values. The future presents us with the prospect of still greater pressures, an alarming thought in the light of our current failure to deal with present ones.

Inalienable Rights?

One of the first biomedical ethical issues to challenge us today may simply be called an ethical issue: namely the subjective or personal right of a human being to life. By "subjective" or "personal" right we mean one that pertains to the individual as a subject, not one that is objectively or formally granted to him by an outside agency, the state. The Declaration of Independence speaks of all men as "endowed by their Creator with certain inalienable rights. . . ." The framers were aware that many societies did in fact alienate (i.e., take away) the individual's God-endowed rights to life and liberty. But in principle these rights were inalienable, justly belonging to the individual because they were part of the endowment of his Creator. Present legal trends recognize only formal rights, granted by the Constitution or other documents, and capable of being taken away when there is no "compelling state interest" in preserving them.

The issue of personal rights versus state-granted formal rights is an issue that transcends the narrow sphere of biomedical ethics. But no sound system of biomedical ethics can be developed until it is agreed that individuals have personal rights that belong to them by virtue of what they are (creatures of God, who so endowed them). If individual rights are thought of as patent grants by the state, then in the last analysis the individual will have no personal rights that he can defend against the will of the state. Consequently he will always suffer loss when there is no compelling state interest in protecting him at the expense of inconvenience to others, particularly to the state itself.

In a fallen world it is not possible for any state to always protect individual citizens and their theoretically "inalienable" rights. But it is one thing for society and the state to be committed to doing all they can to respect and protect the individual while admitting that they simply cannot protect him against the fate that is common to all mankind. It is quite another for the state to make its own "compelling interest" the main criterion for determining whether the individual has any rights to be respected at all.

Christians therefore, before addressing themselves to detailed questions of biomedical ethics, must seek to reestablish the concept of Creator-given rights. We have rights that belong to us because God made us in his own image (Gen. 1:26-27), not because the state grants or concedes them to us. Reestablishing this idea will be possible only when we restore in our society a consensus that certain rights are established, as the Declaration of Independence has it, by the laws of "Nature and Nature's God," not by a social or political convention. The abortion problem, therefore, properly belongs to general ethics and is not specifically a biomedical ethical issue. But attention to specifically biomedical issues will prove pointless unless we can remedy the general ethical breakdown of which our contemporary abortion carnage is a logical result. If we cannot deal with abortion, we have little hope of dealing with more complex issues.

The Question of Intent

As a general rule, criminal law deals with questions of fact, not intent. If I break the law—even if I "didn't mean to"—I must pay the penalty. Ethics, by contrast, does deal with intent. It is necessary for the teacher of ethics to guide us in directing our will rightly, that is, in forming a right intent. The question of intent is particularly important in understanding what is at stake in certain actions. The surgeon who terminates an ectopic pregnancy (when gestation begins outside the uterus) destroys a developing child as surely as the gynecologist who performs an elective suction abortion: however, the intent is different. The surgeon acts to save a woman's life and would, if he possibly could, also save that of the tiny fetus. The gynecologist, by contrast, kills a child that does not need to die, for the sake of the personal convenience, not the life, of the woman. The action is similar, the intent different.

The question of intent always must be involved in the evaluation of a physician's decisions. One physician may administer morphine to a critically ill patient for the relief of great pain; another physician may administer a larger dose as a means of "mercy killing." It is his intent which we must scrutinize. We must also take into consideration the fact that patients respond differently and sometimes unpredictably to medication. The effectiveness of varying dosages cannot always be known in advance, and physicians, being human, may make errors in judgment. For these reasons a legally binding handbook of prescribed medications and dosages for all people in the bewildering multitude of possible physical conditions is an impossibility. So, since the specific behavior of physicians cannot be regulated, we need to be able to assume that the *intent* of a physician is in accordance with Hippocrates' maxim never to inflict injury. The details of what the physician does in an effort to follow this maxim cannot be spelled out in advance, but his motives may be prescribed on the basis of ethical principles. Some of the broad principles of treatment may be regulated by law, but many of the specific actions must be entrusted to his judgment and cannot be prescribed.

The problem of euthanasia—accelerated, "mercy" killing of those already dying—and of what is sometimes erroneously also called euthanasia, the destruction of "valueless" life, must be resolved on the basis of intent and principle, not what is technologically feasible. (The life of a patient may be deemed "valueless" to himself—usually by someone else—or "valueless" to society, especially when society must pay the bills. But the true value of a human life is based on man's creation in God's image, not on the individual's present or future social usefulness.)

Method or Result?

Oklahoma has sought to evade some of the controversy surrounding capital punishment by prescribing death not by hanging or electrocution, but by a lethal injection. The implication of the Oklahoma law is that a "scientific" method of execution removes the objection to capital punishment. But the effect of a lethal injection is precisely the same as the effect of the guillotine, hangman's noose, and electric chair—the death of the victim. The intent, to punish by death, is the same in each case. The new method still kills, effectively prevents rehabilitation of the convicted criminal, and is just as subject to judicial error as any other form of execution. But perhaps many members of the general public will tolerate the use of lethal injections. If so, there is an evident parallel with the trend toward acceptance of "mercy killing" by a doctor—as long as he uses a hypodermic syringe and not a pistol. What ought to be crucial is the result—the death of the patient—not the means used to accomplish it.

In German euthanasia law "assistance in suicide" was considered non-criminal and "killing on demand" was considered criminal. In the first case a physician provided the means, in the other he actually did the killing. The second instance was illegal, even though in both cases death was at the request of the patient, a mentally competent adult.[12] It may be argued—as the Stoic philosophers did—that a man should have the natural right to end his own life. The rival Pythagorean school of philosophy, by contrast, forbade both suicide and assistance in suicide (as well as abortion). This prohibition is reflected in the Hippocratic Oath and is quite consistent with subsequent Christian ethics.

---

[12]See the summary by Helmut E. Ehrhardt, "Abortion and Euthanasia: Common Problems," in *Human Life Review*, vol. 1, no. 3 (Summer 1975).

The majority of candidates for mercy killing no longer fall into the category of mentally and legally competent persons suffering prolonged, intractable pain. Thanks to modern drug therapy, virtually all pain is treatable: no one need choose death as the only way to escape it. The various means of sustaining life (or prolonging death) are such that patients now often can be maintained alive long after they have lost mental clarity and competence. In such cases another person—family, physician, or perhaps in days to come a government inspector—is asked to determine whether the dying patient's life is so devoid of value that he may properly be killed. This represents a usurping of moral authority, the right to decide one's own destiny. The judgment "valueless life" was passed by others on many "thalidomide babies," and a number of possibly affected babies were aborted. Some babies who survived and have grown to maturity, by contrast, have made public their own conviction that their lives do have value.

Killing or Allowing To Die

The crucial ethical question in euthanasia is thus one of intent. The intent to kill a dying patient is wrong. The willingness to allow him to die by not engaging in "heroic" life-sustaining measures, whether at his request if he is mentally competent or in accordance with family wishes if he is not, is both legally and ethically permissible.

The further development of life-sustaining medical techniques will make the dilemma of the terminally ill but somehow surviving patient more common and more complex in the future. Again, the task of the ethicist—pastor, teacher, legislator, scholar—is to establish and defend the *principles* that must be maintained rather than losing himself in a maze of technical questions, such as the definition of death and of "heroic" measures. Answering the technical questions, though necessary, will be insufficient as long as there is no binding consensus on the *goals* that new techniques are to serve.

Genetic Engineering

The frequently-heard term "genetic engineering" covers a variety of procedures, many of which do not actually "engineer" or alter genes. "Genetic counseling" is a term which includes a procedure that is already widespread. Many couples contemplating marriage are tested for rh-factor incompatibility; carriers of hereditary defects may be advised not to marry or at least not to have children. Such counseling becomes an ethical issue only if acceptance of the counselor's advice becomes mandatory. Does society have the right to forbid childbearing—and to require sterilization, or perhaps even forced abortion—to carriers of defective genes?

The prospect of gene alteration, which would produce characteristics in offspring not present in the genes of either parent, confronts us with problems of a different order. In the first place, there is the inevitable problem of failure. The potential danger of harmful mutations far outweighs the possible benefits of harmless ones. Attempts at genetic engineering are virtually certain to produce mutations before achieving the hoped-for results. Our standard for moral conduct, the Bible, does not speak directly to this issue. But much of our widespread reluctance to permit such genetic experimentation seems to be motivated by a less admirable sentiment than following biblical principles: the fear that the genetic "monster" might harm its human makers.

It seems logical to apply here Paul Ramsey's verdict of "unethical experimentation on human beings"—and his concomitant "absolute moral prohibition." We would deplore cases where mutilation was produced in a newborn by surgical or chemical means; it is simply consistent to hold that all "experimentation" which results in the mutilation of the subject is ethically wrong. Genetic engineering also involves, in Malcolm Muggeridge's words, "trespassing against the mortal basis of our human existence," and thus is wrong in principle as well as in practice.

Cloning is a procedure less unpredictable than genetic manipulation, although like it not yet possible in human beings. Here the expected result is a genetic copy of a living individual, producing what have been called "identical twins a generation apart." The mere attempt might well produce monsters; even if it did not, it represents quite a transformation of the biblical mandate given to man and woman to reproduce *sexually* to replenish the earth (Gen. 1:28). Human beings must accept the Creator's way of doing things and refrain from devising alternate methods. (This is not an argument against treating disease. God never suggested that disease is good; healing disease does not *destroy* but rather *restores* a portion of the goodness of creation. Cloning, however, would override the judgment "very good" given by God to sexual reproduction [Gen. 1:31] and attempt to bypass it.) In addition, cloning seems to involve a kind of arrogant self-love—an individual seeks to copy himself, as though he were perfect. This is in opposition to the Creator's plan of reproducing another human being in his image—like and yet distinct—rather than in a man's image.

Artificial Organs, Organ Transplants

"Prosthetic devices" such as artificial limbs have been used for centuries and are ethically noncontroversial. By the same token, the possibility that functioning artificial organs—for example, artificial hearts, lungs, kidneys—may someday be constructed does not appear to present a problem. Organ transplants, such as a kidney from a living donor, are also ethically unobjectionable. Of course, the donation of a vital single organ such as the heart or liver would be tantamount to suicide, and hence not ethically permissible.

The transplanting of organs from just-dead donors does not in itself appear to pose problems.[13] What is problematic, however, is the temptation to "harvest" organs from those not quite dead, or even from physically healthy but mentally "valueless" persons such as the severely mentally retarded, brain-damaged, and the like. The possibility also arises of using organs from persons condemned to death—which suggests the ominous idea that individuals might be condemned to death because their organs are needed for a politically powerful recipient.

Another possible ramification of the organ transplant question is that an individual could have himself "cloned," raise the cloned copy to maturity, and keep him as an "organ bank" for future needs. Since the clone would be a fully human individual, such a procedure would be totally unethical, just as it would be entirely wrong to raise one's child or identical twin as an organ bank for one's own future needs.[14] This procedure would be extremely expensive and would be available only for the very wealthy or very powerful. But, as Ecclesiastes 6:1-12 points out, neither wealth, nor wisdom, nor political power have ever sufficed to create a

---

[13]Lev. 20:19 can be interpreted to apply to this issue, however, as it speaks of defilement by mingling diverse kinds (cattle, seed, fabric).

[14]Late in 1978, a project—not carried out—was planned to have a kidney patient become pregnant and abort the child so that it could provide a genetically compatible kidney for transplantation (*Chicago Tribune*, Nov. 6, 1978).

substantial difference between the ultimate fate of one man and another—at least, not yet.

Expensive life-prolonging techniques and such exploitative measures as forcible organ transplants and the maintenance of human beings solely as eventual organ donors now confront us with the possibility of creating radically different classes of human beings. There may someday be "near-immortals" given superb medical care and a fund of usable organs, and "mere mortals" who must die when their appointed time comes, when they are no longer of compelling state interest, or even when their organs are more interesting to powerful potential recipients than their lives.

The only possible way to forestall such a future, implicit in the technology now being developed, is by establishing a firm basis in law that individuals possess certain fundamental rights as human beings made in God's image—or, in the language of the Declaration of Independence, because they have been "endowed by their Creator with certain inalienable rights." Unfortunately this is not the trend of contemporary legal developments. At the moment, technological possibilities are taking precedence over ethical principles, just as Jacques Ellul predicted. The challenge to biblical Christians, who have a firm basis for their ethical convictions, is to enact laws that guarantee the protection of individual human beings from the new forms of exploitation that modern technology is making possible. We are on the threshold of developments potentially enabling man to "make" or "remake" himself. But man cannot tell *whether* or *how* to remake himself unless he can give a valid answer to the psalmist's question, "What is man, that thou art mindful of him?"

Contributors

Perry C. Cotham currently serves as pulpit minister for the Westwood Church of Christ in McMinnville, Tennessee. He is the author of two other books published by Baker Book House: *Obscenity, Pornography, and Censorship* (1973) and *Politics, Americanism, and Christianity* (1976). Dr. Cotham's graduate degrees were obtained from Wayne State University in Detroit.

John T. Willis, professor of Bible at Abilene Christian University, is an Old Testament scholar, author, lecturer, and translator. Dr. Willis's graduate degrees were received from Vanderbilt University Divinity School. He is the author of one book and numerous articles in various religious journals.

James W. Thompson teaches in the Biblical Studies Center at the University of Texas at Austin. He received his Ph.D. in New Testament studies at Vanderbilt Divinity School and is the author of *Our Life Together* (Sweet, 1977).

Paul B. Henry, former associate professor of Political Science at Calvin College, was elected in November, 1978 to the Michigan House of Representatives. He earned the Ph.D. from Duke University after graduating from Wheaton College. He is the author of *Politics for Evangelicals* (Judson, 1974) and has contributed to several other volumes.

Richard V. Pierard is professor of History at Indiana State University, Terre Haute. He has written or contributed to a number of volumes on Christian political activism, including *The Unequal Yoke: Evangelical Christianity and Political Conservatism* (Lippincott, 1970), *Protest and Politics* (Attic Press, 1968), *The Cross and the Flag* (Creation House, 1972), *Politics: A Case for Christian Activism* (with Robert D. Linder, InterVarsity, 1973), and *Twilight of the Saints: Biblical Christianity and Civil Religion in America* (InterVarsity, 1978).

Letha Scanzoni is a professional writer, the author or coauthor of seven books, the most recent of which are *Sex Is a Parent Affair* (Regal, 1973), *All We're Meant To Be* (with Nancy Hardesty, Word, 1974), *Men, Women, and Change: A Sociology of Marriage and Family* (with John Scanzoni, McGraw-Hill, 1976), and *Is the Homosexual My Neighbor?* (with Virginia Ramey Mollenkott, Harper & Row, 1978).

Jim Reynolds is a counselor and preaching minister for the Southwest Church of Christ in Dallas, Texas. He holds the Th.D. from Graduate Theological Union and is the author of *Secrets of Eden: God and Human Sexuality* (Sweet, 1975).

David O. Moberg is professor of Sociology and Anthropology and chairman of that department at Marquette University. Dr. Moberg is one of the most widely published evangelical scholars today. Among his books are: *The Church as a Social Institution: the Sociology of American Religion* (Prentice-Hall, 1962). *Inasmuch: Christian Social Responsibility in the Twentieth Century* (Eerdmans, 1965), *The Great Reversal* (rev. ed., Eerdmans, 1977), and *The Church and the Older Person* (with Robert M. Gray, rev. ed., Eerdmans, 1977).

W. Stanley Mooneyham, president of World Vision International, spends at least half of each year traveling the world in search of the helpless and needy. He is author of *What Do You Say to a Hungry World?* (Word, 1975). The organization Dr. Mooneyham directs has evangelistic, childcare, and relief and development programs in nearly fifty nations.

Robert G. Culbertson is chairman of the Department of Criminal Justice Sciences at Illinois State University. He was appointed by the governor to the Adult Advisory Board of the Illinois Department of Corrections and has served as a consultant to various law enforcement departments. Dr. Culbertson has contributed articles on corrections to a variety of volumes and journals.

Harold O. J. Brown is currently chairman of the Theology Department of Trinity Evangelical Divinity School. He received the B.D. and Th.M. degrees from Harvard in 1957 and 1959. For the past several years, Dr. Brown has been in the forefront of the campaign against liberal abortion policies; he has served as chairman of the Washington-based Christian Action Council. His articles have appeared in a variety of religious journals and magazines. Among his published books are: *The Protest of a Troubled Protestant* (Arlington House, 1969), *The Reconstruction of the Republic* (Arlington House, 1977), and *Death Before Birth* (Thomas Nelson, 1977).